D0217349

Leading with
Integrity
Character-Based
Leadership

WITHDRAWN

Alan Kolp
Professor of Religion
Moll Chair in Faith and Life
Baldwin-Wallace College

Peter Rea
Chairman, Professor
Division of Business Administration
Baldwin-Wallace College

Cincinnati, OH
www.atomicdog.com

Book Team

Vice President/Publisher	Steve Scoble
Managing Editor	Kendra Leonard
Director of Interactive Media and Design	Joe Devine
Production Coordinator	Lori Bradshaw
Quality Assurance Editors	Tim Bair, Dan Horton
Web Production Editor	Angela Makowski
Marketing Manager	Mikka Baker
Cover Design	Joe Devine

When ordering this title, use ISBN 1-59260-256-8

Printed in the United States of America by Atomic Dog Publishing,
35 East Seventh Street, Suite 405, Cincinnati, OH 45202.

10 9 8 7 6 5 4 3 2 1

Dedicated to our four children

Felicity Kolp
Christina Kolp
Scott Rea
David Rea

With gratitude for who they are and hopes for who they will become.

Contents

Chapter 1

Introduction: Leading Change through Virtue and Value   1

Chapter 2

Character   17

Chapter 3

Chapter 4

Chapter 5

Chapter 6

Chapter 7

Chapter 8

Chapter 9

Prudence   175

Chapter 10

Chapter 11

Chapter 12

Chapter 13

Worth and Worthiness 255

Foreword

This is a first for me. I found my own beliefs and business principles in the words of two professors I had never met—Alan Kolp and Peter Rea. My 42-year business career flashed before my eyes as I read this book. Each chapter highlighted the good and challenged the "questionable good" of my professional achievements. You will go through the same rewarding process.

The hundreds of academic works, educational publications, and business articles I have read, researched, or co-authored over the years have never presented me with direct explanations for the shortcomings of so many top executives around the world. This book does! And it goes beyond that to illustrate the ethical way to achieve record-breaking business results. As you read and re-read—yes, you will—the definitions and tables of do's and don'ts, your most spontaneous objections will rapidly fade. You will join the ranks of those who evaluate the enterprise through the lens of virtuous behavior and who structure management around the basic seven virtues.

Virtuous management is an acquired science, personal to each individual and his or her time line! It begins with one's genetic self, which I define as the gift of nature at birth, via the family learning, the years of basic schooling and higher instruction, through the grueling experiences climbing up the business ladder. Kolp and Rea claim and demonstrate that the rule of behavior for the boss of a five-person team in a small local shop is the same as for the CEO of a giant global corporation. The authors call it *servant leadership.*

European business gurus, catching up with their U.S. counterparts, rushed their own versions of corporate governance manuals to their publishers with titles reading *Virtuous Management* or variations thereof. They wrote in classic academic terminology: They advocate—or, should I say, preach—the old standby concepts of moral responsibility, human integrity, and personal ethics. These three classics are well known to seasoned executives and have been published, rehashed, reformulated, and PowerPointed a million times in most of the 200 business languages used in the world, so that is not the point.

Responsibility, integrity, and *ethics* need to be brought down from their conceptual pedestal and discussed as workable, practical, and understandable principles. No need to be creative—these principles have been around for a long time. In business, we know them as the virtues of courage, faith, justice, prudence, temperance, love, and hope.

Although the Europeans use the qualifier *virtuous,* they never refer to the virtues themselves or to how the virtues play a major role in business. They give long lists of "how-tos" that are as rigid as the function description for the top job in the company, whatever that function may be called. They describe various forms of corporate structures, either one-tier or two-tier. There is little reference to emotion or personal values. But much ink flows to cover the plusses and minuses of reward systems, particularly those including options or profit sharing for directors. In contrast, this book provides executives with a workable set of intellectual instruments and a methodology to create human values independent of location, language, or working culture. At the end of each chapter is even a list of *questions for thought!*

Self-awareness, self-training, and *self-motivation* based on the seven virtues are what the authors want the reader to take away. Kolp and Rea's research is comforting in the sense that their students acknowledge that virtues are acceptable business guidelines. The hundreds who were interviewed recognize the value of extending these tools to the workplace. They claim that sharing their thoughts in various ways with co-workers is indeed possible and accepted. I still refer to virtues but, in fact, it is the business variant that is used in the workplace: *Temperance* becomes *patience, justice* becomes *fairness* or appropriate behavior, and *hope* is the vision for a brighter future. The virtue that scores the highest is *fortitude* at the top echelon or simply *courage* lower in the management pyramid. But what is in a name? Studies show that even in its simplest version people feel they create value.

I think we can all agree with Alan Kolp and Peter Rea that it is regrettable when American businesses need a set of punitive rules formulated in the Sarbanes-Oxley Act to bring corporate behavior back to the basic rules: *transparency, value creation,* and *benefiting our social environment.*

What does it take to be a CEO or CFO today? In my own definition, and it is not different from that of Kolp and Rea, *CEO* stands for six specific areas of simultaneous performance: the CEO is the *Executive* Officer, the *Ethics* Observer, the *Emotions* Manager, the *Education* Provider, the *Excellence* Achiever, and the *Emancipation* Leader. The CFO is the *Financial* counterpart. He or she is the backbone of the corporation and in the "fail-safe" position; the CFO cannot fail.

In the book, Kolp and Rea summarize the performance qualifiers and principles as *servant leadership*. I personally refer to this definition as Kolp and Rea's rule of *virtuous management*. They brought to my table a simple vision and understanding of "character" and "working with virtues." They make these two components a basic "simple life" formula for success in business, which I fully endorse: "leaders at the service of . . . !" Their definition is not specific to religion or creed. Aristotle wrote 2,000 plus years ago, "Success is reward and happiness."

I agree with Kolp and Rea that each executive and each board member must define success for his or her enterprise. This is a corporate decision, addressing both the substance and the form—the "what" and the "how"—with goals quantified in dollars and cents and objectives qualified in human values for all stakeholders. It is an integral part of the company's vision, mission, and tactics.

The book is a breath of fresh air for the executive mindset and an injection of oxygen into the stench of malfunctioning boardrooms. It is a "how-to" manual for the young executive and the seasoned board member alike, the help button to better ways of doing business.

I am happy and proud to have been asked to summarize my personal assessment of this book in the classic form of a foreword. Hundreds of executives worked for me in five global corporations spread over every country in the United Nations. Today I read and re-read this book as a sort of due diligence to my own experience, and yet, I discovered new ways of thinking. The authors have expressed it all so well. Although their premise is academic, I found their book a thoroughly enjoyable read.

This book is being published as the world rides an unprecedented wave of globalization. It is a relentless tide that cannot be reversed. In the political and social arenas, we witness the struggle of the different ideologies; in business and commerce, we see the Asian vs. Western patterns evolving in favor of the sheer numbers of China. China graduates 300,000 men and women in engineering and business each year. Similar numbers apply to India. The United States may no longer be the biggest, but we can still strive at being the best. It is remarkable that this book is published in the United States, by an Ohio-based private publisher, and written by two visionary academics with the title *Leading with Integrity*.

I am confident that, as you work your way through these pages, you will find your own take-aways and that, for the part of your career that is still ahead of you, you will see yourself as a servant leader. I know you will join me in saying, Alan and Peter, well done!

Pierre Jean Everaert
Chairman
InBev SA/NV, the world's largest brewer

Print Edition and Online Edition

Leading with Integrity is available online as well as in print. The Online Edition chapters demonstrate how the interactive media components of the text enhance presentation and understanding. For example,

- Highlighting capabilities allow you to emphasize main ideas. You can also add personal notes in the margin.
- The search function allows you to quickly locate discussions of specific topics throughout the text.

You may choose to use just the Online Edition, or both the online and print versions together. This gives you the flexibility to choose which combination of resources works best for you. To assist those who use the online and print versions together, the primary heads and subheads in each chapter are numbered the same. For example, the first primary head in Chapter 1 is labeled 1-1, the second primary head in this chapter is labeled 1-2, and so on. The subheads build from the designation of their corresponding primary head: 1-1a, 1-1b, etc. This numbering system is designed to make moving between the Online Edition and the print book as seamless as possible.

Supplements

Atomic Dog is pleased to offer a robust suite of supplemental materials for instructors using its textbooks. These ancillaries include a Test Bank, PowerPoint® Slides, and Instructor's Manual.

The Test Bank for this book includes multiple-choice questions in a wide range of difficulty levels for each chapter. The Test Bank offers not only the correct answer for each question, but also a rationale or explanation for the correct answer and a reference—the location in the chapter where materials addressing the question content can be found.

A full set of PowerPoint Slides is available for this text. This is designed to provide instructors with comprehensive visual aids for each chapter in the book. These slides include outlines of each chapter highlighting important terms, concepts, and discussion points.

The Instructor's Manual for this book offers suggested syllabi for 10- and 14-week terms; lecture outlines and notes; in-class and take-home assignments; recommendations for multi-media resources such as films and websites; and long and short essay questions and their answers, appropriate for use on tests.

Seminars that use the text are offered by contacting the authors:
Alan Kolp—akolp@bw.edu—440-826-2172
Peter Rea—prea@bw.edu—440-826-5918

Acknowledgments

Unlike colleges and universities, life is not lived by departments. There is not a business division, a religion department, and the science departments. Life is interdisciplinary. But life does not just happen. Life comes to each person with different measures of predictability and serendipity. Much happens in life that can be acknowledged, to which there is no thought that thanks might be given. Such is not the case for this book. There was a reason it had to be an interdisciplinary effort. And it is imperative that thanks be given.

The origins of the many conversations giving rise to the book are tragic: September 11, Enron, and other business scandals. These tragedies were not simply problems of evil, with which the philosophy department must deal, or mismanagement, with which the business division copes, or even crimes about which the criminal justice department teaches. All of these tragedies were complex human stories that will continue to be discussed from different angles. We acknowledge these events as originating sources of conversations, but clearly, we do not give thanks to them. But they did bring us together in conversations in which each of us realized that our own discipline and life experiences were insufficient to understand, much less explain, what happened.

We also learned perspective, since recent business scandals are outrageous, in part, because they are unusual. Most leaders see the importance in developing character and competence. The difficult challenge is what this looks like and how do you do it.

Necessarily, any collaborative effort is rooted in acknowledgment and deep appreciation for each other. Truly, neither of us alone could have written this book. So we acknowledge the desire, openness, commitment, discipline, and skills we each brought to the task. In the process, good friends became close friends. Above all, we have developed a deep gratitude for each other.

There are others to whom we extend gratitude. There are a number of business, religious, and civic groups that invited us to explore our thoughts. Baldwin-Wallace College also invited us to try out our ideas in classes and other forums. Particularly, the Forum Groups in the greater Cleveland area were seminal spots for early discussions of our ideas, which were being planted like seeds. We are especially grateful to Gerri Hura and Mary Jean Milanko, from the Professional Development Office at Baldwin-Wallace College, who organized corporate groups for us to lead one-day workshops as we began to cultivate those seeds.

Many individuals helped us with ideas and pushed us to think more clearly about our own ideas. For a number of years, Don Lefelar has been a colleague in our effort to do business ethics. John Gordon has been a good listener and contributor of suggestions. We honor the memory of the late David Hoag, who embodied both the competency and character components herein described.

There are always those behind the scenes without whose help this would not have been possible. Connie Hriczik and Jean Haag were always ready to help. And very special thanks go to Ingrid Schumacher for her gracious support and many contributions.

A deep word of thanks goes to Mary Bolton and Julie Rea, whose tireless willingness to edit the book has made it read as well as it does. Surely, these sisters were co-laborers without whom our effort would be poorer. They offered editorial touches that no doubt saved us undue embarrassment. In our thanks, we also include Letitia Kolp.

We would add appreciation to the five people who supplemented our words with their words of endorsement. Pierre Jean Everaert offers seasoned global perspective in his words from the foreword. Robert Joyce eloquently sums up the book. Ram Charan, Michael Feuer, and Larry Spears all deliver encouraging words on our behalf.

No book would see the light of day without wonderful people working with an incredible publishing company. We thank Steve Scoble, who helped us initiate the process. Kendra Leonard and Lori Bradshaw have given us editorial support for which we are grateful. And Victoria Putman has facilitated production of our effort.

We would like to dedicate the book to our four children . . . our future and the hope of the world. Felicity Kolp already is making a global mark with her concern for the poor and involvement in international human development. Christina Kolp is charting a course in the medical world, where she can express her concern to bring healing and well-being to places of sickness and neglect. Scott and David Rea are in high school and are just starting a journey of competence and character, which will be watched with interest and pride.

As you read this book, may you be guided by the words of the Greek philosopher, Heraclitus: Character is destiny.

Alan Kolp
Peter Rea

Reviewers

Thanks to the reviewers of this text:

- Joanne B. Ciulla, Jepson School of Leadership Studies, University of Richmond
- Belinda Johnson White, Morehouse College
- Param Srikantia, Baldwin Wallace College
- Kelleen Stine-Cheyne, Texas A & M University

ήθική

Introduction: Leading Change through Virtue and Value

Outline

In 2004, Chairman and CEO Jeff Immelt informed General Electric's top 200 corporate officers that the $150 billion company must focus on four priorities to remain on top. Three priorities were expected: execution, growth, and great people. The fourth was a surprise, especially since Immelt rated this priority most important: virtue. Immelt stated that, if GE is to be a great company, it must be a good company.[1] GE has added value to shareholders for decades. It remains to be seen if GE will realize its recent goal to develop virtue.

Increasingly, character is nondiscretionary, since businesses win or lose in the marketplace not just due to leadership that knows how to add value but also due to leaders' self-knowledge and ability to collaborate with teams, partners, and the communities in which they operate. More and more, resolving economic problems requires moral solutions.[2]

Character-based leadership needs constant cultivation, especially in light of the complexity of issues and speed of change that confront business, including, but not limited to, the following examples.

1-1 Globalization and Technology

As global trade barriers have fallen, consumer choice has increased, economies have expanded, and inflation has been checked. Increased global trade has developed wealth in China, East Asia, and parts of Eastern Europe. Globalization has improved health care, has spread democracy, and has raised international efforts to struggle for social justice.[3]

The dramatic drop in the cost of technology has increased the speed in which services are delivered and innovation is promoted. In 1950, approximately 1 million overseas phone calls were initiated from U.S. soil. By 1970, phone calls had increased to 23 million; by 1980, to 200 million; and, by 2001, to 6.3 billion.[4] As information and innovation become more diffused, organizations have to replace command and control hierarchies with decision making close to the customer. In fact, corporations that create cultures which focus on pleasing the boss rather than the customer are certain to fail.[5]

We live in a world that is connected, but being wired is not synonymous with creating a global community. The world comprises communities that are largely parochial in outlook, directed by many leaders who are ill-prepared to operate across cultures. The twin towers of globalization and technology have created a hurry-up ethos, but human relationships and understanding cannot be rushed. At a time when speed to market is vital, how can leaders still devote time to building trust, common understanding, and commitment among diverse cultures, which often are dislocated by economic change?[6]

1-2 Corporate Governance, Transparency, and Integrity

Responsible conduct and accountability are on the line as much as most leaders can recall, making integrity a growth market. In a post–Enron, Sarbanes-Oxley, Internet world, integrity is increasingly nondiscretionary in both the profit and nonprofit sectors. An era of transparency and disclosure requires that integrity define an organization's culture. Simply stated, customers, investors, and employees are attracted to organizations they can trust.

Fraud committed by Enron and WorldCom executives, Martha Stewart's stock transaction cover-up, and Strong Mutual Fund late-day trades and market timing are part of this century's business hall of shame, which erased billions in investor wealth. Executives failed to fulfill their fiduciary responsibility, innocent people lost their jobs, suppliers lost what was owed to them, and legal fees skyrocketed. When accurate disclosure about a firm's financial condition is expected, even a whiff of earnings restatements causes share prices to plummet and CFOs and CEOs to lose their jobs.

The glue that holds the capital markets together is trust and integrity. There is debate as to whether investor trust is restored through post–Enron legislation such as Sarbanes-Oxley, actions by attorneys general such as New York's Eliot Spitzer, or voluntary corporate governance reform recommended by business organizations such as the Conference Board. To avoid guilt by association, businesses have responded to general concerns about integrity by instituting or strengthening codes of conduct. Ironically, many corporations involved in malfeasance even had such codes. Some companies have created ethics hot lines and developed ethics programs. Although these measures have benefit, ultimately we must rely on leadership integrity. Customers, investors, and employees seek leaders who can add value (*competence*) and develop virtue (*character*) while they create new products, enter new markets, and reduce costs.

For the sake of perspective, it is worth noting that corporate scandals make headlines precisely because they are unusual and outrageous. Fraud legislation, which has been around since the Depression, and "don't lie, cheat, or steal" pronouncements provide courts and companies with tools to address ethical lapses. Penalties for unethical behavior are important but fall short of aiding leaders who want to conduct business with integrity.

1-3 Redefining the Social Contract

Multinational corporations shed jobs and a just-in-time workforce is growing. Employers want commitment, but job insecurity reigns. Increasingly, people are choosing self-employment to gain some control over their destiny. Since revenue and profitability are uncertain, often the best an employer can offer are experiences and skill development that will keep an employee marketable, should a layoff become necessary. Mergers, acquisitions, cost containment, and reengineering can be necessary evils to remain competitive, although these strategies create distrust in the workplace. However, trust is fundamental to good relationships and sustainable financial results.[7]

In the name of productivity and profitability, will our version of globalization collapse under the weight of burned-out managers, irate employees, and obsolete technologies?[8] How do we balance inflation indices and poverty indices? Export numbers and the pollution index? Economic growth and dislocated cultures and values?[9]

1-4 Leading Change in a Fragmented World

Leading to execute in a fragmented, globally connected world depends on human networks, not computer networks. Strategic issues confronting organizations are too complex and exceed the abilities of a single person or small group. Leading change must become everybody's business. We all have a vested interest in developing our and others' abilities to lead change guided by character. Leaders in high demand are team players who can coach well and who can operate in a variety of cultures. We must invest in leaders who put people before profits.[10]

In 2004, Jeff Immelt said, "The world has changed. Businesses today aren't admired. Size is not respected. There's a bigger gulf today between haves and have nots than ever before. It's up to us to use our platform to be a good citizen. Because not only is it a nice thing to do, it's a business imperative." Benjamin Heineman, a senior vice president for law and public affairs, believes GE must invest in its reputation, "just as there's good will on balance sheets, and just as brand has value, reputation, broadly defined, has enormous value for companies."[11]

1-5 Character-Based Leadership

People are hungry for spirituality, religion, faith, work/life balance—whatever the name, these words speak to a widely felt desire for meaning and purpose. Virtues are discussed openly and people are concerned about the legacy they are leaving.[12]

Character-based leadership provides guideposts to manage turbulent business situations. Who we are and who we want to become define our approach to leadership. Accordingly, the process of developing leadership is the same as developing character. Character-based leadership is developed by our intentions, by our conduct, by people who influence us, and by our experiences.

Enlightened companies are well aware of the advantages of character-based decision making, but how does an organization implement it? What is missing is a practical, "how-to" guide that demonstrates the ways leaders can develop and integrate competence and character. This book does just that.

1-6 Classical Solutions to Today's Business Issues

Over 30 years ago, Robert Greenleaf proposed the idea of *servant leadership,* a particular view of leadership that means that the best leaders make life better for others.[13] In the same spirit, we invite readers to see how the classical virtues can be applied to contemporary business life in ways that promote servant leadership in business. Although many of the varied business philosophies of the past two decades have much to offer corporate leaders, we have chosen to look back two millennia for wisdom that has stood the test of time. This book is organized around the seven classical virtues: courage, faith, justice, prudence, temperance, love, and hope. Identified by Aristotle and supplemented by many others through the centuries, these virtues serve well as business virtues. They effectively serve business because business is ultimately a social enterprise and ethics is ultimately about our relationships with others. This book applies these virtues to common leadership issues that occur at global, corporate, and individual levels.

As business continues to increase in influence over domestic and global affairs, we desperately need leaders who add value guided by virtue. At its best, the for-profit sector creates jobs; it pays taxes for public services; it provides customer products (some of which we want and others that we need); it creates wealth for shareholders, who use the capital markets to fund college educations, homes, and retirements, as well as to grow nonprofit endowments; it forms productive supplier relationships and provides talent to serve on nonprofit boards and donations that support education, health care, churches, and a host of other public services. In the United States, we depend on corporate servant leadership, guided by character and produced by competence, to be socially, environmentally, and financially responsible.

Our contemporary culture treats character and competence as separate attributes. However, we contend that they are intertwined and cannot be pulled apart. When forcibly separated, traditionally they wind up in disparate disciplines of study. The study of character falls into the arenas of philosophy, religion, and psychology. The study of competence falls into the arenas of business and economics. The goal of this book is to integrate concepts that focus on enduring wisdom (virtue and character) with concepts that focus on contemporary business issues (value and competence). Character is about identity—who we want to be and how we can make a life that is bigger than ourselves. Competence is about action—what we need to know and how we execute our ideas to serve stakeholders.

Leadership education must be broader than that typically offered by undergraduate business, MBA, and executive programs and more practical than that offered by either a business or liberal arts education. Although formal schooling plays an important role, much of servant leadership is learned before we ever go to school, or it is learned afterward in the school of hard knocks.

Barriers to learning character and competence are often a product of self-deception, as much as a dearth of experience or education. Socrates proposed that the goal of life is self-knowledge and that a major barrier to self-knowledge is self-deception. We need trusted advisors, candid feedback, humility, and openness to learning if we hope to develop virtue and add value to today's marketplace.

Although being busy might be the next best thing to having a purpose, the classical virtues provide a practical way to consider the noble aspects of servant leadership in business. These virtues have stood the test of time. Clearly, other virtues and other definitions could be identified, but these seven give a sharp focus to thought about the serious leadership issues of our time. With a little imagination, these seven virtues can be applied to the ethical situations most of us experience daily.

Acquiring some insight into each of these virtues and how multiple virtues need to be balanced gets us to the right questions. And having the right questions is crucial for any effective leader. Effective leaders in any arena are those who lead with purpose (character) and lead in a way that keeps business in business (competence).

Aristotle, 384–322 B.C.E.
The Greek philosopher Aristotle, shown here with his mentor, Plato, is responsible for having influenced thought in regard to ethics, the soul, nature, politics, art, and leadership.
Source: © Ted Spiegel/CORBIS

1-7 Aristotle's Question of Success

George Bernard Shaw wrote, "All our progress is but improved means to unimproved ends."[14] Robert Greenleaf's notion of a servant leader builds on Shaw's notion of an unimproved end. Although business is full of change, management gurus, such as corporate strategy and execution expert Ram Charan, view an individual's character as constant, "an unimproved end."[15]

On its face, the notion of servant leadership is easy to embrace, especially if such leaders make our lives better. Most people do not mind doing a good turn if asked, but it is not without reason that we strive for personal success and its associated comforts. We admire successful people who become leaders in their field. Success provides financial rewards to take care of our families and ourselves. Success provides us with status in our corporation and community, in addition to access to the people and resources needed to maintain or build on our success. However, if the only measure of success is material, ultimately the success will be empty. Certainly, there is value in making a living and enjoying creature comforts.

However, possessions and material well-being alone can distract from the deeper focus of servant leadership.

Aristotle framed the question this way: "how will I make my life a success?" His answer was to choose happiness. Specifically, Aristotle said, "All knowledge and pursuit aims at some good . . . and what is the highest of all goods . . . is happiness."[16] He did not use *happiness* to mean pleasure or contentment. Peter Gomes paraphrases a well-known and often quoted definition of happiness by Aristotle when Gomes says, "the exercise of vital powers along lines of excellence, in a life affording them scope."[17] In fact, Aristotle cautioned that the unchecked pursuit of pleasures would blur our understanding of happiness.

Aristotle did not propose that virtue be used to pursue happiness; rather, happiness occurs as a by-product of doing something worthy— when we do what we are meant to do and when we become who we were meant to be. Aristotle defines success within this context of virtue. An inaugural speech for new Phi Beta Kappa members perceptively interprets Aristotle: "Virtue means that you have to consider your contributions beyond yourself. It starts with respect for the dignity of other people and the appraisal of your action on others. It is also something you can cultivate over many years of honest work and lose in an instant."[18]

Aristotle's warning about distorted success was played out by a Houston company that set off an avalanche of distrust directed at corporate leaders. The leaders of Enron were long on ambition and greed but short on integrity and character. For the sake of perspective, it is useful to remember that corporate scandals are not a new phenomenon and that they do not occur frequently. The temptation to abuse power stretches from the corrupt tax practices of the Roman Empire to the 1980s movie *Wall Street*, which made famous the phrase "greed is good."

The news media are attracted to the bizarre and unusual. They are also quick to publicize corrupt business acts that are sensational because those involved were so brazen in their quest for greed at the expense of their responsibility. For the sake of perspective and accuracy, let us again note that, although scandals are spectacular, they are not normal. In principle, most corporations embrace integrity, honesty, and character. But we should not assume that the principles themselves constitute the corporate culture. Michael Hackworth, CEO of Aspirian Corporation, notes that "many business executives think the culture of their organization is what they *want* it to be."[19]

The difficult question is, "How does a corporation actually create a culture based on character?" Legal compliance, ethics codes, and ethics hot lines are important, but these do not necessarily produce virtue.

Virtue is character, and character is a way of life that must develop over time. The bottom line is that character creates and sustains an ethical culture. Again, Hackworth's words are pointed: "In reality, a company's culture is defined by what the top executives actually do. Employees model—that is, they emulate—their boss's behavior. They do what the boss does because they get paid by the boss, recognized by the boss, and eventually, promoted by the boss. That makes the top leader, *ipso facto,* ultimately responsible for the culture of his organization—including the ethical culture."[20]

Can character be taught? Who we are, what we want to become, and how we serve others are central to teachings in the disciplines of philosophy, religion, and psychology. These fields help us reflect on that which is worthy. But the fact is, most of us probably learned about character through our experiences and through role models—parents, friends, church, mosque, or synagogue, and, to be sure, school. Whatever character we learned is now lived out every day in both our business and personal lives. The good news is that learning does not cease when our formal education is finished. We can continue to learn about virtue and develop character. Although we will never achieve perfection, we can hope to make progress.

Business has a self-interest to promote this kind of lifelong learning. Corporate personnel want to avoid ending up on the front page of *The Wall Street Journal* for financial fraud, consumer deception, environmental degradation, sexual harassment, or contracts with suppliers that use sweatshops. And so, most corporate leaders are *not* corrupt, if only because they understand that no one wants to invest in, buy products from, or sell supplies to someone who cannot be trusted.

1-8 Servant Leadership and Competence

Character is vital, but equally so is the need for competent leadership. A well-intentioned incompetent likely wants to satisfy stakeholders but can be clueless about how to do this. Such ignorance can cause unintended negative consequences, as did inept Willie Loman in Arthur Miller's play *Death of a Salesman,* who just did not know how to get things done.

The acid test of competence is result. A competent leader is capable of adding value to customers, employees, and suppliers, as well as to shareholders and the communities in which the firm operates. A competent leader knows how to execute.

Greenleaf developed his idea of servant leadership because he believed our nation suffered from a crisis in leadership. Too often, governments did not govern, schools did not educate, health care did not make people healthy, churches did not promote a spiritual life, foundations did not build stronger communities, and businesses did not create wealth in ways that served the communities in which they operated. Although the role of leadership has always determined a society's quality of life, in the past 100 years we have come increasingly to rely on institutions and, therefore, on institutional leaders.

Prior to the twentieth century, most people were farmers, merchants, or professionals operating in communities where the role of government was quite small. Today quality of life is determined by the quality of leadership in our colleges, governments, hospitals, places of worship, schools, and foundations, as well as in the for-profit sector. Business leadership is significant, as communities depend on the profit sector to create jobs, pay taxes for public services, create wealth for shareholders, provide good products and services to customers, develop strong supplier relationships, and provide leadership and resources to nonprofit boards, all while fulfilling their social responsibilities to take care of the planet and to treat their stakeholders ethically.

The 1990s were a golden era for business, as the stock market climbed to unprecedented levels, jobs were created, tax revenues soared, and the corporate world became a source of answers to the problems of poor schools and poor governments. If the nonprofit and government sectors were ineffective, many believed this could be resolved if only they were "operated more like a business." In other words, business leaders were presumed to be competent and would make a difference.

Whether the shift in public opinion was just or unjust, as the twenty-first century opened, the business world was tainted with distrust. The names of Enron, WorldCom, and Tyco all came to mean "serve yourself," rather than servant leadership. In these cases, leaders appeared all too competent in serving their personal interests, while revealing serious questions about their character. Boards, regulators, and the media flunked the competence test in their oversight responsibilities. Even though they did not benefit personally from their own incompetence, they failed to execute their responsibilities.

As was the case with character, so we should ask about competence: can it be taught? Even though competence presupposes innate talent and ability that cannot be taught, various competencies can be taught. When we talk about "making a living," we usually have in mind the arena of business. A viable business depends on competence—the ability to add value to stakeholders. Libraries are full of books and universities are replete with courses on strategy and leadership development. A similar wealth of wisdom is offered in organizational structure, incentive systems, business process design, succession planning, culture change, accounting, finance, and marketing. Competencies can be learned.

Thus, how is it that many well-intentioned leaders fail to deliver results? Execution is not only the biggest issue facing business today; it is also largely an unexamined issue. Competence is easier to learn than to put into practice. Again, simply knowing something does not mean acting on that knowledge. If character is currently the unimproved end, then, for genuine progress to be made, competence must be the improved means.

Leadership is essential to corporate success and extraordinarily rewarding to those who can get things done. Leadership can also be exhausting and sometimes even dangerous to the leader. Those who are threatened by change can lash out at the one leading the charge to change. The litmus test of effective leadership is skill at introducing and managing change. Virtue and character provide leadership with moorings from which to navigate the problems inherent in leading change. Adding value or competence is the acid test of whether leaders can move beyond intentions to deliver results. The inspirational compass to guide business has virtue and character as its true north. The commitment and capacity to serve others requires perspiration and competence.

1-9 Barriers to Individual Servant Leadership

Character is a way of living and is concerned more with what we do than with what we think. Impediments to ethical conduct include "blind spots"—it is easier to see the fault in others than to see the flaws in oneself. We also can underestimate our strengths or competencies. The point of an executive development tool, such as a 360-degree evaluation, is to help us see ourselves as others see us. As mentioned earlier, Socrates cautioned that, although the goal of life is self-knowledge, the barrier to this goal is self-delusion. Langdon Gilkey, Sigmund Freud, and a multitude of other theologians, philosophers, and psychologists warn against our creative capacity to deceive ourselves and rationalize our behavior, while others see us as self-serving. In other words, we all have a "lawyer within," who argues our own case, which can make us oblivious to our blind spots.

We need discernment to combat self-delusion, so that we can see the difference between fleeting satisfactions that distort the meaning of success and sustaining virtues that can see us through difficult times. Harvard Professor Peter Gomes distinguishes between issues of worth and issues of success in a chosen field. Gomes warns us with the 1914 observation of Harvard President Lowell that the world is full of people who have what they want but are neither happy nor satisfied.[21]

If our blind spots are the initial impediments to servant leadership, surely individual and corporate busyness is a close second as a barrier. "Being busy" is seldom an end in itself, but it often corrodes the end human beings seek. Most of us would say the point of life is that it has meaning or purpose. Busyness does not guarantee a meaningful life; in fact, it often erodes the attainment of a meaningful life. According to Gilkey, the phrase "meaning in life" is best understood when we "take it to refer simply to a sense of wonderful purpose in what we do and the life we lead. A man possesses a sense of 'meaning' when he feels there is a vital connection between the goals he values and the activities and relationships in which he is involved."[22]

Perhaps the trick is to differentiate being busy from engaging in busyness. Typically, being busy is important, as we seek to make meaning in life. Much of our early life is busy developing character and acquiring basic skills, knowledge, and experience to become competent. We create goals in life, engage in activities, and develop relationships—which, we hope, to use Gilkey's words, give us "a sense of wonderful purpose."

However, we all know how easy it is to slip from being busy into engaging in busyness. Our life goals become lost or set too high. Instead of getting where we wanted to go, we begin to feel that life has become a treadmill. In busyness, our activities drain us instead of sustain us. They begin to seem less like nurture and more like torture. If we persist in this high level of meaningless activity, relationships that were initially inviting and energizing become as lifeless as a creek dried up in summer's heat. The channel may remain, but there is no flow of vitality.

1-10 Barriers to Corporate Servant Leadership Built on Character and Competence

Although most people can express what they personally believe, it is uncommon for businesspersons to express clearly why and how they live out their virtues in a corporate setting. Usually, an emphasis on profitability is far clearer to employees than ideas about virtue. Ask businesspeople how they learn about their corporation's virtues and they will respond with stories, symbols, and names of leaders who reveal the sometimes unwritten priorities. Beyond a moral imperative to include virtue as part of profitability goals, good businesses see a practical benefit of adding virtue: everyone wants to invest in, buy from, and work for companies that can be trusted.

1-11 The Clarion Call

Over 2,000 years ago, Aristotle laid the foundation for liberal arts education by asserting that ethics involved developing character. The process of ethical formation provides individuals with a clear moral compass—and the seven classical virtues serve well as such a compass. A liberal arts education teaches how to live a worthy life through virtue and character. A business education teaches how to make a living by adding value and acquiring competence.

The connection between developing character and adding value is rarely explicit, but the purpose of this book is to illustrate to students, executives, and people in general how to see the links between virtue and their daily business and personal experiences. There is no foolproof method of teaching character-based leadership. However, with a proper introduction, the development of character can be applied to contemporary business issues in a way that is relevant and time-tested.

Character-based leadership flows from who we are and how we express our character. Case studies are valuable for learning about ethical problems, but if they are used exclusively the treatment of ethics begins to feel like an intellectual abstraction, providing no clear guidance in how to live a meaningful life. Ethics is learned more from life experiences than from classroom experiences. However, a classroom can help us reflect on and practice the role that awareness and discipline play in responding to barriers that inhibit the development of character. The details of how to close the gap from unawareness to awareness, from awareness to attention, and then from attention to action will be addressed throughout this book. However, whatever method is used, the point is to recognize that character does not happen by accident.

Consider the WorldCom fiasco. On one hand are the leaders, CEO Bernard Ebbers and CFO Scott Sullivan, and on the other middle manager Cynthia Cooper, an auditor and one of three *Time* magazine 2002 "Persons of the Year." In an interview, a *Time* editor asked Cooper, "If the culture comes from the top, how is it that you three didn't fall prey to it?" Cooper reflected this way: "I think it comes back to value and ethics that you learn through your life. My mother has been a tremendous influence on me."[23] Cooper's next words serve as a clarion call to all: "There's a responsibility for all Americans—teachers, mothers, fathers, college professors, corporate people—to help and make sure the moral and ethical fabric of the country is strong."[24]

Chapter Quiz

1. Which of the following is *not* one of the seven classical virtues?
   a. courage
   b. harmony
   c. prudence
   d. faith
2. Which of the following philosophers identified the seven classical virtues?
   a. Kant
   b. Mills
   c. Aristotle
   d. Socrates
3. The study of character falls into all of the following areas of study *except*
   a. philosophy.
   b. business.
   c. religion.
   d. psychology.
4. Which of the following philosophers proposed that the goal of life is self-knowledge and that a major barrier to self-knowledge is self-deception?
   a. Mills
   b. Kant
   c. Socrates
   d. Aristotle
5. According to Aristotle, which of the following is true about virtue?
   a. It is used to pursue happiness.
   b. It is a by-product of happiness.
   c. It creates happiness.
   d. It is tangentially related to happiness.
6. According to Hackworth, who defines a company's culture?
   a. employees
   b. management
   c. top executives
   d. corporate board
7. Which of the following is true about competence?
   a. It can never be taught.
   b. It can always be taught.
   c. Some of it can be taught.
   d. It can be taught only if character is present.

8. What is the biggest barrier leaders face in terms of delivering results?
   a. employee confusion
   b. employee fellowship
   c. strategy coherence
   d. strategy execution

9. Character is most concerned with which of the following?
   a. action
   b. thought
   c. result
   d. motive

10. According to Gilkey, humans possess a sense of meaning when there is a connection between which of the following?
    a. goals and results
    b. goals and activities
    c. results and activities
    d. results and relationships

Note: You can find the correct answers to these questions by taking the quiz and then submitting your answers in the Online Edition. The program will automatically score your submission. If you miss a question, the program will provide the correct answer, a rationale for the answer, and the section number in the chapter where the topic is discussed.

Web Exercises

Visit the Martha Stewart corporate website (http://www.marthastewart.com/page.jhtml?type=page-cat&id=cat18819) and take a look at some of the information provided on corporate governance, including the Code of Business Ethics and Conduct (http://media.corporate-ir.net/media_files/irol/96/96022/CorpGov/Conduct.pdf). What kinds of leadership values are present? Are any missing? Early in the Code, it states, "If an applicable law conflicts with a policy in this Code, you must comply with the law; however, if a local or foreign custom or policy conflicts with this Code, you must comply with the Code." What do you think this indicates about the company's view of servant leadership and the other topics introduced in this chapter?

Visit http://www.sarbanes-oxley.com and select two or three stories posted there that interest you. What kinds of barriers to servant leadership do you find in these examples?

Endnotes

1. Marc Gunther, "Money and Morals," *Fortune*, November 15, 2004.
2. Warren Bennis and Joan Goldsmith, *Learning to Lead* (Boston: Basic Books, 2003), xii–xv.
3. James Kouzes and Barry Posner, *Leadership Challenge* 3rd ed, (San Francisco: Jossey-Bass, 2002), xx–xxi.
4. Henry Mintzberg, *Managers, Not MBAs: A Hard Look at the Soft Practice of Managing and Management Development* (San Francisco: Barrett-Koehler Publishing, Inc., 2003), 153.
5. Joseph Stiglitz, *Globalization and its Discontents,* (New York: Norton, 2003), 216.
6. Ibid., 214.
7. John Gordon. *An Empire of Wealth: The Epic History of American Economic Power,* (New York: Harper Collins, 2004), 404–05.
8. Ram Charan and Jerry Unseem, "Why Companies Fail," *Fortune*, May 27, 2002, 53.
9. Kouzes and Posner, xx–xxi.
10. Ibid.
11. Gunther, 2–3
12. Kouzes and Posner, xx–xxi.
13. Larry C. Spears and Michelle Lawrence, ed. *Practicing Servant Leadership: Succeeding Through Trust, Bravery, and Forgiveness* (San Francisco: Jossey-Bass, 2004), 11.
14. Peter J. Gomes, *The Good Life: Truths That Last in Times of Need* (San Francisco: HarperSan Francisco, 2002), 3.
15. Charan and Unseem, 53.
16. Aristotle, "Nichomachean Ethics," *The Basic Works of Aristotle,* ed. Richard McKeon (New York: Random House, 1941), 937.
17. Gomes, 58.
18. Ibid., 43.
19. Michael Hackworth, "Only the Ethical Survive: Leadership in Fairness and Honesty Makes Good Business Sense," *Issues in Ethics* (Markkula Center for Applied Ethics, Santa Clara) 10, no. 2 (1999): 11.
20. Ibid.
21. Gomes, 3.
22. Langdon Gilkey, *Shantung Compound: The Story of Men and Women under Pressure* (New York: Harper & Row, 1975), 193.
23. Richard Lacayo and Amada Ripley, "Persons of the Year: Coleen Rowley, Cynthia Cooper, Sherron Watkins," *Time*, December, 30 2002–January 6, 2003. http://www.time.com/time/personoftheyear/2002/poyintro.html#.
24. Ibid.

ήθική

Character

2

Outline

Cynthia Cooper of WorldCom, Sherron Watkins of Enron, and Colleen Rowley of the FBI were selected by *Time* Magazine in 2002 as "Persons of the Year." The front cover identified them in bold letters: "The Whistle-blowers."[1] This is an apt description.

A whistleblower is someone who reveals a wrong. This is its powerful function for business ethics, but it is also a limitation. One would like to assume that most people involved in business are not doing wrong things, because basically they are good people. Typically, good people do not need any more knowledge. The real question is whether they have the courage of conviction to act on what they know is "right" or "good." Generally, most people think they know what is "right" or "wrong." And they claim they know the difference between "good" and "bad." In a word, they say they have character. One might ask how many "good" people not directly involved in Enron's or WorldCom's fraud knew others were wrong but failed to act the way Cooper and Watkins did. Perhaps the word whistle-blower too often means "snitch" or "rat." This is unfortunate since the word should define courage and responsibility.

Can you imagine leaders making any other statement than they want people of good character who do the right thing? The company might attempt to "produce" good business characters by teaching them ethics. Certainly, this is not bad and probably is effective in many instances. However, not all businesspeople take ethics classes. And every teacher knows that, just because students or executives took a class, it does not mean they learned everything in the class. In the same vein, just because people complete an ethics class, it does not mean they are ethical.

As already suggested, ethics and character can be taught. But the teaching typically happens in the world's classroom, rather than in an educational building. Indeed, it is more appropriate if we say that character is "formed" and teaching is one aspect of this formation. Character formation is closer to learning ethics than most people think.

2-1 Looking Backward to Go Forward

In choosing character-based leadership, we place ourselves on an ancient path. Management fads come and go, but the way character will be discussed in this book can be traced back to Aristotle, Plato, and Socrates.

Character always involves ethics; indeed, character is ethics. The Greek word for "ethics" (*ethos*) can be translated as "character." In addition, *ethos* also means "custom, manners, habit." Seeing this connection enables one to understand that ethics should not be reduced simply to an issue of behavior, sometimes encapsulated in a list of "do's and don't's." Rather, ethics is one's character that is expressed in the world.

Character is more than behavior; character is one's way of both being *and* doing in the world. This is why, when we use English, it is a richer discussion to talk about character than ethics. Usually, ethics denotes an act or action. It tends to be limited to ethical concerns. But character entertains not only the question "What do I do?" but also the equally important question "Who am I?" This is why we want to explore character, rather than simply ethics (although in the Greek language they are one and the same).

Character is not an abstract concept. Abstract concepts are created by bright, creative minds, which are to be celebrated but which also need to be grounded. In his book *The Secular Mind,* Harvard psychiatrist Robert Coles narrates his fascinating visit in 1973 to the Covington, Louisiana, home of physician-novelist Percy Walker. Walker was a man with an amazing mind, but he cautioned, "The abstract mind feeds on itself, takes things apart, leaves in its wake all of us, trying to live a life, get from the here of now, today, to the there of tomorrow."[2] Walker's last phrase is the crux of the matter: all of us are "trying to live a life." That is a given. And character is simply a way of describing how every one of us can best "get from the here of now, today, to the there of tomorrow." Doing that with character is not always a given.

One further comment from Walker suggests why character and ethics are bound together when talking about people trying to live a life—in business, at home, and in the community. "Let me try this on you: we ought to stop, every once in a while, and ask ourselves who we think we are. I'm not just talking about 'existentialism,' here; I think I'm talking about moral self-examination—as in exactly who do you think you *are!*"[3] Clearly, by "moral self-examination" Walker means more than "what" we do in the world or even "how" we do it. He means, as he says, "exactly who do you think you are?" This is a character question.

"Who" we are is our character. Once more, if we go to the root meaning of character, much is revealed about how we "get" character. The English word is a transliteration of the Greek word *charakter.* We can note the verb for character means to "cut, notch, engrave, or impress." This verb tells us that no person comes with character as a finished product. Rather, character is formed—we are notched and impressed. Character is made, not inherited. We are not born with it, it develops. From our birth, various ways of looking at our world and understanding our place in it are cut into the fabric of our being. Ways of being and acting are impressed upon us from a variety of sources. Quite literally, we *become*—our character "comes to be."

2-2 Classical Virtues

Aristotle summarized character formation in his opening words on ethics: "Every art and every inquiry, and similarly every action and pursuit, is thought to aim at some good."[4] Simply put, character formation is the making of good people. When we are taught character, we learn about our *ethos,* our ethics.

Students and executives can tell stories about ethical and unethical leaders who have shaped them. They understand the need for integrity and ethical conduct. However, they are less likely to be clear about the meaning of virtue. This observation implicates the classical virtues as the beginning point for teaching character.

We offer seven marks of character, the seven classical virtues—courage, faith, justice, prudence, temperance, love, and hope—to understand aspects of character. They provide focus for both our personal life and our corporate life, because they profoundly describe a way of life. They can shape how we relate to others with whom we work or help us change the way we relate to others.

Courage is the beginning place, because without it nothing would be done and no risk taken. The word *courage* is rooted in the French for "heart," *coeur.* This can be pushed back to Latin, *cor,* which also means "mind" or "soul." This is not simply philosophy class stuff; it is also the stuff of the business world—or it should be. Lubrizol is a multinational corporation with over $3 billion in sales. Lubrizol's *Ethical and Legal Conduct Guidelines* defines the price of moral courage: "do what is right even when it is likely to cost us more than we want to pay and more than we think is fair. It occasionally requires us to stand up and be counted . . . to demonstrate the courage of our convictions."[5] Lubrizol says it is not enough simply to be competent; we must also have character. However, we are wiser about managing risks successfully if we are competent. When we have previously managed trouble, we instill courage in others and ourselves.

Faith is trusting something or someone. Faith transcends the individual; it vests us in something or someone outside ourselves. The Latin words for "faith" (*fides* and *fiducia*) clearly point to its role in business. Bearing one's fiduciary responsibility is more than an economic or legal duty—it is an act of character. To be without character can lead to corporate actions that land one both on the front page and in jail. Corporate leaders who demonstrate they can add value for shareholders (competence) must also be trusted (character) to attract capital. Who wants to invest in a company led by management that cannot be trusted?

When fiduciary responsibilities are not met, shareholders demand justice. "Law and justice" is often thought of as a legal issue, which it is. But justice is primarily seen as virtue, as a dimension of character. As virtue, then, justice develops in legal, political, and religious directions. Hence, law derives from justice or, better, expresses what is just.

Two terms take us to the core meaning of justice. The first term is *fair*. Justice is always concerned with "what is fair." The other term comes from the Latin word *aequus,* "equal." Servant leaders struggle with equality issues that have to do with impartiality and evenness. To be just does not mean every person has to have the same portion, but there has to be a fairness. Executive compensation, affirmative action, equal opportunity, and reduction in workforces are all justice issues.

Some people will appropriately be paid more than others, but how can these decisions be made fairly? On what basis and according to whom do we conclude stock options, as an example, are warranted? The virtue justice should guide the purpose of decisions such as executive compensation. However, competence is also needed to understand the complexity of executive compensation plans.

The fourth virtue is prudence. Ironically, *prudence* used today might more readily describe the economic manager than the virtuous person. A quick look at the Latin words behind this term, *prudens* and *prudentitia,* show that they can translate as "sensible, reasonable; foresight and common sense." In the business world it would be hard to find a more prudent person (in virtue and value sense) than Warren Buffett. In 1965, if you had invested $10,000 in Buffett's company, Berkshire, you would have earned $500,000 by 1999.[6] These results demonstrate that Buffett's investment competence is to be prudent.

Prudence is linked closely to the fifth virtue, temperance, which means moderation, balance, and self-control. It is rooted in the Latin *tempus,* meaning "time, season, right time." A creative way to bring the virtue of temperance into play as an aspect of creating value is the Balanced Scorecard (BSC), developed by Kaplan and Norton to find the balance among seemingly contradictory stakeholder aspirations. Temperance requires extraordinary competence to execute strategies that satisfy customers, owners, employees, suppliers, and other business stakeholders.

Within the business world, the sixth virtue, love, can be scary or irrelevant, unless, as we suggest, it has the perspective of care, compassion, and mercy. The Latin for "care," *cura,* also means "concern, attention" as well as "supervision." Other words for care are *sollicitudo* and *diligo,* meaning "diligence." A virtuous person is a caring person—compassion and mercy add nuances to care. Outplacement services and severance packages are acts of compassion to employees who lose their jobs for reasons beyond their control. The practical benefit is that laid-off workers who are treated well are less likely to sue the company, and those who remain have more faith they will be treated well, should they be the next to go. Mergers and acquisitions often fail to enhance shareholder wealth, at least in part due to employees' focusing on pleasing their boss to preserve their job rather than focus on serving customers. It is not without reason that employees will focus on self-preservation if they conclude no one is looking out for their interests.

Compassion also requires competence, as illustrated in the research on *emotional intelligence,* which we will later cite. Interpersonal skill and the capacity to read others' emotions, to regulate our emotions, and to demonstrate empathy are competencies needed to create a high-performance team.

Hope, the final virtue, is the lure of the future, the pull of the potential, and hope is always realistic. If it is fantastic (a fantasy), investors should watch their wallets. Hope is expectation, often with appropriate apprehension. It is easy to see how this may lead back to other virtues, such as prudence and temperance. Real hope is always confident. Confidence counterbalances apprehension. A well-formulated strategy is built on realistic hope that the company can achieve a more prosperous future built on its "core competencies."

2-3 Teaching Character

Having determined *what* is to be taught, we now determine *where* character is taught. There are two simple answers. First, and most important, character is taught everywhere. Every encounter and experience has the potential positively to form character—or to cause malformation. Such encounters and experiences tend to be informal. Second, character is taught more formally as an ethics component of any class. It might be an undergraduate philosophy class, an MBA business ethics class, or an executive seminar.

Ask folks in a group to describe where and how they learned ethics and rarely will the answer be "in the classroom." This does not mean the classroom is unimportant; rather, it means that the classroom is not the first place for learning character. Nor is it the sustaining learning place for ethics.

Think how much character is taught before kindergarten or even pre-school. Imagine all the "teachers" we have before we encounter our first classroom teacher. When we are young, we do not get lectures, but there are lessons all over the place. People learn ethics as part of early character development. They share stories of their parents' teaching and modeling. They talk about the influence of grandparents, as well as neighbors, friends, and bosses who model behavior. For some, a church, synagogue, or mosque had a significant *forming* influence. Sometimes they talk about when they were tested and how they responded.

Basically, character is *formed*. To be sure, it includes information, but it is more than intellectual knowledge. Forming character, then, is ethically "notching" or "marking" a person.

When ethics is taught in the classroom, often the formation comes by information. We learn ethical principles, such as "treat others as you want to be treated," and we use case studies to demonstrate real-life complexities and how to think ethically. But this can get tricky. We must always remember that knowledge does not necessarily lead to good action. Perhaps most of us have personally experienced the discrepancy of knowing the good while being "up to no good."

Adrian van Kaam distinguishes *informative thinking* from *formative thinking*.[7] Informative thinking has to do with information. No doubt, a tremendous amount of learning takes place because of the information we receive. But information is not necessarily "formative." For example, every MBA program teaches students how to "formulate" strategy or how to set a future direction for an enterprise. Strategy formulation includes an analytical approach with a focus on competitive advantage and a qualitative approach about creating a shared sense of team and why people resist change. Although information about formulating strategy is helpful, it does not prepare us for the challenges leaders confront in executing a strategy. This information does not help leaders realize how the responsibility of setting and executing strategy will change them and the way people relate to them. Knowing how to formulate a strategy is different from thinking and acting strategically. Information alone does not always make a difference in who we are.

Formation, on the other hand, always makes a difference in who we are and what we do. Formation has to do with the way our world and people in our world shape and mold us. We are never a finished product. Even if we seem to have it together, we have to keep it together. "Deformed" would be an appropriate way to describe how we lost it, or maybe never had it.

All of us know what we mean when we say something is deformed. Often, deformation has to do with physical appearance. But deformation also applies to the nonphysical. A "bad character" literally is a character who has been deformed. From the perspective of good or right, it is not normal. It is quite possible to be competent in business but deformed in character. In fact, the competent leader who lacks character is capable of causing great harm. Such leaders may know how to formulate and execute strategies—how to get people to do what they want—but are deformed in their character.

The goal is to become a person of character, rather than a person who knows ethical principles. Principles are important but, too often, teaching ethics becomes simply an informational exercise. As important as it may be to teach students and executives about issues such as sexual harassment, sustainable economic development, and financial disclosure, the deeper question is "How do we develop character?" To know the good does not necessarily mean that we do the good. People with character do the good.

2-4 Leadership and Culture

Much of what forms us is not a matter of choice. Our character formation begins with the culture into which we are born. In their classic work, *Habits of the Heart,* Robert Bellah, et al., acknowledge "So long as it is vital, the cultural tradition of a people—its symbols, ideals and ways of feeling—is always an argument about the meaning of the destiny its members share. Cultures are dramatic conversations about things that matter to their participants."[8] Those of us who live in the United States are culturally formed with an "American character," which is different from a European or Chinese character. And there are subcultures within the American culture—for instance, black, Hispanic, New England, and southern cultures. In fact, there are subcultures within every nation. For example, Brazil has enormously different regional cultures. Wealth in the southern part of Brazil is similar to Belgium, and poverty in the northeastern region is similar to India; in fact, Brazil is sometimes renamed "Belinda." Each of these subcultures has its own symbols, ideals, and ways of feeling. These necessarily are learned, but seldom do we sign up for a class in order to learn them.

Corporate culture is vital to strategic success, since there are both healthy and unhealthy cultures. *Corporate culture* is a short-cut for describing the way of life in a particular business. Specific corporate cultures also have their symbols, ideals, and ways of feeling. To go to work for a particular business means beginning another formation process—an enculturalization. An entrepreneurial culture, for example, forms people to be innovative, to think like owners and not like employees, to manage the business and not assets. Surely, the culture in Silicon Valley is different from that of many Fortune 500 corporations or nonprofit organizations.

This is not the place to describe and analyze the idea of corporate culture as it is manifested in the way of life of a particular business. *Corporate* comes from the Latin *corpus, corporis,* which translate as "body, individual, or person." Hence, we all know that the business company is a "corporation"—that is, it is the individual body. IBM is a different body (corporation) than Dell. A corporation has character, just the same as an individual. Furthermore, the company character goes a long way in determining the corporate culture.

In an earlier era, every company, or corporation, had a "soul" or a "heart." And people knew what that meant. Although important, if economic gain and individual success are the only descriptions of character, then we lose sight of the historic way to lead a life of character. If leaders feel the pressure to perform and rationalize that they are only enhancing shareholder wealth or their own, then the results are companies like Enron, which lost any sense of what it means to lead with character. Again, it might make sense to say Enron lost its soul.

Kevin Rollins, CEO of Dell
As the head of Dell, Inc., Rollins worked to create a company with a clear conscience.
Source: Courtesy of Dell Inc.

Indeed, this book relies on a classical education that is centuries old to form character. And it shows that character formation—individual or corporate—always has to do with soul and heart. That this direction makes sense is captured in a *Nightly Business Review* interview with the CEO of Dell, Inc., Kevin Rollins. This segment of the show stated, "Rollins sat down with New York Bureau Chief Scott Gurvey to talk about Dell and its program to create an ethical and successful corporate culture, called the soul of Dell."[9] Rollins noted that "the soul of Dell" will be the concern in the future for every responsible, competent company. The corporation that has lost its soul also loses its sense of responsibility and that is exactly what Rollins recognized in the interview. Corporations depend on leaders and employees alike to take responsibility and act on character. Leaders cannot do it alone. Rollins said, "Clearly in light of what has gone on the last couple years, that there's no way that Michael (Dell) and I can be responsible for everything that goes on in the company."[10] The key is that all of Dell's employees assume responsibility for the corporation's conduct—the character of Dell's culture. As we will see later in this chapter, responsibility develops as the key manifestation of character.

Rollins elaborated on the connection between responsibility and culture: "But if we engage all, you know, 40,000 of our people and empower them to be responsible, they'll keep us safe and keep us clean and pristine as a company. And so it's part of the soul of Dell, the winning culture."[11] Interestingly, Rollins did not call the 40,000 people "employees." Certainly, there is nothing wrong with the language of "employee." But if one thinks more in terms of "people," one has a better sense that people also have souls and that soul is the heart of character. And character is what results in responsibility.

It is also fascinating that the one thing Rollins and Dell think they can do with 40,000 people is to empower them—to empower them to be responsible. Clearly, this is presumptive. But the presumption is not whether these leaders can make the people responsible. Rather, Rollins and Dell have to presume that the people already are—or will become—people of character, because only if they are people of character will they likely choose to be responsible. Based on this presumption, then, the two leaders can empower.

Scott Gurvey noted that Dell was already doing much of the reporting work required by Sarbannes-Oxley and other legislation. "Yes, we really had," said Rollins. "In fact, we started the soul of Dell prior to a number of the corporate scandals. . . . But it was very good timing to reinforce the value of ethical behavior, living to a code of conduct, to a higher standard, as we call it."[12] The really good news here is that Dell Computer was not born with soul; Rollins claimed it was the people who "started the soul of Dell." So can every corporation and every person become a soulful one. That is what this book is all about: character formation and soul making.

In fact, character formation and soul making are two of the chief tasks of leadership. As much as at any other time in history, our post–Enron world demands a connection between leadership and character and between leadership and ethics. This is exemplified in an article by Nannerl O. Keohane, ex-president of Duke University, who was instrumental in establishing the Center on Leadership and Ethics at Duke. She says leadership "manifests itself in three types of behavior . . . as problem-solving, as making things happen and as taking a stand."[13] It is the last type of behavior that is relevant here: leadership as taking a stand. Keohane elaborates: "We need good ways to help leaders understand the robust value of ethics in leadership, not as an add-on, but as an essential component of success."[14]

Finally, Keohane makes the connection that is at the heart of this book—namely, the connection between leadership and character. She affirms that "character, whether in leadership or life more generally, means taking responsibility for what we know to be true." She adds that "leaders cannot be like scouts, way out in front of the rest. . . . But leaders must be willing to be visibly in the vanguard, in touch with their followers but able to act on conviction, even when not everyone in the organization agrees with them."[15]

Although most corporations have mission statements, few employees know what they say and fewer still act on them. Johnson and Johnson's use of its credo to respond to the Tylenol crisis is more the exception than the rule. Johnson and Johnson set the standard in corporate responsibility in pulling Tylenol from the shelf when a killer had laced the product with cyanide. Johnson and Johnson put people before profit.

The struggle is to close the gap between pronouncements and responsible conduct. Awareness is about knowing what is right, and discipline is about doing what is right. The quest is to figure out how to cultivate a culture in which our words become our deeds. Leaders shape and develop business culture by incorporating what they know to be true: responsibly acting on conviction. That is leadership from and with character.

2-5 Character and Culture Formation

Each individual is formed by a number of cultures, from his or her country of origin to the family into which he or she is born. All of these cultures have a kind of formative destiny: to be a white male born in the U.S. Midwest means to be an American, but not exactly the same kind of American as a Chinese-American female born in San Francisco. But eventually, both may wind up working for the same company in the Silicon Valley.

Our formative cultures are shapers of our identity and even destine us in particular ways. However, they do not predestine us. Everyone has choices.

Victor Frankl survived three years in a Nazi death camp. As he expected, people who were treated like animals behaved like animals. What was less clear was, when someone was hungry, why would he or she share food? When someone was cold, why would he or she share a blanket? He observed that those who responded well to their horrible ordeal were not necessarily wealthier or more educated, more sophisticated, more cultured, or even more religious.

Frankl concluded that being responsible is the essence of human existence. For example, by taking responsibility for our life, Frankl showed that we can demonstrate optimism in the face of tragedy by turning suffering to achievement and guilt to change for the better. It is always possible to determine what is a responsible action. Our struggle is always for a worthy goal, rather than a tensionless state. Our meaning is not given with our identity, but it is made out of real-life experience. If we know the "why" of our existence, we can bear almost any "how." He believed that what matters is not what we expect from life but, rather, what life expects of us. Ultimately, life is about finding the right thought and right action in our circumstances in a moment. Frankl said that everything can be taken from us except one thing: our final freedom to choose our attitude and our response to any circumstance we confront.[16]

Our character is never finally "made," inasmuch as we are always in process. Even though it sounds awkward, every person is "self-making." This recognizes that our learning—our forming—is never done until our death-day.

A core part of our character formation is the way we act. Character is more than who we are; it is also what we do. And this is the ethical aspect: character expressed. If character is our lifelong "self-making," our ethical behavior is also always in process. Of course, habits are part of the process. Habits are nothing more than acts repeated over time in predictable ways without forethought. In a sense, habits are destiny. But habits are not pre-destination; they can always be altered or even eliminated.

In fact, our ability to reason morally develops as we mature. Lawrence Kohlberg's three levels of moral reasoning reveal how we develop our critical thinking to resolve ethical dilemmas through maturation and education:

1. *Pre-conventional.* At this level, most children, many adolescents, and some adults see the world as black-or-white, right or wrong; authority figures know what is best, given the situation. Eventually, individuals start to look out for their own interests. They conclude that, if people are nice and obedient to authority, they can get what they want.

2. *Conventional.* At this level, adolescents and adults look to cultural norms for moral guidance. People's moral reasoning is largely

defined by others' expectations. The goal is to win approval from others by being "good." Rules are followed to maintain social order.

3. *Post-conventional.* At this level, moral reasoning is based on a personal code. The emphasis is no longer on external forces, such as punishment, reward, or social roles. People adhere to a social contract that benefits others, although this contract is abandoned when rules do not serve others. This evolves to a universal code of ethics, such as justice and compassion.[17]

Kohlberg's stages demonstrate that, as we grow, we have more experiences and become more experienced. Our world gets bigger, the questions get harder, and the decisions often get more complex. As leadership responsibility increases, leaders must satisfy an increasing number and a more complex group of stakeholders. As responsibilities grow, leaders make bigger and bigger decisions, often with less and less information, that impact more and more people. Furthermore, political posturing, a lack of appreciation among staff for the strategic import of a given decision, and the sheer volume of decisions that have to be made in a given day all conspire to limit the information available to leaders. Courage and confusion are common leader experiences. Leaders end up with decisions that others do not want to make because the decision will take courage or because the answer is unclear.

One time-honored place where leaders can develop their moral reasoning is the college classroom. Most colleges and graduate programs have courses in ethics. It is becoming more difficult for any graduate to get an MBA or M.D. without taking at least one course in business ethics or medical ethics. These classes teach both ethical content and moral reasoning.

There is much to be said for this approach. Knowledge is a crucial component of character development. Although this book takes an approach different from that of a traditional ethics course, it is important to have some sense of the content of a traditional approach. As a way to lead into the importance of responsible leadership, we will briefly examine the two traditional ways of teaching ethics, organized with the metaphors of root and fruit. Neither opposes our approach to teaching ethics as a component of character formation; to the contrary, character formation includes understanding ethics from both metaphorical perspectives.

2-6 Ethics As Root of Character: Deontology

The metaphor of root to describe the relationship of ethics and character means that one understands ethics to originate from deep within each person. Indeed, one might argue that this metaphor suggests that ethics is at the core of character, that character grows from ethics. Furthermore, ethics as root suggests that there is always "something there" to explain how character is formed and how it is expressed. In the classical Western tradition of ethics, this root metaphor lives in a couple of versions of deontology.

The heart of the word *deontology* is the *onto* part. This is a Greek word for "that which is" or "being." Hence, deontology has to do with what already exists or what already is there. This perspective on moral philosophy typically holds that there is at least one, if not more, preexisting rule or principle which should govern human action. Although there are variations within the theory, adherents of the prevailing deontology theory are called by one writer *rule-deontologists*.[18] William Frankena elaborates when he says they "hold that the standard of right and wrong consists of one or more rules—either fairly concrete ones like 'We ought always to tell the truth' or very abstract ones like Henry Sidgwick's Principle of Justice."[19]

Deontology theory values the human right to act on principle, regardless of the consequence. It emphasizes origination or intention of action, rather than outcome or consequence. This is why the metaphor of root is instructive. Ethical decision making is rooted in a principle and our intention to act from that basis.

Because the rule or principle is already there, ethical learning is more an issue of discovery than discernment. The rule is there to be found. And when it is found or learned, it becomes an obligation to action. In this light, one can understand the classic maxim of Socrates: to know the good is to do the good. Obligation is the key to human behavior. Duty takes precedence; one has a duty to follow the rule. This perspective also enables us to understand why someone would be a conscientious objector and engage in civil disobedience. Even if the public at large does not agree with his or her action, the person feels duty-bound to follow his or her own conscience—that is, the principle behind the conscience.

Corporate ethics programs often include ethics codes, ethics training, and hot lines, all designed to identify "the right thing to do." Once that is known, then the individual is duty-bound to act in a way that is consistent with the rule.

2-7 Ethics As Fruit of Character: Teleology

To move from deontology to teleology is indeed like talking about a plant from the perspective of fruit instead of its root. The metaphor of fruit focuses the discussion in moral reasoning on the issue of results and outcomes. Character may have to do in part with core issues, but the ethical decision making is governed by end results, not beginning points.

Unearthing the meaning of teleology makes clear its thrust. *Teleology* is a combination of Greek words. The operative word is *telos,* which means "end, finish, and goal." Teleology theory is not looking for an ethical or moral principle to apply in action. Rather, what winds up being ethical or moral is the outcome, the result, of a particular action. For example, this theory does not begin with a preexisting understanding of what the good is. The good might be something as general as the stakeholder model—satisfy as many stakeholders as possible. Only when one knows what would satisfy each stakeholder can one know how to proceed.

Without doubt, the dominant representative of teleology theory is utilitarianism. Utilitarianism defines right actions as those that maximize utility—that bring the most benefit to the most people. Utility, or usefulness, is the goal, or the end, of ethical action. Simplistically, one might even say deontology is a principled approach and teleology is a product approach. Frankena's definition of utilitarianism neatly summarizes these elements: "The sole ultimate standard of right, wrong, and obligation is the *principle of utility* or *beneficence,* which says quite strictly that the moral end to be sought in all that we do is *the greatest possible balance of good over evil* (or the least possible balance of evil over good)."[20]

Utility is the fruit of character manifested behaviorally. Ethical learning for a utilitarian is not the discovery of a principle to apply in moral decision making. Rather, the learning is the reasoning with respect to the end; which moral action will bring the greatest good? It is not a principled decision but one made always with respect to a particular situation. It is more like discernment than discovery. The need is to figure out what to do in any particular situation to ensure that doing good outweighs the bad.

The stakeholder model represents one approach to corporate strategy and/or business ethics. It is an enlightened self-interest approach in that leaders assume they will benefit if those who have a stake in the corporation also benefit. The figuring out, or discernment, requires a clear sense of the enterprise's stakeholders, what would satisfy them, and how the firm would know it had succeeded. Of course, what stakeholders want may not be what they need, and what they need is often changing, so discernment can prove difficult.

2-8 Conclusion

Certainly, deontology and teleology are not the only two theories in moral philosophy. Most ethics textbooks also deal with egoism, distributive justice, relativism, and virtue ethics. Indeed, ethicists will see some connections between this book and virtue ethics, which is why virtue ethics need not be detailed now.

The key for this book, however, is not choosing a particular ethical theory to apply in a business setting. To the contrary, the key is to see how character is formed, so that ethical actions result. Those actions may come from principles rooted within, or actions may be shaped by the desired result of the greatest good for a particular situation. Again and again, the central question for character development is not which ethical theory guides one's action. Rather, the central question asks how ethical responsibility grows as a core aspect of character formation. Continued concern for ethical responsibility keeps the focus on the practical instead of the theoretical.

To the general question "What makes a good business leader?" this book always has two answers. The good business leader is competent and has character. We assume that everyone can learn both aspects to become good business leaders. But because we are all human, shortcomings and failures are inevitable. That is why the hope is for "good" business leaders—not perfect ones. We want leaders of character. Now we need to look at how leaders of character develop competence.

Chapter Quiz

1. The Greek word *ethos* can be translated into all of the following *except*
   a.   character.
   b.   faith.
   c.   custom.
   d.   habit.

2. Which of the following is *not* true about character?
   a.   It encompasses only behavior.
   b.   It is more than behavior.
   c.   It can be taught.
   d.   It involves ethics.

3. Which of the following is true about ethics and character?
   a.   Neither can be taught.
   b.   Both are innate.
   c.   Both can be taught.
   d.   Only character is innate.

4. Which of the following virtues transcends the individual and is vested in something or someone other than the individual?
   a. faith
   b. hope
   c. love
   d. prudence

5. Which of the following types of thinking "always makes a difference in who we are and what we do"?
   a. informative
   b. synthesis
   c. formative
   d. selective

6. Which of the following statements is true about having character and knowing ethical principles?
   a. Having character is more important than knowing ethical principles.
   b. Having character depends on knowing ethical principles.
   c. Knowing ethical principles creates character.
   d. Knowing ethical principles ensures character.

7. Character belongs to which of the following?
   a. the individual
   b. the corporation
   c. the individual only
   d. a and b

8. Which of the following statements is true about culture?
   a. It shapes the individual.
   b. It predestines the individual.
   c. It rarely affects the individual.
   d. It is universally uniform.

9. According to Kohlberg, which level of moral reasoning is based on a strict interpretation of right, wrong, and obedience to authority?
   a. conformity
   b. conventional
   c. pre-conventional
   d. post-conventional

10. According to Kohlberg, which level of moral reasoning is based on a personal code, social contracts, and universal code of ethics?
   a. conformity
   b. conventional
   c. pre-conventional
   d. post-conventional

Note: You can find the correct answers to these questions by taking the quiz and then submitting your answers in the Online Edition. The program will automatically score your submission. If you miss a question, the program will provide the correct answer, a rationale for the answer, and the section number in the chapter where the topic is discussed.

Questions for Thought

1. Share a story that demonstrates a time when you learned ethics.
2. Can you recall an early lesson in life when one of the classical virtues was at play? Please explain.
3. Identify a relatively recent work or professional experience when one of the classical virtues was at play.
4. Explain the difference between teleology and deontology. Do you tend to prescribe one view over another? Why?
5. Have you ever had a classroom or school setting where ethics was taught? Why did you or didn't you learn ethics during your educational years?
6. Do you think a newborn baby is ethical? If so, how? If not, when and how does a person become ethical?
7. It seems clear that people do learn about ethics. How do you think people grow ethically?
8. This chapter assumes that to be a responsible leader is to be an ethical leader. Explain why you agree or disagree with this assumption.
9. Select a person who, in your mind, exemplifies character.

Web Exercises

Visit the Berkshire-Hathaway site (http://www.berkshirehathaway.com) that contains Warren Buffet's letters to his shareholders. Read several letters and consider what values Buffet expresses to his shareholders. What kind of character does he exhibit? What aspects of that character are visible in his business dealings?

Visit Dilbert's Biggest Weasels of 2004 at http://www.dilbert.com/comics/dilbert/shop/html/weasel_poll_results.html. What kinds of character do the "Biggest Weasels" have in common? Do you agree with the poll results? Having read about character, how would you define a weasel, or someone lacking in character?

Endnotes

1. *Time*, December, 30, 2002–January 6, 2003, front cover.
2. Robert Coles, *The Secular Mind* (Princeton, NJ: Princeton University Press, 1999), 127.
3. Ibid., 129.
4. Aristotle, "Nichomachean Ethics," *The Basic Works of Aristotle*, ed. Richard McKeon (New York: Random House, 1941), 935.
5. *Ethical and Legal Conduct Guidelines* (Wycliff, OH: The Lubrizol Corporation, 2002), 6.
6. Larry Kanter, "Brilliant Careers: the Oracle of Omaha, " *Salon*, http://www.salon.com/people/BC/1999/08/31/Buffett.
7. Adrian van Kaam, *Fundamental Formation*, vol. 1 of *Formative Spirituality*, 4 vols. (New York: Crossroad, 1983), xvii.
8. Rober Bellah, Richard Madsen, William M. Sullivan, Ann Swidler and Steven M. Tipton, *Habits of the Heart: Individualism and Commitment in American Life* (New York: Harper & Row, 1985), 27.
9. "One on One with Dell CEO-Elect Kevin Rollins," *National Business Review*, April 3, 2004, http://www.NBR.com/transcript/2004/transcript030404.html#story3.
10. Ibid.
11. Ibid.
12. Ibid.
13. Nannerl O. Keohane, "Heroes and Leaders in the 21st Century," *Exchange: The Fuqua School of Business Alumni Magazine*, 17, no. 1 (2004): 20.
14. Ibid., 21.
15. Ibid.
16. Victor E. Frankl, *Man's Search for Meaning*, (New York: Perceus, 2000).
17. Lawrence Kohlberg, "Stages of Moral Development," 1971, http://www.xenodochy.org/ex/lists/moraldev.html.
18. William K. Frankena, *Ethics* (Englewood Cliffs, NJ: Prentice-Hall, 1963), 15.
19. Ibid.
20. Ibid., 29.

ἱκανότητα

Competence— Adding Value

3

Outline

Competence informed by character, character enhanced by competence—this chapter looks forward to identify the strategic issues facing corporations and looks backwards to consider the wisdom of proven approaches to the challenges of leadership.

Society rightfully expects more from corporations than profitability, yet profitability is important, because it offers society more order and stability than do layoffs, shoddy customer service, missed earnings, or bankruptcy. Negative corporate events such as these can be caused by limited competence rather than by limited virtue.

If corporate responsibility is the goal, then competence is the means. Corporate responsibility depends on adding value to customers, shareholders, and employees and doing it with virtue. To add value, competent leaders must acquire the knowledge and skill to create a competitive advantage, understand the strategic issues they face, and know how to execute for results.

Finally, competence is about worth in the sense of value and materiality. By adding value, competence seeks to make the business product and enterprise worth more. Some people do seem to be born with innate talents and aptitude for competency in business. But even in these cases, the gifted individual still has things to learn and experiences to be had. In other words, he or she needs to be educated.

However, educating for business competence alone is shortsighted and possibly even risky. If competence seeks to add worth to a company, so does character deal with worth. Indeed, people of high character are worthy people. This use of worth language draws on the realm of virtue. Character develops people of worthiness. Indeed, the language of worth and worthiness will be used in Chapter 8 to summarize the teaching of this book.

It has already been affirmed that character is taught. For most of us, this learning began long before we entered the classroom, but it was education nonetheless. Education also continues in the classroom. A good liberal arts education fosters ethical growth and development, even if the curriculum does not have a specific ethics class. The classic liberally educated person has the basic orientation to become a person of character, a person of worth. For any business company or organization, this is a person of worth—worth in both senses: worthiness of character and worth in value-added competence. No business leader is sought or kept if he or she is worthless.

3-1 Contemporary Strategic Issues Call for Broadly Prepared Leaders

Consider the competencies needed in leading a company to compete effectively when facing business challenges such as the following:

- *Leading of change.* Senior leaders and boards struggle to create an external, customer-driven organization when it is comprised of functional experts who are resistant to change and who can see only the parts and not the whole.

- *Restoration of investor trust.* Increased public scrutiny and regulation are the legacy of a post–Enron world. Building trust with customers and employees in an environment of transparency and financial prudence is an issue that confronts all publicly traded companies and, increasingly, privately held firms and nonprofits.

- *The big margin squeeze.* At the beginning of the twenty-first century, corporations are struggling to retain customers, confront downward pressure on prices, and generate profit. Small- and mid-capital manufacturers in the United States must compete with off-shore, low-waged companies and must sell to large retailers that reward high volume in exchange for low margins. How do leaders control costs and allocate limited resources wisely to produce earnings in an environment of uncertain growth?

- *Industry overcapacity.* Overcapacity is common in most industries. For example, in financial services the repeal of the Glass Seagall Act increased industry competition and consolidation. As a result, insurance companies can now buy banks, banks can buy security firms, and, to be competitive, small credit unions must serve their communities with excellent service.

- *Health care crisis.* For-profit and nonprofit health care organizations struggle to balance increasing health care quality and access while decreasing costs. Dramatic cost increases are driven by factors such as nursing and doctor shortages, malpractice insurance, technological advancements, and pharmaceutical innovations at a time when government reimbursements are declining, even though demand for health care increases as America ages.

- *The value chain.* Domestic and global logistics involve a complex mix of traditional transportation and warehousing combined with new tools such as global satellite tracking and the Internet, designed to execute just-in-time delivery despite the security challenges since 9/11.

- *Outsourcing.* Firms struggle to evaluate what, why, and how to outsource functions that are not part of their mission and core competencies.
- *Partnerships, mergers, and acquisitions.* Leaders create and manage a daunting mix of international strategic alliances, minority investments, partnerships, mergers, and acquisitions rather than the traditional monolithic corporation.

Ultimately, competence is about responding to strategic issues such as these, by getting results that contend with global competition profitably and responsibly. Volumes are written about strategy, innovation, and leadership development. There is no shortage of tools and methods to design organizational structures and processes that drive performance to lead change that creates customer-focused cultures. However, when all is said and done, many well-intended leaders often say more than they do. The simple question is "Why can some leaders get things done but others cannot?"

Sometimes the problem is that the strategy is wrong, but executed brilliantly. Sometimes a strategy looks better on paper than it plays out in reality. And sometimes the strategy is wrong and the execution is weak.

Sound strategy involves a careful assessment of customers, competitors, and company capabilities. Those who are developing strategy need to engage key stakeholders and primary customer contacts by asking questions and learning. Along the way, sound working relationships are developed, while the strategists get a reality check about the firm's capabilities. Leaders need to understand whether people cut across functions easily and treat each other with candor and respect, or whether gamesmanship and delusion rule. If internal politics trump customer service, leaders must develop a reality check for the decision-making process—one that promotes honest, constructive discourse.

Strategy and operations must be inseparable. Leaders must view the world from 50,000 feet, as well as 50 feet. Strategy is often too shallow or too operational. For a strategy to result in serving customers better than competitors do, while still making a profit, the right people have to be in the right job following the right processes. In other words, "it's the people, stupid!"[1]

Successful execution depends on selecting and evaluating people whose capabilities match the organization's strategies. A leader might be brilliant at marketing and adept with operations but unskilled as a strategist. All leaders have chinks in their armor, so the issue is whether weaknesses can be improved. If this is not possible, can one person's strengths offset another's limitations?

3-2 Separate Silos: Business Education and the Liberal Arts

Worth is the focus of competence and worthiness is the focus of character. In the human person, they are one. But in a college or university setting they tend to be separate. Competence is the primary focus of business faculty and character is the primary focus of the liberal arts.

However, the notions of making a living and leading a life that is worth living are inevitably intertwined. Consider the competencies discussed by business education and the liberal arts. If we want leaders who are competent and who possess character, then we need to integrate, rather than separate, a practical business education with a moral foundation. Indeed, integration—integrity—is the name of this book.

3-2a Business Education: Undergraduate and MBA Students

Undergraduate and MBA students seek a business education to become competent. First, they determine what they are suited to do, recognizing that this may change as they grow and gain experience. Second, they develop requisite or adequate abilities or qualities. Then they develop the capacity to perform. Business school curriculums define competence as the acquisition of both knowledge and skills such as the following:

Knowledge
- Ethical and legal responsibilities in organizations and society
- Financial theories, analysis, reporting, and markets
- Creation of value through the integrated production and distribution of goods, services, and information
- Group and individual dynamics in organizations
- Statistical data analysis and management science as they support decision-making processes throughout an organization
- Information technologies as they influence the roles and techniques of management
- Domestic and global economic environments of organizations

Skills
- Communication abilities
- Ethical understanding and reasoning abilities
- Analytic skills
- Use of information technology
- Multicultural and diversity understanding
- Reflective thinking skills[2]

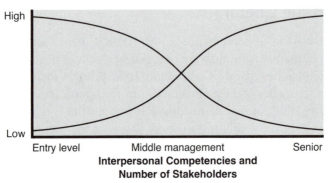

Figure 3-1
Knowledge and Interpersonal Competencies
by Level of Management

Source: Adapted from Kerzner, Harold, *Project Management: A Systems Approach to Planning, Scheduling and Controlling,* 8th ed. (New York: John Wiley & Sons, 2003).

Competence means something different for undergraduate and MBA students than for senior leaders. Experience is an important addition to knowledge and skill. Entry-level professionals may well be smarter than senior leaders but lack the experience to direct the future of a company.

The level of complexity of a particular leadership situation and the number of stakeholders served determine a leader's responsibilities. Figure 3-1 illustrates that technical knowledge is more important in entry-level positions and interpersonal skill is more important in middle and senior leadership positions.

Successful senior leaders set direction by using exceptional interpersonal skill in working with multiple stakeholders and in developing high-performance teams. Middle managers shape and execute strategies and develop and manage teams. Entry-level employees focus on managing themselves and technical areas, such as sales, accounting, or human resources. Although entry-level positions involve working in teams, the number of stakeholders served is usually limited. Small companies rely more on generalists. Increasingly, leaders at all levels and in all organizations of all sizes must create sound processes, so that different functions, alliances, and joint ventures collaborate. The challenge is often to create a sense of team among people who do not work closely with each other but whose collaboration is vital to corporate strategies.

The greater the responsibility, the more leaders are involved in strategy (doing the right thing) than operations (doing things right). However, leaders at all levels need to understand the strategic issues that confront a corporation, since adaptation to these issues is preeminent to sustainability. In addition, the strategic issues that confront a company determine the competencies needed to adapt, to innovate, and to lead change effectively.

A business education contributes to a graduate's success in his or her chosen career, but it does not ensure that the newly educated person will be competent. One reason is that, increasingly, companies must engage a wider range of constituencies on a wider range of issues. Economic development, social justice, and regulatory issues are thrust on the corporate plate, wanted or not. It is at this juncture that the liberal arts prove their merit. The practical benefits of a liberal arts background are the insights into theology, history, and culture that are necessary for leaders to understand business and ethical issues such as those embedded in sourcing materials and labor globally or to enter foreign markets for the purpose of economic growth.

3-3 The Liberal Arts

Entry-level, middle-level, and senior leaders all need to be competent in understanding the human condition and the appropriate responses to the situations common to corporate life. All leaders struggle to balance conflicting priorities between what they want and what they need to do; between personal aspirations and responsibilities to family; and between their friends and the community, nation, and planet. While we support a culture of altruism that opposes self-serving behavior, the latter (**SELF-SERVING BEHAVIOR**) typically has greater attraction than the former (**ALTRUISM**). To this point, Sigmund Freud, in *Civilization and its Discontents,* offers a cynical view of our need to see humankind as good: "To make a low bow to the deeply moral nature of mankind; it will help us to be generally popular, and much will be forgiven us for it. Maybe we are tough on those who criticize people since we like to view ourselves as benevolent or to at least think other people think of them this way."[3]

Freud goes on to express concern with an educational system that was failing to prepare students to cope with a selfish world:

> In sending the young into life with such a false psychological orientation, education is behaving as though one were to equip people starting on a polar expedition with summer clothing and maps of the Italian lakes. In this it becomes evident that a certain misuse is being made of ethical demands. The strictness of those demands would not do so much harm if education were to say: this is how men ought to be, in order to be happy and to make

others happy; but you have to reckon on their not being like that. Instead of this, the young are made to believe that everyone else fulfills those ethical demands—that is, that everyone else is virtuous. It is on this that the demand is based that the young, too, shall become virtuous.[4]

We need to heed Freud's admonitions. Clearly, there are bad characters out there. And to be sure, the world is a rough, often nasty place to do business. Simply to acquiesce with this view of people and the world by saying, "That's how it is," is to "buy the culture." The price of not emphasizing character, however, is naïveté. That would mean we *de facto* teach the young to become what we fear the most—selfish.

Philosophers, theologians, and ethicists have long debated the question of whether humankind is basically good or evil. Biology, in contrast, is clear that selfishness is built into our DNA to ensure survival of the species. The paradox is that enlightened self-interest reveals that altruism can be in our best interest. Cooperation can be an effective way to compete. Excessive concern for family and friends can create a backlash of complaints about favoritism. Excessive concern for the interests of a company, community, or country can cause backlash due to charges of exploitation and nationalism.

For example, multinational corporations and organizations, such as the World Trade Organization, are increasingly being accused of inadequate concern for human rights, poverty, and environmental degradation. Fair or unfair, perceived or real, corporations must respond to anti-business sentiments regarding self-serving conduct and operation at the expense of the local community. In other words, protests and increased regulation are bad for business. How might corporations cooperate to win the hearts and minds of the communities in which they want to do business?

Should we give to or take from only those we know? And how shall we deal with those we do not know? *Enduring Love,* a book by Ian McEwan, describes four men who hear cries for help from a man and a boy trapped in a large gas balloon adrift in the wind. All four grab a rope that trails the balloon along the ground. Just when rescue seems likely, a swirling wind pushes the balloon over a cliff. Three men let go and one hangs on but soon falls to his death, giving his life needlessly; the boy and man later land safely.

One of the three survivors reflects on his choice: "This is our mammalian conflict, what to give to others and what to keep for yourself. Treading that line, keep the others in check and being kept in check by them, is what we call morality. Hanging a few feet above the Chilterns escarpment, our crew enacted morality's ancient dilemma: us, or me."[5]

3-3a   A Colonial Answer to Narrow Business and Impractical Liberal Arts

Will higher education answer the call to integrate ethics into business education? Will the humanities and social sciences have much to contribute to finding a job? Liberal arts faculties tend to believe that graduates who enter business make a "Faustian bargain," selling their soul (virtue) for material gain. Put simply, many liberal arts faculty believe business lacks virtue.

This contemporary view of the liberal arts contrasts sharply with its historic mission, as established during colonial times. Benjamin Rush, a close friend of John Adams, signer of the Declaration of Independence and founder of several colleges and universities, wanted higher education to produce citizen leaders. Rush and another famous colleague, Thomas Jefferson, shared a practical vision for the liberal arts—that the liberal arts should prepare responsible young graduates to work in commerce and government, as well as cultural and religious institutions.

Rush rejected the elitist British system of education that preserved the advantage of the wealthy and acknowledged no responsibility to advance society. Rush was harsh in his criticism of colonial institutions that did not accommodate the fact that "the business of the principal part of the inhabitants is to obtain the first and most necessary means of subsistence."[6] Rush called for a useful education to be grounded in the liberal arts, while exploring political and commercial activities of the day. Graduates would possess the "virtue needed to build a just, compassionate, economically sustainable democracy."[7] Rush advocated a liberal arts education that would be "useful and applicable" to all students. He explicitly stated concern for the business sector: "There is but one expedient left whereby we can save our sinking country, and that is by encouraging American manufacturers. Unless we do this, we shall be done forever."[8]

Today many liberal arts colleges deny this history or, worse, actively demean the field of business. Interestingly, their view is more consistent with the British tradition than the inclusive legacy proposed by America's founders. President William Durden of Dickinson University believes the time has come to prepare students for corporate leadership by rejecting both the narrowly focused vocational education common to most business schools and the ideological liberal arts programs that eschew practical applications. He says, "It is time to educate graduates whose hubris and exaggerated ambition are tempered and balanced by studies that aim to challenge one's understanding of oneself and to prepare one to function intellectually and morally in a complex world." A liberal arts education does not ensure integrity or selflessness, but it does offer a foundation for the development of character. Rush and Jefferson would agree with Durden's stance that the compartmentalizing of liberal arts and business inhibits the intellectual and moral development of students.[9]

3-4 Competence—How Does One Develop It?

Is there an evaporating pool of talent capable of coping with strategic issues such as leading change, restoration of investor trust, margin squeeze, industry overcapacity, health care problems, value chain management, outsourcing, and partnerships? Leader confidence has been shaken by intense competition, increased public scrutiny, and the need to respond effectively to rapid change. In the mid-1990s, 50 percent of leaders believed they could lead competently. Five years later, only one-third believed they possessed the requisite leadership competencies.

Increasingly, competent leaders will have to become extraordinary strategists. They will have to respond effectively to relentless change and possess the capacity to build relationships and talent. In contrast, the fatal flaws of leaders include a reluctance to take risks, an inability to understand colleague and/or customer concerns, difficulty in coping with business and people issues, and arrogance. Twenty-first-century leadership calls for strategies that respond to complexity, ambiguity, and intense performance pressure such as few individuals can handle solo. Competent leaders, therefore, have no choice but to build teams. It has been suggested that, because the demands of leadership are becoming so great, corporations may find that the best candidates do not want the job.[10]

Small business owners do not face the same complexity of strategic issues that confront global corporations, but the breadth and depth of the competencies needed to market, finance, and manage staff of even a modest venture exceed the abilities of most people. The wise small business owner relies on staff and professional services such as accounting and legal counsel. In addition, he or she relies on informal business associates and business advisory boards to acquire the competencies needed to lead and operate the company.

It does not happen by accident that some companies comprise adequate numbers of competent leaders. How do they do it? Companies that create succession plans that attract, develop, and retain leadership follow practices such as these:

1. Reward risk taking and tolerate failure in granting significant responsibility to their most talented leaders. Provide candid and

constructive feedback designed to promote a performance-based culture that constantly evaluates its practices.

2. Identify and select future leaders for professional and community experiences that will address their strengths, needs, and career potential. These companies are less hierarchical than most and have more flexible organizational structures.

3. Design reward systems that support leadership development, flexible career paths, and customized compensation packages.

4. Expect senior leaders to accept the responsibility of leadership development by encouraging emerging leaders to participate in executive education, by demonstrating a long view to development before expecting returns, and by encouraging mentoring.

5. Approach leadership development similarly to strategic decisions: identify the "best bets," invest aggressively, and manage risk.[11]

Although corporate support of leadership competencies is important, wise leaders also take full responsibility for their own development. Small business owners have no choice but to accept such responsibility. As we said in the previous chapter, with people of good character, competent people must also choose to excel through good habits and disciplines such as these:

1. Reflect on strengths and weaknesses and seek feedback to improve performance.

2. Pursue continuing education to live out a commitment to lifelong learning.

3. Demonstrate a consistent work ethic by preparing well for meetings and projects.

4. Become involved in community activities, recognizing that more responsibility can often be acquired serving on a nonprofit board than in most entry-level positions.

5. Develop authentic professional relationships built on mutual trust and support with mentors, peers, and colleagues.

Finally, experience may be the most effective method of achieving competence. Formal education can develop skills such as working with others and thinking critically and can impart knowledge in areas such as accounting. Certainly, academic study provides an environment for being reflective. Although formal education is important, it does not provide the skills and knowledge necessary, for example, to establish a sales and procurement office in Brazil to test a market and to source materials. Like character, competence is often learned through trial and error. Good

Michael Jordan
Is there any question about competency here? Probably
not. What about humility?
Source: © Reuters/CORBIS

mentors and first-hand experiences provide insights into competitive
advantage and performance. Competent businesspeople have the ability
to formulate or execute a competitive advantage, regardless of their level
of responsibility. The task of creating a competitive advantage defines
what competent leaders do.

3-5 Educational Incapacity—the Competence of Humility

Formal education or the education that comes from professional experience can be a liability rather than an asset. For example, one instructor
who teaches chemistry cringes when she hears a student say, "I want to go
to medical school and become a doctor, so I can be rich." Bright, experienced people can be more interested in comfort and stability, more confident that their way is the best way, and less open to change and learning.
Part of being competent is recognizing that education—formal and infor-

mal—can cause blind spots that inhibit the ability to add value and develop virtue.

Adding Value—Consider why you buy clothes from a retailer rather than through the Internet or catalogues, even if the latter is more convenient. Why do retailers who are losing business to the Internet and catalogues not understand that their competitive advantage is in letting people try on clothes? Their facilities and staff discourage anyone from trying on clothes and fail to offer comfortable fitting rooms. Experienced retailers are well qualified in the field of merchandising but blind to their primary competitive advantage—the fitting room. Every business has its own version of the fitting room—while education and experience blind it to the need to adapt to new circumstances.[12]

Developing Character—Consider whether ethical competence can be achieved through ethical frameworks and analyses of cases. Kierkegaard suggests that our moral challenge is to understand that blind spots convince us to rationalize our actions as being ethical, even though we are self-serving. In other words, the competence to develop character depends on our ability to detect when we choose pleasure over service to others. We need to acquire competence to understand the impediments to a moral life, with self-deception topping the list. Character can be taught and learned by being honest in understanding ourselves, our interests, and human nature. Recognition of our moral blind spots is essential to doing the right thing.[13]

The benefits of formal education and professional experience need to be tempered by an awareness of the risks of educational incapacity. Effective leadership balances the confidence founded in formal and informal education with humility based on our infinite capacity to deceive ourselves.

3-6 Competitive Advantage

Competent leaders must have the ability to formulate and execute a competitive advantage that serves customers better than competitors do while making a profit. The principle of comparative advantage can be examined and understood at both the country level and the corporate level.

3-6a Comparative Advantage of Nations

As the old joke goes, in European heaven the Swiss are the diplomats, the French are the cooks, the Germans are the engineers, the Italians are the lovers, and the English are the police. The convoluted European hell is where the Swiss are the lovers, the French are the diplomats, the Germans are the police, the Italians are the engineers and the English are the cooks. Certainly, we can find exceptions to these characterizations, yet there is truth in the comparative advantage of Swiss chocolate, French wine, German beer, Italian pasta, and English desserts. When Britain produces cloth and Portugal produces wine, and there is consumer demand for each, both countries are advantaged as long as they trade freely with each other. It was around the beginning of the nineteenth century that David Ricardo, a British economist, used this example to coin the term *comparative advantage*. In essence, the idea is that all people benefit when each nation sticks to what it does best, as long as barriers to trade are minimal.[14]

Various countries approach their free trade and competitive advantage very differently, as Thomas Friedman illustrated when he compared the way the United States, Europe, Japan, emerging economies, and Russia sell gas. In the United States, the purpose of the gas station is to sell gas cheaply and efficiently. A customer must clean his or her own windows and put air in the tires, but gas can be had for only $2.30 a gallon. The frills are gone. In the European gas station, there may be more amenities. Union contracts, which make gas more expensive, may also be in play. Taxes clearly are elevated. Here gas may cost almost $5.00 a gallon. In Japan a customer might get even more attention than in Europe. One might be greeted warmly and feel well served. Taxes are still a significant issue, and one still pays $5.00 a gallon. In the emerging economy station, gas may even be cheaper than in the United States. And in Russia, gas is only 50 cents a gallon, but there might not be any. The black market might be a factor and drive up the price per gallon. Clearly, these economies have their own set of trying circumstances.

European and Japanese market economies differ from the U.S. free market in that they are willing to pay higher taxes and accept associated regulations for the benefit of more protection from market forces. It is difficult for emerging economies to adopt American-style capitalism, because they lack the basic infrastructure of established rule of law, banking systems, capital markets, roads, and public services.[15]

Since no one wants to buy a mediocre or, worse, a defective product, consumers benefit from competitive pressure placed on businesses to deliver products at fair value and services that are unique and desired by the market. This benefit often comes at the cost of dislocated workers and cultures.

Maximizing the benefits of free trade and limiting its costs require that competent leaders form legitimate partnerships with local communities. Competent leaders take the first step in this partnership process by listening to the community. Oil executives operating in Angola were upset with a speaker who pointed out that the country was a breeding ground for terrorism because of the gap between the quality of the executives' lives and that of the locals. The indignant executives stated that they were creating wealth. The speaker responded that, although this was true, locals believed the industry had disrupted their culture, damaged their environment, and exploited their resources. When the executives asked for advice, the speaker told them to ask the Angolans. Although local communities make laws formally to grant businesses permission to operate, a shared understanding between a corporation and the communities in which it operates is more effective and enduring than legislation. Competent leaders ask permission and listen to the concerns of local communities to ensure the sustainability of their businesses.[16]

3-6b Creating a Corporate Competitive Advantage

Numerous models and approaches explain how corporations can create a competitive advantage. A fundamental approach can be built on three questions:

1. On what basis will the corporation compete? In other words, what customer benefit can a company offer that competitors cannot easily match?
2. Is the firm's economic model sustainable? In other words, is the corporation's business model profitable?
3. Does the corporate strategy capture the passion of employees sufficiently? In other words, can the leaders of the corporation inspire people to change, either out of desire to excel or out of fear of failure?[17]

Billy Beane, the general manager of the Oakland Athletics baseball club, created a competitive advantage using a viable economic model that captured the passion of his employees—baseball players, coaches, scouts, and executives. In 2002, Beane had $40 million to spend on 25 baseball players. His competitor, the New York Yankees, had $126 million to spend on 25 players and perhaps another $100 million in reserve. On what basis could Oakland compete for employees? "What you don't do, is what the Yankees do," said Beane. "If we do what the Yankees do, we lose every time, because they're doing it with three times more money than we are."[18]

Oakland evaluates baseball players differently than do teams such as the Yankees. Using analytic tools and statistical models, Oakland signs players who perform well on the field but who are undervalued by other teams. Despite having one of the lowest payrolls in baseball, Oakland has won more regular season games during the past few years than any other team except the Atlanta Braves.

Oakland has created a competitive advantage in the marketplace for players with a distinct business model that has targeted competent but undervalued athletes. The Yankees, on the other hand, have created a competitive advantage by acquiring more resources than their competitors. Each team has relied on its unique strengths—and both have been winners, demonstrating there is not just one way to run a business.

3-6c Competitive Advantage Equals Growth

Growth is a product of competitive advantage, and it is the foundation of economic development—more profits, more jobs, more taxes, more technology transfer, more worker training, more philanthropy, and more executives serving on nonprofit boards.

Too often, incompetent leaders embrace a strategy of endorsing the status quo, while they fail to promote strategic thought and action that would create a competitive advantage.[19] Strategic planning typically generates reams of paper that describe the industry and the company's competitive situation and conclude with recommendations to increase revenue by serving new market segments and to improve profitability by cutting costs. These documents are prepared by executives who communicate poorly and who possess conflicting agendas.[20]

Corporate growth is influenced by the way a firm defines its business. Consider the classic question of whether railroad companies are in the train business or the transportation business. Although the need to transport goods increased throughout the twentieth century, most of the growth was in trucking and air transport, rather than rail. The rail companies defined themselves according to their product, rather than their customers' needs.[21]

Typically, growth is achieved by selling more products to current customers, thus earning a higher percentage of a customer's wallet, rather than by attracting new customers. Coca-Cola's growth strategy was to earn a greater percentage of each customer's stomach, when it determined it was in the beverage rather than the cola business. It planned to earn a higher percentage of beverage purchases by adding bottled water and citrus drink lines to complement its soft drink products, thus growing its market share and profits.[22]

Companies can also grow by serving end users. For example, the end user for a trucking firm that ships materials to a manufacturing company is likely to be a retailer and then, ultimately, a consumer. Although the trucking company has no direct contact with retailers and consumers, services such as warehousing, just-in-time delivery, and all that goes with logistics management provide potential growth opportunities if the corporate leader understands and delivers on services valued by the end customer.

3-7 Competence Equals Performance

To come full circle, competence is about getting things done. Senior leaders are pulled in the struggle to satisfy multiple stakeholders, who often have conflicting priorities. Ultimately, organizational results hinge on attracting the right people and creating a high-performance team. Therefore, the questions that should drive the priority of people and processes include the following:

1. Do the executors have the prerequisite ability and discipline to get results?
2. Do the executors also develop the strategy and understand it?
3. Do the executors have the information needed to assess customer satisfaction relative to competitors?
4. Do the executors have the feedback, support, and training they need to develop their abilities?
5. Do the executors have a proven record of overcoming obstacles?
6. Do the executors have access to resources proportionate to opportunities so that operating budgets are tightly linked to strategic priorities?[23]

Each of the seven virtues will be a building block in forming the character and developing the competency to make the kind of leader Bossidy and Charan describe. Their book, *Execution: The Discipline of Getting Things Done*, concludes with advice for senior leaders recently appointed to a new position of responsibility. The following words summarize Chapters 2 and 3, on character and competence, as we prepare to examine each of the seven classical virtues.

Make sure your team stays on top of your customers' needs, their buying behaviors, and changes in those behaviors. Always look for ways to improve your results by introducing initiatives that drive results and bind your people together. Sharpen your intellectual honesty—see things as they are, not as you want them to be. It will be hard at times to know how you are doing. You need confidants to help you keep your head straight.

You need access to wisdom, candor, and help, so that you can keep growing and learning. The new job is stressful, so lead a balanced life. Do not get too low or high. Some people grow in their jobs and some swell. The best are never too busy being "big honchos" to pay attention to important details and stay close to their people. They are never too high to listen and learn.[24]

Chapter Quiz

1. The result of the Glass Seagall Act in the financial services industry is an example of which strategic issue?
   a. leading change
   b. margin squeeze
   c. industry overcapacity
   d. outsourcing
2. Which of the following statements is true?
   a. Worth is the focus of character.
   b. Worth is the focus of competence.
   c. Competence is the primary focus of liberal arts.
   d. Character is the primary focus of business studies.
3. Technical knowledge is most important to which of the following groups?
   a. corporate board
   b. senior management
   c. middle management
   d. entry-level employees
4. According to Ian McEwan, morality is which of the following?
   a. acting on morals
   b. having the right motives behind actions
   c. balancing internal goals with external pressures
   d. balancing what we give to others and what we keep to ourselves
5. In terms of leaders who believed that they possess the requisite leadership competencies, which of the following is true?
   a. More leaders in the mid-1990s than in the early twenty-first century believe they were competent.
   b. Fewer leaders in the mid-1990s than in the early twenty-first century believe they were competent.
   c. The percentage of leaders who believe they were competent were the same.
   d. The percentage of leaders who believe they were incompetent were the same.

6. Which of the following is the most effective method of achieving competency?
   a. education
   b. experience
   c. mentorship
   d. training

7. According to Kierkegaard, what is our moral challenge?
   a. to understand our ethical obstacles
   b. to understand the impediments to a moral life
   c. to understand our morality in real-world scenarios
   d. to understand our character

8. The story about the Oakland Athletics baseball team provided in the chapter illustrates that the team's management used which of the following as a competitive advantage?
   a. revenue
   b. fan basis
   c. talent evaluation
   d. geographic benefits

9. Corporate growth can be a product of all the following *except*
   a. competitive advantage.
   b. absolute advantage.
   c. serving end users.
   d. defining the business scope.

10. Ultimately, organizational results hinge on which of the following?
   a. attracting the right people
   b. having the economic capital
   c. creating a high-performance team
   d. a and b
   e. a and c

Note: You can find the correct answers to these questions by taking the quiz and then submitting your answers in the Online Edition. The program will automatically score your submission. If you miss a question, the program will provide the correct answer, a rationale for the answer, and the section number in the chapter where the topic is discussed.

Questions for Thought

1. How would you define business leadership competence?
2. Is business competency alone sufficient to be an effective leader? Explain why or why not.
3. What is or could be the value of a liberal arts education to a business leader?
4. What does a business perspective have to teach the traditional liberal arts perspective?
5. Is competence simply a business issue, or is it a broader issue in nonbusiness arenas?
6. How would a business leader who did not have a liberal arts education go about acquiring the knowledge and skills associated with this educational perspective?
7. What is competitive advantage?
8. How does an individual or a corporation develop a competitive advantage?
9. How does a business leader create a shared vision and high-performance team?

Web Exercises

One way of developing competence discussed in the chapter was that of joining and becoming active in organizations created for professionals in your area. Check out one example, the National Small Businesses Association (http://www. nsba.biz). How would being part of this organization help you be a more competent employee? What resources does it provide for small business managers? How would being a member of the American Pharmacists Association (http:// www.aphanet.org//AM/Template.cfm?Section=Home) help the manager of a drug research company?

The American Management Association offers nearly 20 seminars (http:// www.amanet.org/seminars/index.cfm) for professionals in areas ranging from critical thinking skills to senior executive training. Take a look at their offerings. Based on the area you hope or plan to work in, which seminars would help increase your own competence?

Endnotes

1. Larry Bossidy and Ram Charan, *Execution: The Discipline of Getting Things Done* (New York: Crown Business, 2002).
2. AACSB International, 2002, http://www.time.com/time/personoftheyear/ 2002/poyintro.html#.
3. David Barash, "The Conflicting Pressures of Selfishness and Altruism," *The Chronicle of Higher Education,* July 18, 2000, sec. B8.
4. Ibid., sec. B 10.
5. Ibid.
6. William Durden, "The Liberal Arts as a Bulwark of Business Education," *The Chronicle of Higher Education,* July 18, 200, sec. B 20.
7. Ibid.
8. Ibid.
9. Ibid.
10. *Conference Board 2,* no. 13 (2002).
11. John Beeson and Ann Barrett, "Companies Facing Pressures to Develop New Breed of Corporate Leaders," *Conference Board 2,* no. 13 (2002).
12. Edith Weiner and Arnold Brown, *Insider's Guide to the Future* (n.p.: Boardroom, 1997).
13. Gordon Marino, "Before Teaching Ethics, Stop Kidding Yourself," *The Chronicle of Higher Education,* February 20, 2004, sec. B5.
14. David Ricardo, "On the Principles of Political Economy and Taxation," http://www.systemics.com/docs/ricardo/principles.html.
15. Thomas Friedman, *Lexus and the Oliver Tree: Understanding Globalization* (New York: Doubleday, 2000).
16. Charles Handy, "Creating Wealth Is Not Enough," *Conference Board 2,* no. 13 (2002).
17. Jim Collins, *Good to Great: Why Some Companies Make the Leap . . . and Others Don't* (San Francisco: HarperCollins, 2001).
18. Michael Lewis, *Money Ball: The Art of Winning an Unfair Game* (New York: W.W. Norton and Company, 2003), 119.
19. Henry Mintzberg, *The Rise and Fall of Strategic Planning: Reconceiving Roles for Planning, Plans and Planners* (New York: Free Press, 1994).
20. Kim W. Chan, "Value Innovation: The Strategic Logic of High Growth," *Harvard Business Review,* January/February 1996.
21. Theodore Levitt, "Marketing Myopia," *Harvard Business Review,* September 1, 1975.
22. Bossidy and Charan.
23. Ibid, 184.
24. Ibid, 269.

ἡγεσία

The Nature and Development of Leadership

4

100 Years of Leadership Research

Outline

Leadership is the art of accomplishing more than the science of management says is possible.[1]

Colin Powell

Lance Johnson concluded, "After you have done a lot of deals, you recognize that to develop a business takes a team approach. It's more important to me that the business is successful than who wears the biggest hat."[2] Johnson made small industrial parts using a method called investment casting. In 2000 he sold the business because the process could no longer compete economically with offshore manufacturers, especially in China. He researched methods where he could compete and identified a process called metal injection molding. This process uses hydrogen plasma ovens to heat metal injection molded parts to more than 1,000 degrees Centigrade. The business he sold had become a commodity with associated low margins. The business he created is valued added with associated high margins.

Johnson created a competitive business opportunity, but he needed help with strategy and operations, in addition to capital. He was willing to give up ownership control to access the expertise and capital of Glengary, a private equity firm. Glengary invests only in leaders who will listen and who want access to a talented group of operating partners in addition to capital. Glengary's operating partners, who are seasoned leaders, along with experts in accounting and law, plus college professors with experience in growing businesses, surround the entrepreneur with talent and expertise in areas such as finance, tax, legal, engineering, operations or sales.

In exchange for Glengary's investment, Johnson turned over the chief executive responsibilities to one of Glengary's operating partners, Rick D'Angelo. D'Angelo was educated as an organic chemist and learned about leadership, strategy, marketing, and business development at General Electric (GE). After a successful career at GE, D'Angelo explored buying his own company. He learned about Glengary's unique approach to early-stage investing and decided to become an operating partner working with several companies rather than be limited to operating just his company.

Steve Haynes and Tom Tyrrell are Glengary's managing and operating partners. Haynes had a successful career in public accounting and investment banking. His excitement to pull together a deal was sobered by his realization that early-staged companies could not grow for two reasons: (1) the company founding leaders often took on too much debt and (2) the founding leaders were often creative but lacked leadership competencies, expertise in team building, finance, marketing, selling, or strategy to analyze and execute growth opportunities.

Tyrrell was CEO of American Steel & Wire, where his leadership was recognized by *Inc.* magazine's 1988 Northeast Ohio Entrepreneur of the year award. He led five start-ups or consolidations of metal companies ranging in value from $250 million to $1.5 billion. His experience in working with investment bankers and venture capital firms was extensive. Tyrrell was disturbed that venture capital companies were often limited to financial returns of about five years and lacked concern for sustainability after a company was sold. Accordingly, venture capital firms limited their investment to finance, ignoring human investment in the leadership of the fledging company.[3]

Hyanes and Tyrell formed a unique venture capital firm that invests financial and human capital with a deep commitment to social corporate responsibility. Glengary combines the talents of someone like Johnson with experts like D'Angelo along with legal, accounting, and educational support. The model consists of Glengary investing a relatively small amount of capital, operating partner time/talent, and services such as legal and accounting in return for ownership in the company. Glengary opens its operating partner meetings to Baldwin-Wallace College undergraduate and MBA students to help educate the next generation of entrepreneurial leaders. Glengary measures success by financial return as well as its contribution to education, to local jobs created, to clients created for professional firms, and to value of new products to customers in the region, nation, and world.

Even if you adhere to the leadership theory that people involved with Glengary were somehow born to be leaders, you will have to admit those leaders are not born ready to be leaders. No one is born knowing how to sell a company unable to compete against Chinese manufacturers and, then, create a new injection molding company. No one is born knowing how to make a transition from technical expertise to leading and building a team. These skills are largely learned on the job. A dearth of experience stifles leadership development. The right kind of experience increases, but does not assure, leadership development.

Leadership demands a significant period of preparation, a period of human development. This is true even for those gifted with remarkable leadership talent and motivation. More than two millennia ago, "in the Republic, Plato set out his vision for training leaders for the ideal political state. Starting with good raw material, he felt, was critical to the success of his program. But he also believed that training and work experience were critical. His candidates would undergo rigorous studies of arithmetic and geometry, with a healthy dose of athletics for balance. Afterward came work experience in public office or the military."[4]

We would do well to listen to Plato's sage advice. "Throughout their many years of preparation, Plato would have tested the candidates to determine which ones should advance to the next level of study and work experience. Finally, at age fifty—yes, fifty—Plato's candidates would be ready to rule."[5] Two more important recognitions emerge here. First, some kind of testing is normal before handing over the leadership responsibilities to someone. Insofar as possible, it is important to know that a person is competent to lead. Second, competence typically comes with some seasoning. Although it may be difficult to judge, common sense suggests that there is a time when a potential leader is "ready." We may quibble with Plato's suggested age of 50, but we don't quibble with the idea that leaders go through a developmental process, which readies them.

Ironically, despite over 2,000 years of leadership study and practice, and despite 100 years of social science research, there is much we do not know about leadership. In the past century, the scientific method has been applied to leadership in an attempt to simplify leadership into manageable variables.[6]

A century of empirical research also reveals that leadership is more art than science. However, research does help us understand what we know and don't know about leadership. This appendix will examine research into the nature of leadership by focusing on four key concepts: power, leadership traits, behaviors, and situations. Since everyone is a leader to some degree and can further develop his or her abilities, this research will be examined from the perspective of developing leadership competencies.

4-1 What Is Leadership?

Based on your experiences and observations, whom would you define as a leader? Could you gain agreement with a group of friends on a definition of leadership? After reviewing thousands of studies, *The Handbook of Leadership Theory, Research and Managerial Applications* (1990) uncovered no widely accepted definition of leadership. Clearly, common themes emerge such as the ones just identified: power, traits, behaviors, and situations. Most scholars and practitioners also allow that leadership involves "the process of influence."[7] Since to some degree everyone influences others, everyone potentially is a leader. And most have a vested interest in improving leadership abilities and investing in the leadership development of others.

The study of leadership does not guarantee good leaders. And effective leaders might never have read a leadership book. Understanding research on leadership is not necessary in order to be an effective leader, but surely some application of leadership theory and insights into the kind of experiences that develop leadership can further develop competence.

Whether leaders are born or bred has been the focus of about a century's worth of leadership research. In the late 1800s to mid-1940s, researchers tended to believe that leaders were born, not bred. Research and practice assumed that innate abilities shaped human personality and behavior, regardless of the situations. IQ tests became the hunter traits and the prey. More than 40 years of research and several hundred studies examined the difference between leaders and followers. Researchers concluded that traits did play a role in leadership, but no clarity emerged regarding that role.

The next major phase of leadership research (the mid-1940s to the early 1970s) shifted to the study of behaviors, rather than traits, for two reasons: (1) behaviors are more observable, objective, and accurate than traits and (2) behaviors can be developed and taught, while traits are innate or developed early in life. The Ohio State University and University of Michigan studies identified important leader behaviors, such as initiation of structure and consideration of people. Additionally, they demonstrated that behaviors can be learned. However, behavioral research had the same limitation as the earlier trait research. It assumed an overly simplistic view of leadership, failing to account for the complex situations that leaders experience.

In the final phase—from the 1970s to the present—research confirmed that no best leadership style fits all situations, so contingency theory rules our day. In the 1970s, theories attempted to combine trait, behavioral, situation, and contingency theory to explain successful leadership. This research concluded the following:

1. Different leadership traits, behaviors, and styles can be effective in a given situation.

2. The ability to become the next Gandhi is limited to a few, but people can learn to become good leaders.

3. While a host of factors determine organizational fate, leaders clearly have positive and negative impacts on performance.

4. Leadership needs to be understood in context, since examining leader behavior or the situation in isolation provides an incomplete picture.[8]

Now we begin an examination of each of these four salient characteristics of leadership: power, traits, behaviors, and situations.

4-2 Power

Power is about real or imagined influence over others. Power is the capacity to change our future. As we have already seen for twenty-first-century leadership, managing change is the crucial issue. All else hinges on this. Power also has to do with influencing the degree to which change actually happens. Power does not flow exclusively downhill—that is, from leaders to followers. Followers influence leaders, just as leaders influence followers.

Probably, most successful leaders intuitively understand power, yet even those who have led successfully would benefit from the research conducted on four organizational sources of power: legitimate, reward, coercive, and information. These concepts articulate what leaders know in practice and, if reflected and acted upon, could increase leader understanding and use of power.

1. *Positional or legitimate power* can be readily understood—for example, a colonial nation has more power than the nation it occupies. Lee Kuan Yew ruled Singapore from its inception from 1959 to 1990 with a personality described as "living by the conflict theory of management: you either dominate or are dominated." Lee experienced the power of British colonial rule and then an oppressive Japanese occupation during World War II. As the world's longest-ruling prime minister, he used his power to create a per-capita income higher than England, the world's busiest port, and a global center for manufacturing for a tiny country almost devoid of natural resources. In 1994 an American teenager convicted of a crime was sentenced to be caned. Despite U.S. and international pressure, Lee held firm in using corporal punishment since Singapore's crime rate was among the lowest in the world. Lee argued the U.S. was too permissive, had lost its moral compass, and, therefore, should not impose its power and culture on other nations.[9] Of course, power requires more than authority associated with the position of a colonial power or prime minister. This is easily demonstrated by those who hold positions of authority but who fall short of Lee's abilities to advance his fellow countrymen's economic, educational, and health care progress.

2. *Reward power* is the real or perceived potential for power to control the desires of others—merit pay or promotions, computers, cars, or travel expenses. Other examples are office and parking spaces and the power to intercede on behalf of others. Frequently, leaders erroneously think followers want what the leaders want. Supervisors might believe that the best way to motivate workers is through money, when actually the opportunity to make a difference is more highly valued. An overemphasis on rewards can lead to compliance rather than commitment. It might also cause resentment if employees feel manipulated.

3. *Coercive power* is the opposite of reward power, since influence is achieved through punishment or removal of positive results. Compliance officers fine or fire stockbrokers who violate Securities and Exchange Commission regulations. Supervisors fire employees who violate human resource or ethics policies. The mere perception of coercive power can be as effective as its use. For example, a police officer can drive in traffic with effect without writing a speeding ticket. Like reward power, coercive power can be used well or poorly.

4. *Information power* results from having knowledge that people need or want. For instance, the financial information created and distributed by a chief financial officer is a source of considerable power.

Often, more than one source of power is operating simultaneously in any given leadership situation. Clearly, the issue of power in leadership is not limited to one theory of leadership or to one style of leadership.

We need now to turn from organizational sources of power to three sources of personal power: expert, referent, and prestige. Each operates in concert with one or more of the previously mentioned organizational sources of power.

1. *Expert power* occurs when someone knows more than others. Expertise is different than positional power. A computer technician may well have expert power but have no positional power in a company.

2. *Referent power* concerns whom it is we know. Fear or admiration can be projected onto those who know people of influence. An executive secretary might use his or her power with the boss to put in a good

word for a friend who is in danger of losing a job due to performance problems.

3. *Prestige power* reflects status or reputation earned through success in adding value and/or in developing character. Jimmy Carter is a good example of someone with prestige power. He no longer has the positional power of the presidency, but he carries exceptional worldwide prestige power because of his reputation for integrity, even among those who disagree with his politics.

A critical question is when to lead from each base of organizational and personal power. A middle manager on the corporate fast track must decide whether to challenge a boss who humiliates those needing a job too scared to stand up to the abuse. A senior leader with largely unchecked positional power must decide if a large, deferred retirement bonus negotiated five years ago for an estate plan is warranted now that the company is laying people off. Reflecting on how he learned when to lead from each base of influence, Mark Kirk noted the role his mentors had played. Kirk started his career as a public accountant, was a CFO before he was 30 and had become a CEO by age 40.

As a newly appointed CFO, Kirk flew to Europe with his CEO to raise capital for his company. Succeeding sooner than expected, they sought an earlier flight home from Zurich. Their request for an earlier flight brought good news and bad news. The good news was that two tickets were available. The bad news was that one ticket was in coach and the other was in first class. The CEO purchased the tickets and asked Kirk if he had ever flown first class from Europe. Kirk indicated he had never flown from Europe before. The CEO handed him the first-class ticket and squeezed into the back row of the plane. The CEO's gesture of appreciation for a job well done earned Kirk's loyalty, a loyalty that was reinforced each time Kirk saw his superior exercise strength of character by letting someone else "ride first class."

But Kirk watched as the same CEO pounded the table, using his positional power to get results. He was a leader who understood when to lead from character by personal sacrifice and when to lead from position, demanding action when corporate well-being was at stake.

Kirk also learned a different lesson about power from a man named Cliff, who worked deep in the bowels of an aircraft company. A brilliant engineer, Cliff was a worldwide expert on aircraft lighting systems. No wise leader would consider a new product in this field without seeking out Cliff in his tiny, cramped, hidden office. Cliff led through his competence alone.[10]

While these stories about Kirk and Cliff illustrate positive uses of power, the Milgram study revealed the potential for people with authority to abuse power. The Milgram study asked subjects to help a student memorize facts. The subject administered electric shocks to a student in an adjacent room when that student made a mistake. Subjects increased the voltage and continued to shock learners, as required by an authority figure. Seventy percent of the subjects continued to shock students simply on instructions to do so, even when students cried and complained of heart conditions. This study revealed how far people will go when directed by an authority figure, even though their actions result in injury to another person. This is a graphic illustration of how power can influence others to do what they know is wrong.[11]

4-3 The Limits of Our Knowledge about Power

Based on various studies of power, we can now reasonably draw four generalizations.

1. Effective leaders use all sources of power. They understand the pros and cons of each source and select the appropriate base of power in any given situation.
2. Effective leaders know how to use power to influence others, but they are also open to being influenced by followers. Leaders who rely more on referent and expert power motivate and satisfy followers more than those who did not. The result is less absenteeism and better performance.
3. Some leaders view power as a zero sum game: there is a finite amount of power. If power is shared, everyone gets a smaller piece of the "power" pie. Others see power as making the pie bigger. The popular word to describe power sharing is *empowerment*. Leaders share power through delegation and participative management, but final responsibility still rests with the leader.
4. Effective leaders are willing to use coercive power when deemed necessary. Power is increased when leaders identify available rewards, determine which rewards are valued by followers, and, as much as possible, administer rewards for performance equitably.[12]

Research on power helps us understand its sources and, by implication, how power can be acquired and used. Now the association of power with the virtues must also be recognized.

Mintzberg contends that in practice too much power resides with CEOs who manage by numbers at the expense of art and craft. He proposes that leadership should balance the use of science, art, and craft:

Perspective	Science	Art	Craft
Bases	Logic (oral)	Imagination (visual)	Experience (emotion)
Reliance	Facts	Creativity	Practical experience
Concerns	Replication	Novelty	Usefulness
Decision making	Deductive	Inductive	Iterative
Strategy	Plan	Vision	Venture
Contribution	Systematic analysis informed by inputs and assessments	Art informed by insights and visions	Craft informed by actions and experiments

Source: Adapted from Mintzberg, p. 93.[13]

Mintzberg criticized a CEO style that relied on science and numbers to the exclusion of art and craft. He concluded that not since the 1930s has the focus on short-term share price, at the expense of production of bet-

George Washington, Military Leader and First President of the United States
Washington knew the perils of taking on a leadership role and understood the limitations of his power.
Source: Library of Congress, Prints and Photographs Division, LC-USZ62-7585.

ter products, improvement of customer service, or the completion of innovative research, been so pervasively driven by CEOs with a scientific perspective. He posits that too many CEOs play with other people's (shareholders') money, cost employees jobs through layoffs, destroy long-term market capitalization, and then walk away, enriched by golden parachutes. He believed the business press and business schools have conspired to perpetuate the myth of the "heroic CEO" who supposedly achieves remarkable results single-handedly. He wonders how, by himself, IBM's CEO Gerstner added more than $40 billion to the firm's market value. Since he did not have a lab next to his office, how did Merck's CEO, Gilmartin, generate drugs to replace those whose patents had expired? Mintzberg asserted that the very characteristics resulting in the appointment of MBAs to senior leadership undermine their performance once in power.[14] "They are too smart, too fast, too confident, too self-serving, and too disconnected. Many of the white knights of heroic management turn out to be the black holes of corporate performance."[15]

In contrast, the association of virtue is clearly seen in the example of George Washington as he pondered the sustainability of democracy of this young nation. His ultimate act of delegation and empowerment exemplified the way in which power, guided by virtue, works. Having fought a war against a tyrannical monarch, George Washington recognized that blind allegiance to authority was dangerous. In 1796 he also understood that, even if his authority as president were respected, the future of the United States depended on the peaceful transfer of power. While there was support for Washington to serve beyond his eight years, he concluded that he had achieved as much as his limited power would permit. He humbly thanked the nation for entrusting him with the country's leadership. Prudently, he stated that his long desire to retire coincided with the nation's need for a peaceful transfer of power. He wrote:

> Friends and Fellow citizens:
> The period for a new election of a citizen, to administer the executive government of the United States, being not far distant—and the time actually arrived when your thoughts must be employed in designating the person who is to be clothed with that important trust—it appears to me proper, especially as it may conduce to a more distinct expression of the public voice, that I should now apprise you of the resolution I have formed, to decline being considered among the number of those out of whom a choice is to be made.[16]

To summarize the application of power to leadership development, individuals should evaluate which base of power is the source of their influence, which needs further development, and the degree to which power was used wisely (see Table 4-1).

T a b l e **4-1 Source and Use of Leader Power**

Source of Power	Strengths in Using This Base of Power	Areas to Improve This Use of Power	Wisdom in Using This Power
Positional or legitimate power			
Reward power			
Coercive power			
Information power			
Expert power			
Referent power			
Prestige power			

4-4 Some Leaders Are Born to Greatness

This chapter opened by considering whether those involved with Glengary were born to be leaders. If they were, then these leaders were born with certain leadership traits. Traits are a second fundamental topic of leadership, to be explored as we just did with power.

Based on your experience, what traits would you associate with effective leadership? When they hire leaders, executives likely have a set of traits that they believe predict performance. They also have opinions of whether these traits can be developed. Executives may be confident in their hiring abilities, but Peter Drucker cautioned that, far too often, executives are wrong.

> By and large, executives make poor promotion and staffing decisions. By all accounts, their batting average is no better than .333. At most, one-third of such decisions turn out right; one-third are minimally effective; and one-third are outright failures. In no other area would we put up with such miserable performance; indeed, we need not and should not. Managers making people decisions will never be perfect, of course, but they should come pretty close to batting 1.000.[17]

4-4a Leadership Traits and Behaviors

Colin Powell looked for traits and behaviors such as intelligence, judgment, loyalty, integrity, high energy, a balanced ego, ability to execute, and, most important, the competency to see around corners. He was uneasy when a person's resume and past experience were given more consideration than who the person was today or what he or she would contribute tomorrow. He believed it is easier to train a bright novice in the fundamentals of business than train someone to have integrity, judgment, energy, balance, and drive to get things done.

Typically, the traits or attributes that Powell described are associated with personality. Personality is usually a matter of perspective. We can view personality from our perspective or from the perspective of others. In part, personality is defined by the impression we make on others. We form impressions by asking questions such as "What kind of a person is this leader? Impressions help us decide whether this person is someone with whom we want to work. We use personality characteristics to describe others: kind, aloof, determined, intense, shy, bright, candid, and so on.[18]

Clearly, the picture of personality becomes complicated if we assume that much of who we are may be the result of inner development. In this sense, personality can be defined by reference to our inner consciousness. This issues forth as motive. In many instances, theorists have posited unconscious elements that also determine who we are. Motives can only

T a b l e **4-2 The Five-Factor Personality Model**

Dimensions	Traits	Behaviors
1. Adjustment	Self-control	Open to feedback
	Steadiness	Calm under pressure
2. Agreeableness	Empathy	Cares about others
	Friendliness	Pleasant disposition
		Desire affection with others
3. Dependability	Achievement orientation	Ambitious
	Credibility	Consistent words and actions
	Conformity	Avoids trouble
	Organization	Makes "to do" lists
4. Intellectance	Openness	Travel to foreign countries
5. Surgency	Dominance	Takes responsibility
	Sociability	Large group of friends

Source: Adapted from Hughes, Ginnet, and Curphy, p. 171.[19]

be inferred, but behavior can be observed. Hence, after World War II, behavior became the key to understanding traits. Behavior expresses personality traits. Accordingly, leadership research focused on traits that are observable through behaviors.

There is a practical benefit of interpreting traits through behaviors rather than projecting unseen and unobservable motives. Using behaviors means saying, "I thought we agreed that you would send me a report by Monday and you didn't contact me until Wednesday to let me know the report was not done." Using motives means suspecting that you are lazy and undependable for not completing a report when you said you would. However, we should not discount motive, but rather recognize that motive is harder to measure.

Some leadership theorists assume that traits and behaviors make the key difference in leadership performance. Most other theorists only agree that they make some difference. The question, then, is how are traits predictive and is it possible to evaluate traits? Second, how do we evaluate behavior? While no perfect list exists, a common and helpful grouping (dimensions) is referred to as the five-factor model of personality. On a scale of 1 (low) to 10 (high), rate yourself in Table 4-2 on the five dimensions, traits, and behaviors.

Adjustment

The traits associated with adjustment include self-control and the ability to regulate emotions when people are subjected to stress, adversity, and criticism. Cool under pressure and calm under fire are common adjustment behaviors. Characteristics include the ability to not take failure personally, while other people become tense and full of angst and begin to blame others. Thick-skinned leaders can help a group respond effectively to pressure and adversity.

Agreeableness

The traits associated with agreeableness include friendliness, concern for others, and the desire to be affiliated with others. Agreeable people exhibit behaviors to get along rather than to get ahead. "Emotional intelligence" is exhibited through empathy, openness, and optimism, while those who are not agreeable exhibit behaviors such as insensitivity, aloofness, and pessimism. Agreeableness is vital to leaders who depend on competence to create high-performance teams.

Dependability

Dependability describes more about how we work, rather than how we work with others. Dependable leaders are effective planners, have a strong work ethic, and are conscientious. Those lower in dependability tend to be more creative, impulsive, and less concerned about rules and commitments.

Intellectance

This odd term refers to openness to new experiences, curiosity, and imagination. This characteristic is exhibited through behaviors such as travel, involvement in the arts, sports, reading, and learning about other cultures. In contrast, lower intellectance behavior includes narrower interests and a preference for preservation of the status quo over innovation. Intellectance should not be confused with intelligence, since bright people are not necessarily curious.

Surgency

Another odd term, *surgency* refers to self-confidence, ambition, and desire for power. An individual who is high on the surgency scale is more likely to be outgoing, competitive, and decisive. In contrast, a person low in surgency would prefer to work alone and would have little interest in influencing or competing with other people.

Since traits and behaviors remain relatively constant over time, it is important that leaders and their organizations have some insight into their self-rating of adjustment, agreeableness, dependability, intellectance, and surgency, yet, given the batting average for selecting leaders, as noted by Peter Drucker, reflection and self-knowledge may be anything but common. Too often, leaders, and/or those who hire leaders, place people in situations that highlight weaknesses or fail to compensate for leader weaknesses.[20]

4-4b Leadership and Intelligence

It should come as no surprise that there is a correlation between intelligence and leadership effectiveness. While we hope intelligent people apply for leadership positions, how do we define and measure intelligence? It is easy to assume that intelligence tests are valid and that they actually measure what they say they measure. However, intelligence, or aptitude, tests often are challenged on the basis of cultural and language, gender, and socio-economic bias. Furthermore, there are many variations of intelligence, which a single test is not able to define and measure.

With these significant limitations in mind, research has demonstrated a positive relationship between intelligence and a leader's competence to learn fast, to draw sound assumptions and conclusions. There also is a correlation between higher intelligence and the likelihood of creating a compelling vision and developing strategies that realize the leader's vision. Such people are more likely to solve problems better and to forecast future problems. We conclude that some level of native intelligence is necessary, but not sufficient, to create effective leadership.

The triarchic theory of intelligence includes three elements: analytic ability, practical intelligence, and creative intelligence. Analytic ability is what we often define as intelligence. This dimension refers to the ability to comprehend relationships among issues, as well as to reason inductively and deductively. Standardized test scores are the most common vehicles used to measure analytic ability, yet standardized tests are limited because some people are good test takers but struggle to cope with life. Then others are poor test takers but lead organizations brilliantly. In other words, some people have "practical intelligence," or what is more commonly referred to as "street smarts." They know how things get done and they have the ability to get things done that an intelligence test does not measure.

Creative intelligence is the competence to see patterns before others do, or to create work that is unique and useful. We often attribute creativity to the arts. Composers can hear an orchestra in their head and, then, score what they imagined. Similarly, entrepreneurs imagine unmet customer needs and create business opportunities that meet these needs. While many creative people are intelligent, their creativity is sometimes limited to a specific field, such as an insightful artist who has no sense of business, or an entrepreneur who is brilliant at identifying unmet customer needs but who is musically tone deaf, or a writer who is able to use words that capture exactly how we feel but who is innumerate.[21] How would you rate your analytical, practical, and creative intelligence? Can you identify specific experiences that helped you gain insights into your strengths and weaknesses in addition to ways you might further develop?

4-4c Leadership and Emotional Intelligence

Another form of intelligence is emotional intelligence, measured as one's emotional quotient (EQ), the competence to connect with others through empathy and self-awareness. We can consider that leaders are hired for their IQ and promoted or fired for their EQ.[22] Additional dimensions of emotional intelligence include self-motivation, persistence in the face of adversity, ability to regulate emotions, ability to adapt, and ability to relate and get along with others by understanding our feelings and the feelings of others.

Emotional intelligence purports that leaders who get results free people through positive emotions to do their best.[23] While the role of emotions in leadership is not novel, the contribution of the concept of "emotional intelligence" organizes and labels ideas that have been widely known. Can you identify experiences when the organization where you worked found itself in trouble when led by people who were insensitive, were unaware of their impact on others, and lacked interpersonal competence?

As with intelligence tests, researchers do not agree on the definition of emotional intelligence. Emotions are like personality traits; they are not easily changed. And psychologists tell us that emotions generally are complex. Clearly, leaders who have effective interpersonal competence and ambition and who can control their emotions are often advantaged. Is this anything more than common sense? Is it old wine in a new bottle? Similar to trait theory research that has been conducted for nearly a century, emotional intelligence represents new packaging of old concepts.[24]

To summarize research on traits and behaviors, evaluate in Table 4-3 the strengths and weaknesses of your traits and behaviors.

T a b l e **4-3 Leadership Trait Evaluation**

Traits	Behaviors	Strengths	Areas to Improve
Self-control	Open to feedback		
Steadiness	Calm under pressure		
Empathy	Cares about others		
Friendliness	Pleasant		
Achievement	Ambitious		
Credibility	Words and actions consistent		
Conformity	Avoids trouble		
Organization	Makes "to do" lists		
Curiosity	Travel to foreign countries		
Dominance	Takes responsibility		
Sociability	Large group of friends		
Intelligence	Analysis		
	Practical		
	Creative		
Emotional intelligence	Self-motivation, persistence in the face of adversity, regulates emotions, adaptable and relates to others		

4-5 Some Leaders Have Greatness Thrust upon Them

4-5a Leadership and Motivation

A crucial question about the nature of leadership asks why we do what we do. What motivations drive behavior? As we just saw, we may not be able to observe motives, but since leadership is about motivating ourselves and others to achieve goals, we need to understand its complexity. Content and process motivation theories offer insights into why we do what we do. While these theories offer a way to generalize what motivates people, leaders must deal with the reality that motivation is personal. That which motivates one person will not necessarily motivate another.

This fact requires the leader to spend significant effort and time in understanding someone's motives. For example, researchers and business leaders who attempt to measure employee satisfaction only uncover indirectly whether people are satisfied or unsatisfied with their job. And even if someone says he or she is satisfied, we do not therefore know why he or she is satisfied. Some people are easily satisfied, while others are seemingly impossible to please. Some might be motivated by material gain, while others are charged by making a difference. Some are reflective, proactive, and articulate, so they can express why they are satisfied or dissatisfied with a job, while others are unaware, reactive, and unable to express their satisfactions and dissatisfactions. As for a trait, we cannot observe a motive and then simply backtrack on a clear path that would explain a person's unmet need. We can measure behavior, such as employee retention. We can surmise the motivations of people who stay or leave a job based on observable behavior, yet tracing and understanding motives that led to this behavior are elusive.

4-5b Content Motivation

Can we explain why people behave in particular ways, based on their needs? Content motivation attempts to identify employee needs, so that leaders might align employee interests with corporate objectives.

Hierarchy of Needs

Are some needs more important than others? In the 1940s, Abraham Maslow declared that unmet needs motivate human beings. He organized motives by the well-known hierarchy of needs—physiological, safety, belongingness, esteem, and self-actualization (see Figure 4-1). His conclusion was based on four assumptions:

1. Motivation is only driven by unmet needs.
2. Needs are arranged in a hierarchy from basic to complex.
3. Lower-level needs must be met before higher-level needs.
4. Needs can be classified into five categories.

- *Physiological needs* are basic, such as needs for air, food, housing, and relief/avoidance of pain. Applied to a work setting, basic needs include salary and working conditions.

- *Safety needs,* such as the need for security, are desired once physiological needs have been met. Applied to a work setting, needs include safe working conditions, cost-of-living salary increases, job security, and benefits (medical insurance and retirement).

- *Belongingness needs,* such as those for love, friendship, and acceptance, are desired once safety needs have been satisfied. Applied to a work setting, these needs include being accepted at social functions, conversing around the coffee pot, and, especially important, feeling included in a work team.

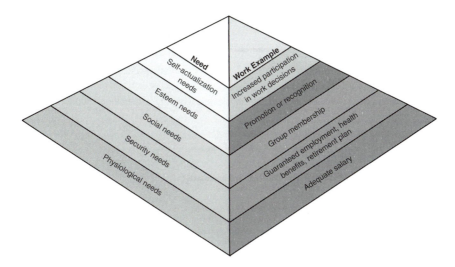

Figure 4-1
Maslow's Hierarchy of Needs

- *Esteem needs*, such as those related to ego, status, and recognition, are desired once belongingness needs have been satisfied. Applied to a work setting, these needs include titles, merit pay, satisfaction, career advancement, and input into making decisions.

- *Self-actualization needs*, such as the need to develop our potential, are desired once esteem needs have been satisfied. Applied to a work setting, these needs include leadership development, the opportunity to create, and the ability to control our destiny.

Maslow's research helps us understand basic human needs. We should note, however, that his notion of a hierarchy has been challenged. For example, it is possible to meet belongingness needs and still not have basic physiological or safety needs met. People can also revert to a lower-level need. Despite these limits, Maslow's hierarchy still provides leaders with a general sense of the relative needs of a given group of employees.[25]

4-5c Two-Factor Theory

To what degree are we motivated by extrinsic (external) or intrinsic (internal) factors? In the 1960s, Frederick Herzberg purported that people are motivated by two categories of factors—maintenance factors and motivator factors. The former refers to satisfaction with external factors, such as pay, security, status, working conditions, and relationships. The latter refers to satisfaction with internal factors, such as achievement,

Maintenance Factors

High extrinsic motivators   Low extrinsic motivators
(Maslow's three lower-level needs: physiological, safety, and belongingness)

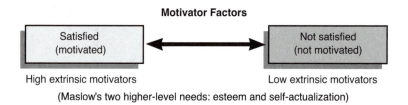

Motivator Factors

High extrinsic motivators   Low extrinsic motivators
(Maslow's two higher-level needs: esteem and self-actualization)

Figure 4-2
Herzberg's Two-Factor Theory
Source: Adapted from Lussier and Achua, p. 79.[26]

recognition, challenge, and growth. Herzberg concluded that these satis-factions can be considered and measured on the two dimensions as shown in Figure 4-2.

Herzberg reported that maintenance factors are a source of dissatis-faction. Leaders are not likely to satisfy or motivate employees based on money and benefits, but they can eliminate these issues as a source of dis-satisfaction. Herzberg recognized that, although pay is important, it is not motivationally as powerful as some intrinsic factors. In an era of empow-erment and team building, leaders who delegate and seek input are meet-ing an intrinsic source of employee satisfaction. These kinds of issues play directly into the discussion of the various virtues. For example, the issue of justice may be an issue in employee satisfaction, if the employee under-stands that receiving a fair wage is acceptable, even if not every person in the company receives the same wage. In fact, injustice would be equal wages for every person in the organization independent of responsibility or performance.

4-5d Process Motivation

Why do people have different needs and how do they go about satisfying these needs? While content motivation theories identify and try to under-stand people's needs, process motivation theories attempt to understand why needs differ, why needs change, how people try to meet their needs, and how they know they are satisfied. Equity theory, expectancy theory, and goal setting theory all attempt to answer these questions. We will examine each in turn.

Equity Theory

As its name implies, equity theory speaks to corporate justice, one of the seven virtues. People compare their inputs—effort, expertise, and skills—and outputs—compensation, promotions, recognition—with their colleagues' inputs and outputs. Do you think the virtue justice is objective? Equity theory postulates that fairness is perception. For example, employees who inflate their performance or overestimate what others earn will be dissatisfied. On the other hand, employees might be satisfied until they learn, whether the information is true or not, that someone is earning more for the same effort.

The problem with equity theory is that it is difficult to know how employees define equity and how they view their inputs and outputs. Of course, leaders should avoid real and perceived perceptions of playing favorites and attempt to use appraisal systems fairly to evaluate pay for performance. However, do you think appraisal systems are objective or a formal way for supervisors and employees to communicate about their perspectives and perceptions?

Expectancy Theory

Are people motivated when they believe they can accomplish a task, they will be rewarded, and the effort is worth it? Expectancy theory offers this conclusion: motivation = expectancy × instrumentality × valence. *Expectancy* refers to the perception that there is a high probability that effort and ability will enable a person to accomplish an objective. If we do not think a task can be completed, we do not try. *Instrumentality* refers to the belief that performance will result in a reward. The more faith we have that performance will result in a reward, the higher our motivation. *Valence* refers to increased motivation based on the value we place on the reward.

While on the surface this theory seems to make sense, research results have been inconsistent. Clearly, context also matters and expectancy theories cannot always take the context into account. For example, expectancy theory works best with employees who have an internal locus of control and who perceive that they control their destiny.

T a b l e   **4-4 Personal Motivation Evaluation**

Motivation	Met	Unmet	Importance
Maintenance			
Salary			
Working conditions			
Job security			
Benefits			
Motivator			
Member of a team			
Recognition			
Merit pay			
Career advancement			
Opportunity to create and control destiny			
Opportunity to develop character			

Goal Setting Theory

Simply stated, this theory concludes that specific and challenging goals are motivating, especially for people who have a high need to achieve. Goals should be clear, specific, and measurable and have a time table. Motivation and commitment are increased when goals are difficult yet achievable and when teams participate in setting goals.

Goal setting is the most validated motivation research. Difficulty arises, however, when we want one goal and reward another. For example, while corporate strategy depends on long-term growth, investors reward quarterly earnings. While corporations have increased their attempts to knock down silos and increase teamwork, performance evaluations often reward individual effort. While hospitals want doctors and nurses to report medical errors, malpractice attorneys and insurance companies drive up costs for those who are honest. While corporations want cost control, budgets are often cut, with no reward when departments save money.[27]

To summarize research on motivation, reflect in Table 4-4 on your career goals and evaluate how these goals are influenced by your motivations.

4-6 Leader Situations

After decades of trait research in the first half of the 1900s, the focus turned to understanding how situations, leader and follower behavior, and performance are related. In the late 1940s, Ohio State University researchers interpreted about 150 statements and concluded that leaders show strength in two dimensions: consideration and initiating structure. *Consideration* refers to leader support of subordinates. Here we see behaviors such as demonstrating concern by speaking up for subordinates' interests, caring about their personal situations, and expressing appreciation for performance. *Initiating structure* refers to leader focus on goals and achievement. For example, this includes establishing standards, creating deadlines, and monitoring performance.

In the 1960s, University of Michigan researchers identified leader behavior that contributed to effective group performance. Rather than describe leader behavior, this research theorized that leaders can emphasize employee or job-centered behavior, but not both. In contrast, the Ohio State researchers believed that consideration and initiating structure can emphasize both.

These Ohio State and University of Michigan studies were the first step in describing what leaders do. Blake and Mouton extended these studies by creating the Leadership Grid that profiles leaders on two dimensions: concern for people and concern for production. This method concludes that the most effective leaders demonstrate both concern for people and concern for production. Studies have supported and contradicted this conclusion, based on whether production measured employee retention, employee perception of production, and other elements.[28]

Another important question is how leaders view human nature. Whether or not leaders have thought deeply about human nature, their thoughts drive their behaviors, which become habits, and ultimately define their character. Do you think people are basically lazy or that people want to work? According to McGregor, if you believe the former, you hold the view of Theory X. If you believe the latter, you believe in Theory Y. Theory X managers view employees as lazy, as requiring coercion, autocratic leadership, threats, and punishment. Theory Y managers view employees as people who like work and, therefore, do not need close supervision if they are committed to the task.[29]

Figure 4-3
Fiedler's LPC Leadership Style
Source: Adapted from Lussier and Achua, p. 143.[30]

4-6a Leadership and Contingency Theories

Leadership research now suggests that traits, behaviors, and situations all need to be taken into account, but the appropriate style is contingent on the situation. In other words, contingency theory means "it depends." One size does not fit all, so leaders need to adapt their style to the situation.

Contingency Leadership Theory and Model

In 1951, Fred Fiedler discovered that leadership styles are relatively constant, since leader traits and behaviors are relatively constant. Contingency leadership evaluates leader style (task and relationship orientation) with the situation (leader/member relationship, task structure, and position power). While leaders can adapt to a situation to some degree, their dominant style is either task or relationship. Fiedler's least-preferred co-worker (LPC) leadership style (a scale of 1 to 10) asks, "Are you more task- or relationship-oriented?" (See Figure 4-3.)

When observed in simulations and on the job, leaders tend to perform in a way that is consistent with their stated preference.

Situational Favorableness

Fiedler's research asks how and to what degree does the situation enable a leader to influence followers. The more control the leader has over followers, the more favorable the situation is to the leader. Situational favorableness is defined by three variables:

1. The relationship between leaders and followers is the most powerful situational factor. Are relationships favorable (cooperative and collegial) or unfavorable (antagonistic and fractured)? Do followers trust, respect, accept, and have confidence in the leader?

2. Structure is second in influence to leader-follower relations. Are tasks structured or unstructured? Do employees perform routine tasks that are clear and easily understood? The more structured the situation, the greater the leader influence.

3. Position power is the weakest factor. Does the leader have power to reward and punish, hire and fire, offer raises and promotions?

Fiedler thinks leaders can make changes easier by changing the situation rather than their style, since preferences are more difficult to change than the situation. For example, if relationships are poor, then the leader needs to rely on emotional intelligence. The leader can make a difference by taking an interest in followers, listening carefully, and personally getting to know people. Providing more or less structure, clearer or less clear standards, tighter or looser deadlines is easier to do than changing the leader's style.

One can see that Fielder's model is a variation on the University of Michigan studies and that it draws on trait and behavioral theories. Furthermore, contingency theory has received mixed results, since some situations are not easily prescribed and, in some cases, it is the style rather than the situation that should be changed.

4-6b Leadership: Path-Goal Theory

In contrast to Fiedler's perspective, this perspective focuses on whether leaders should adapt their styles to fit the situation. House claimed that leader behavior influences follower satisfaction.[31] Therefore, leaders should be directive, supportive, participatory, or achievement-oriented based on the situation to maximize satisfaction and performance. By developing a clear path to achieve individual and organizational goals, the leader impacts follower motivation. The leader also can increase the rewards desired by followers when they reach their goals. In other words, leaders clarify the path to guide followers in how they can achieve what they want and what the organization wants. Leaders first diagnose the situation according to a series of follower perceptions:

1. Authoritarianism—the degree to which followers defer to a leader for what and how tasks should be done

2. Locus of control—the degree to which followers believe they or others can control reaching a goal

3. Ability—the degree to which followers have the ability to achieve goals

Another way to examine the situation is from the perspective of environmental variables. These include task structure, formal authority, and work group:

1. Task structure—the degree to which tasks are repetitive
2. Formal authority—the degree to which the leader has power
3. Work group—the degree to which followers contribute to job satisfaction and relationship among followers

Based on these three variables leaders select one of four styles:

1. Directive—leaders provide structure when followers seek direction from authority, when followers have external locus of control and low ability, or when tasks are complex and desire for authority and satisfaction is high.
2. Supportive—leaders provide high consideration when followers do not want autocratic leadership, have internal locus of control, and have high ability or when environmental tasks are simple, authority is weak, and followers do not provide job satisfaction.
3. Participative—leaders include followers in decision making when followers want involvement, have an internal locus of control, their ability is high, and the task is complex.
4. Achievement-oriented—leaders set difficult but realistic goals, set high expectations, and reward performance when followers are open to autocratic leadership, have an external locus of control, and have high ability. This is effective when the environmental task is simple and authority is strong.

A meta-analysis that included 120 studies revealed that path-goal theory was statistically significant, but results were far from conclusive. Given their complexity, it is difficult to apply these ideas. And it is difficult for managers to know what style best fits a given situation.[32]

Perhaps part of the complexity of using path-goal theory to predict behavior is due to the fact that leadership is relational. Sometimes we are in the "in-group" and sometimes we are in the "out-group." The former involves mutual respect, trust, and an expectation that professional relationships and obligations will continue to grow. Followers enjoy the leader's attention and support and, in turn, receive challenging and interesting assignments. In exchange for being in the in-group, followers work hard, are loyal to the leader, perform at a high level, are highly satisfied, and experience low stress.

In contrast, the leader might perceive out-group members as less motivated and less competent, interact with them less, provide few opportunities to perform, and promote them less often. Their role tends to be limited to a formal job description and there is little or no expectation of high performance, commitment, or loyalty. Whether or not the leader's perceptions are fair, the follower is likely to live up to the expectations. Those in the out-group are more likely to take punitive actions against the organization.

In achievement-oriented cultures, such as the United States and Germany, followers are often measured on competence, performance, and commitment. Formal human resource policies focus on fairness, equal opportunity, and the hiring and promotion of the most qualified. In other cultures, such as the Middle Eastern and French, evaluation is often based on social class and birth. Managers hire people they know and who are recommended by people they know. Skills and competence are secondary to personal recommendations. In Hong Kong and Malaysia, leaders are expected to take care of their own people. In many Arab countries and nations such as Afghanistan, leaders surround themselves with family and clan members who can be trusted and who are loyal. Outsiders are hired to help, but access to the in-groups is based on community factors.

Even in the United States, research suggests that people often associate with those who have similar backgrounds and share their values and beliefs. To counteract this potential bias, leaders need to reach out to employees with whom they do not usually interact. Without a conscious effort to seek out new people, in-group members work well together but ignore input from outsiders. To overcome this bias, organizations might consider the following guidelines:

1. Pick in-group members based on competence and character.
2. Periodically evaluate in-group criteria for competence.
3. Assign tasks to the most skilled, regardless of group membership.
4. Set clear performance-related guidelines for in-group memberships.
5. Keep members fluid to allow movement in and out of groups.[33]

4-6c Leader Substitute

Ricardo Semler is president of a Brazilian company called Semco. His firm relies on well-trained workers who have access to financial and salary information. Workers control when they work and vote for who will be their managers. This structure and culture results in a company that can be operated with a half-dozen senior managers.[34]

Saturn has been ranked among the top-performing divisions at GM, and its employee and customer satisfaction have been among the best in the industry. In part, this success is attributed to self-managed teams, in which supervisors, inspectors, time clocks, and union stewards have been replaced by teams responsible for quality, cost, production, and people. Management and union leaders support the notion that mistakes are part of taking risks. Compensation is linked to meeting quality and productivity goals.[35]

Semco and Saturn are examples of the Substitutes for Leadership Model (SLM). SLM suggests that, when the task is clear and followers are experienced, they are not likely to need leaders to structure their behavior. In some cases, leaders lack power or a dysfunctional culture limits a leader's influence. For example, a manager's influence is limited when they reside in a state different from followers, lack authority to provide meaningful rewards, or deliver resources.

SLM is appealing because the approach combined with technology shares information throughout the organization, reduces layers of management, and makes telecommuting and outsourcing possible. SLM provides a way to free leaders to be more strategic or to empower followers when leaders lack influence. However, like LMX, the model has not been tested extensively.[36]

4-7 Transactional versus Transformational Leadership

MIT's Myron Tribus stated, "The ultimate curse is to be a passenger on a large ship, to know that the ship is going to sink, to know precisely what to do to prevent it, and to realize that no one will listen."[37] In the 1990s, this is how some IBM executives probably felt as they tried to wake up the company to the threat of desktop computers' increasingly using a tool called the Internet. IBM lost $15 billion over a three-year period and managers were taking even less risk than usual. IBM understood how to make and market mainframe systems, but the speed with which Internet applications and software were being adopted was faster than any senior manager had experienced. However, after five years of turmoil, IBM emerged more flexible and capable of competing in the Internet world. In 1999, a quarter of IBM's $82 billion in revenue was Internet-related, contributing to the stock's increasing by 20 points.[38]

Why do people oppose change, even when it is in their interest to adapt? Perhaps they resist loss. By telling people what they need to hear and not what they want to hear, leaders put themselves in harm's way. The leader may have a passion for a better future, but followers focus on the losses they are being asked to accept.[39] However, in a connected world where tariffs are falling, dealing with change is nondiscretionary. GE's Jack Welch cautioned that, if internal change is slower than external change, the end is in sight and the only question is when.[40] Corporations, non-profits, and governments need transformational leaders to help organizations adapt at or faster than the speed of shifting market conditions.

Transformational leadership differs from transactional leadership. The latter involves an exchange of one thing for another—that is, work for pay. Transformation involves the creation of a new form or structure, a change in conditions, or a radical change in outward form or inner character. Transformational leaders prod followers to rise above their self-interests or to redefine their narrow interests to work together.[41]

In the late nineteenth century, Harvard President Charles Eliot often fought with eminent professors, outspoken students, displeased parents, meddling politicians, and presidents of competitor institutions. He inherited an institution whose courses were boring and whose professors were inaccessible and inexperienced. Harvard focused on compulsory chapel and student discipline, while ignoring issues that confronted the country, such as slavery.

In the late 1860s, Eliot was a 35-year-old chemistry professor who had not excelled. He was not particularly warm. Harvard denied him an appointment for a prestigious chair. He left Harvard, toured Europe, and accepted a teaching position at MIT. Few would have guessed that Eliot would be elected Harvard president by a vote of 16 to 8 in May 1869 and would serve Harvard's longest presidency (until 1909).

But Eliot was a transformational leader who admitted Catholics, Jews, African Americans, Chinese and women (Radcliff College). To attract better talent, he increased professor salaries. He strengthened Harvard's professional schools and created new programs in business and education. He abolished compulsory chapel and permitted students to choose their courses. Other presidents raised funds and pursued similar strategies, but Eliot was uniquely clear in his goals and means, enabling Harvard to respond to the economic and political issues of the day. While he was often criticized as being independent, actually he depended on the faculty he attracted, the wealthy Bostonians who funded his vision, and an increasingly progressive American culture. As a transformational leader, Eliot managed to help followers understand the benefits of enlightened self-interest—to work together for common goals as a way to create individual opportunity.[42]

While transactional leadership is part of transformational leadership, the latter includes factors such as

1. *Intellectual stimulation (new ideas and empowerment).* Leaders challenge followers to solve problems and question assumptions. Leaders expect followers to perform at a level not imagined previously. An emotional bond between leaders and followers supports, encourages, and creates a sense of team. Followers are empowered to test their abilities and ideas.
2. *Charisma and inspiration (overcome resistance to change).* Followers are more open to change if leaders offer an inspired vision.
3. *Individual consideration (motivate and encourage).* Leaders and followers develop a personal relationship whereby followers feel they are treated fairly, although not necessarily equally. Followers are motivated and encouraged, since their interests, skills, and values are aligned with the organization's needs.[43]

A couple hundred studies have revealed that transformational leaders are better than transactional leaders in leading change and getting results. In fact, laissez-faire leadership is negatively correlated with effectiveness. In contrast, transactional leaders motivate followers by setting goals and promising rewards for performance that supports the status quo. The significant limitations of these studies is that they do not take into account factors such as the leader's understanding of the industry, business operations, market trends, finance, and strategic ability to cope with stress, negotiate contracts, and execute.[44]

The most important task in understanding leadership is to understand human change. It is key to everything.[45] Obviously, leadership would be far easier and safer if organizations tackled only the issues for which solutions were already known. But change makes this unrealistic. Change is demanding.

> The dangers of exercising leadership derive from the nature of the problems for which leadership is necessary. Adaptive change stimulates resistance because it challenges people's habits, beliefs and values. It asks them to take a loss, experience uncertainty, and even express disloyalty to people and cultures. Because adaptive change forces people to question and perhaps redefine aspects of their identity, it also challenges their sense of competence. Loss, disloyalty and feeling incompetent: That's a lot to ask. No wonder people resist.[46]

To help organizations adapt, transformational leaders may or may not be charismatic. Behind our English word for *charisma* is the meaning, "inspired gift or favor." Charisma involves relationships among people. While charismatic leaders are transformational, not all transformational leaders charismatically achieve results. For example, GE's Jack Welch took on conflict and change and was extraordinarily focused in achieving results, but he is not considered a charismatic leader.[47]

Charisma is a double-edged sword, since ultimately transformational leadership is a moral exercise that should raise the standard of human conduct.[48] In the 1990s, David Koresh was bright, curious, and energetic and had a strong need to be the center of attention, but he was not leading from a moral purpose. He loved church and religious radio programs. He joined the Branch Davidians, a group that had split from the Seventh-Day Adventists. Over four years, by convincing followers he was a living prophet and that Armageddon was coming, he became the group's leader. He prepared for the end of the world by acquiring handguns, assault weapons, and explosives. He made members watch violent war movies and put them through long fasts. In April 1993, his leadership resulted in the death of approximately 60 adults and 25 children, many of whom were killed with a single shot to the head.[49]

Perhaps the most profound way to conclude the discussion on transformational leadership and charisma is with Martin Luther King's *I Have a Dream* speech. It rings with a clarion call to our better nature:

> This will be the day when all of God's children will be able to sing with new meaning—my country 'tis of thee, sweet land of liberty, of thee I sing; land where my fathers died, land of the pilgrim's pride; from every mountain side, let freedom ring—and if America is to be a great nation, this must become true. So let freedom ring from the prodigious hilltops of New Hampshire. Let freedom ring from the mighty mountains of New York. Let freedom ring from the snow capped Rockies of Colorado. Let freedom ring from the curvaceous slopes of California. But not only that. Let freedom ring from Stone Mountain of Georgia. Let freedom ring from Lookout Mountain of Tennessee. Let freedom ring from every hill and molehill of Mississippi, from every mountainside, let freedom ring. And when we allow freedom to ring, when we let it ring from every village and every hamlet, from every state and every city, we will be able to speed up that day when all of God's children—Black and White men, Jews and Gentiles, Protestants and Catholics—will be able to join hands and to sing in the words of the old Negro spiritual: Free at last, free at last, thank God Almighty, we are free at last.[50]

4-8 If We Have the Experience, Do We Understand Its Meaning?

The research on why some leaders succeed and others fail can be summarized briefly by stating that those who succeed know how to reflect, learn, and adapt and those who fail do not know how to reflect, learn, and adapt. Successful leaders avoid becoming too comfortable and they develop new behaviors to cope with new responsibilities.

All leaders are in danger of meeting a new challenge with old behaviors inappropriate to the new situation in which they find themselves. The behavior associated with successfully demonstrating technical expertise is different from the management of technical workers. The behavior associated with being excellent at working through details to control an outcome is different from delegation to others. Managing an audit unit effectively is different from thinking strategically to build an audit practice.

Flaws and blind spots unnoticed before a promotion to a leadership role can become glaring. A salesperson's inability to build a team does not matter when he or she serves customers well, but it does matter when promoted to sales manager. An engineer's arrogance does not matter when the result is high technical standards but does matter when people do not want to work with an egotistical manger.

When leaders assume increased responsibility, they benefit from understanding the need to change behavior—perhaps the very behavior that led to their promotion. Consider the behavior and skills needed at different levels of leadership responsibility:

1. *Manage yourself.* Can young managers learn to be responsible for their conduct, performance, and development in their first professional position? A successful transition from college to an entry-level leader position often requires learning about personal strengths and weaknesses and building healthy working relationships.
2. *Lead others.* Can leaders make the turn from managing their performance to managing the performance of others? A successful transition requires setting standards and delegation.
3. *Lead multiple departments.* Can leaders master increased scope and complexity as measured by size of budgets, people, and markets? A successful transition requires leaders to create a team among people more expert in an area than they are.
4. *Lead a division.* Can leaders handle an increase in the number of stakeholders served and profit and loss responsibility? Leading a division requires that leaders accept accountability even though performance will depend on people and events beyond their control.
5. *Lead an enterprise.* Can leaders provide strategic, operational, and people skills to satisfy key stakeholders? A successful transition requires that leaders develop the competence to lead change and transform an organization to adapt to external markets.[51]

Interestingly, independent of function or industry, successful leaders learn similar lessons from the same challenges and derailed leaders do not learn from their experiences. Ineffective leaders often have the experience and miss the meaning. Successful leaders are active learners. They keep notes on interesting ideas, seek feedback and mentors and ask probing questions: "What am I learning?" "What do I need to do differently?" "What habits have made me too complacent?"

Experience does not ensure leadership development, but a dearth of experience certainly does little to create better leaders. The following experiences are especially helpful in developing leader competence and character, especially those that broaden leaders' perspectives to include customers, shareholders, vendors, and the community.

1. *Learning from bosses and other people.* Learn how integrity or lack of it influences competence to lead.

2. *Challenging jobs.* Start-up operations, turnaround situations, or completing important projects under pressure all require that leaders can cope with stress and learn quickly to work with difficult people.

3. *Civic engagements.* Sometimes leaders find it difficult to acquire strategic or important project work in their jobs. Serving on nonprofit boards or volunteering for a strategic assignment can build a leader's expertise and professional network—do well by doing good.

4. *Coursework.* Academic experiences can build leader competencies and character through reflection. Courses provide a forum for comparing abilities and character to those of others in order to build self-confidence. Faculty and peers also help leaders gain insights into different perspectives.

5. *Hardships.* We may learn more from our failures than our successes. Making mistakes, being in dead-end jobs, being fired, or firing someone can teach humility. Personal tragedy and suffering can force inward reflection on our humanity, resilience, and flaws.

6. *Leaps in scale or scope.* Increase in the number of people, budget size, functions, markets, or products requires team building and delegation. Leaders are forced to move from doing a job to seeing the job gets done, generating commitment, and letting go of control.

7. *Projects and task forces.* Plant closing, acquisitions, work with a board, and tight deadlines on vital projects all require working with unfamiliar people and subjects. Leaders must ask the right questions, rely on the expertise of others, find a mentor, and develop character.

8. *Start-ups.* Today's economy demands that leaders understand innovation and growth. Creating new products or entering new markets involves less history, fewer rules, and increased ambiguity. Leaders must plan, build teams, execute, learn from mistakes, and produce. These experiences teach leaders about the burden of their responsibilities and ways to take intelligent risks.

9. *Turnarounds.* Turning a profit from a unit bleeding red often requires overcoming dysfunctional teams or nonaligned departments. These

T a b l e   **4-5 Evaluate Leadership Experiences to Develop Competence and Character**

Experience	What Competencies Did You Learn?	What Did You Learn about Character?	How Could You Acquire This Experience?
Learning from bosses and other people			
Challenging jobs			
Civic engagements			
Coursework			
Hardships			
Leaps in scale or scope			
Projects and task forces			
Start-ups			
Turnarounds			

experiences teach leaders the skill to balance the need to be tough enough to create change, with the need to be compassionate to ensure productive working relationships.[52]

Over the course of a career, leaders experience inept bosses, assume responsibility for solving tough business problems with a cranky or dysfunctional team, and have the distasteful task of firing a long-term, loyal employee. The best leaders change because they have to respond under pressure. Since successful leaders learn, adapt, and reflect on their experiences, consider in Table 4-5 how experiences that best develop leadership influence your growth. Also determine which experiences you should pursue to develop further your leadership competencies and character.

4-9 Conclusion

There is a leadership crisis that can be seen all around us. At least in modern times, citizen and employee anger and cynicism directed at political, civic, and corporate leaders who are not trusted are at record levels. There is a serious lack of leadership for many positions. There are two burning questions in every age that are especially acute in our present age—who will be our leaders and how will they be developed? There are many answers to these two questions. This chapter focused on the important features of leadership theory. While leadership theory is an evolving science, the good news is that research has revealed that leadership can be learned.

In that sense, leadership is not simply the domain of those born to be leaders, yet one feature of leadership that is not always treated in leadership theory, but that is crucial to effective, long-term leadership, is character. And when a person develops character and acquires competencies, then there is a leader ready to lead change and truly make a difference in a business, in the community, and in our world. A leader without character and competence is either a pathetic person or a dangerous person—and perhaps both.

Leadership is character. Character develops and deepens as we collaborate with others, earn trust, gain commitment, and build a shared vision. Our era of turmoil and change calls for character-based leadership.

Chapter Quiz

1. The Ohio State University and University of Michigan studies in leadership showed that:
   a. leadership was only an inborn trait
   b. leadership could be learned
   c. leadership came only from having strong father figures as a child
   d. leadership ability has a direct correlation to IQ level
2. The four organizational sources of power are:
   a. legitimate, reward, coercive, and information
   b. reward, coercive, information, and secretive
   c. financial, reward, legitimate, and information
   d. information, financial, political, and coercive
3. When one person knows more than others, the power that person has is:
   a. referent power
   b. prestige power
   c. executive power
   d. expert power
4. Which of the following is an example of referent power?
   a. Jack plays golf with Sandy, the head of his company. When promotion time comes around, Jack mentions that his assistant Alissa has been putting in especially long hours and doing good work.
   b. Karen knows more about the company's real-estate holdings than anyone else, and is happy to share her knowledge.
   c. Bertram used to work for a high-powered law firm in Germany, and continues to get speaking engagements in Europe, talking with managers in various fields there.
   d. Patricia is a former Ambassador to Trinidad and is helping Errol as a consultant on a project involving Caribbean culture.

5. The five factors of the Five Factor Personality Model are:
   a. empathy, friendliness, ambition, dominance, and adaptability.
   b. adjustment, agreeableness, dependability, intellectance, and surgency.
   c. self-control, willpower, mannerisms, sociability, and drive.
   d. credibility, conformity, consistency, steadiness, and organization.

6. Surgency refers to an individual's:
   a. ability to motivate and empathize.
   b. personal curiosity and desire to learn.
   c. methods of rewarding and punishing.
   d. self-confidence and ambition.

7. In achievement-based cultures, employees are evaluated on the basis of:
   a. loyalty and obedience.
   b. social class and family position.
   c. competence and performance.
   d. ability to care for others.

8. The SLM theory states that:
   a. when the task is clear and followers are experienced, they are not likely to need leaders to structure their behavior.
   b. if workers are asked to multitask, they are likely to need leaders to structure their behavior.
   c. when the task requires leader-follower interaction on the team level, followers are not likely to need leaders to structure their behavior.
   d. if the leaders are experienced at laissez-faire management, the followers will embrace the model and are not likely to need leaders to structure their behavior.

9. "Charisma" means:
   a. the gift of tongues.
   b. inspired gift or favor.
   c. inspired speech or idea.
   d. the gift of comfort.

10. A good example of a company under transformational leadership is:
   a. a company where the employees are working towards an IPO or similar event.
   b. a company where the employees are switching from a strict schedule to a flextime program.
   c. a company where the employees are united to create a new vaccine.
   d. a company where the employees are moving from a primarily temporary workforce to a more permanent situation.

Note: You can find the correct answers to these questions by taking the quiz and then submitting your answers in the Online Edition. The program will automatically score your submission. If you miss a question, the program will provide the correct answer, a rationale for the answer, and the section number in the chapter where the topic is discussed.

Questions for Thought

1. What kinds of leadership traits do you think you have? How do you identify them? What kinds of shortcomings do you feel you have that might hamper your leadership abilities? How can you overcome these?
2. There are many kinds of power. Which kinds are best for what situations? Which kinds do you find yourself dealing with the most?
3. Emotional intelligence is a much-discussed topic in business today. What helps someone develop a high "EQ"? What are methods of helping your employees become better leaders through evaluation of their EQs?

Web Exercises

Visit the Emotional Intelligence consortium at http://www.eiconsortium.org/ and read any of the articles discussing EQ and business practices. Is there a consensus on how emotional intelligence plays into successful business dealings? For even more information on emotional intelligence and to participate in a study, go to http://eqi.org/toc2.htm.

Visit several sites that promote leadership development, such as http://www.mapnp.org/library/ldr_dev/ldr_dev.htm, http://www.heartlandcenter.info/, and http://www.leadershipnow.com/. What common things do these groups want to teach? What are their goals? What would you add or remove from their training programs, based on what you have read in this chapter? How is leadership best learned?

Endnotes

1. Colin Powell, http://www.fertilizerworks.com/html/market/Leadership.PDF.
2. Mary Vanac, "A Different Kind of Venture Capital," *The Plain Dealer*, January 9, 2005, sec. G6.
3. Ibid., sec. G1 and G6.
4. Henry Mintzberg, *Managers, Not MBAs* (San Francisco: Barrett-Koehler, 2003), 199.
5. Ibid.
6. Afsaneh Nahavandi, *The Art and Science of Leadership* (Upper Saddle River, NJ: Prentice Hall, 2003), 32.
7. Charles Manz and Christopher Neck, *Mastering Self-Leadership* (Upper Saddle River, NJ: Prentice Hall, 2003), 2.
8. Nahavandi, 37–38.
9. Arthur Shriberg, David Shriberg, and David Lloyd, *Practicing Leadership: Principles and Applications* (New York: John Wiley & Sons, 2002), 117–18.

10. Mark Kirk, "Competence, Character and Positional Power," Baldwin-Wallace College, Berea, OH: January 23, 2004.
11. Stanley Milgram, "Behavioral Study of Obedience," *Journal of Abnormal and Social Psychology* 67 (1963): pp. 371–78.
12. Richard Hughes, Robert Ginnett, and Gordon Curphy, *Leadership: Enhancing the Lessons of Experience* (New York: McGraw-Hill Irwin, 2002), 121.
13. Mintzberg, 93.
14. Ibid., 118.
15. Ibid., 119.
16. Jacob Needleman, *The American Soul: Rediscovering the Wisdom of the Founders* (New York: Tarcher/Putnam, 2002), 113.
17. Hughes, 79.
18. Powell.
19. Hughes, 171.
20. Ibid., 171–73.
21. Ibid., 186.
22. Daniel Goleman, Richard Boyatzis, and Ann McKee, *Primal Leadership: Realizing the Power of Emotional Intelligence* (Boston: Harvard Business Press, 2002).
23. Ibid.
24. Hughes, 198.
25. Robert Lussier and Christopher Achua, *Leadership: Theory, Application, Skill Development* (Thomson, Southwestern, 2004), 76–77.
26. Ibid., 79.
27. Ibid., 81–85.
28. Hughes, 208–11.
29. Shriberg, 28.
30. Lussier, 143.
31. Hughes, 377.
32. Ibid., 142–46.
33. Nahavandi, 166–71.
34. Ibid., 173.
35. Lussier, 321.
36. Nahavandi, 173–75.
37. Hughes, 389.
38. Ronald Heifetz and Marty Linsky, *Leadership on the Line: Staying Alive through the Dangers of Leading* (Boston: Harvard Business Press, 2002), 21–23.
39. Ibid., 26–27.
40. Hughes, 406.
41. James MacGregor Burns, *Transforming Leadership: A New Pursuit of Happiness* (New York: Atlantic Monthly Press, 2003), 24.
42. Ibid., 68–70.
43. Nahavandi, 236–37.
44. Hughes, 420.
45. Burns, 17.
46. Heifetz, 19.
47. Lussier, 340.
48. Burns, 2.
49. Hughes, 404.
50. Ibid., 409.
51. M. McCall and M. Lombardo, *Off the Track: Why and How Successful Executives Get Derailed,* Technical Report no. 21 (Greensboro, NC: Center for Creative Leadership, Greensboro, NC.
52. Robert W. Eichinger and Michael M. Lombardo, *Twenty-Two Ways to Develop Leadership in Staff Managers,* report 144 (Greensboro, NC: Center for Creative Leadership, 1990).

ἀνδρεία

Courage

5

Outline

5-1 Courage (Fortitude)

It is likely that most people think they know exactly what courage means. But do they? The word is rooted in the French *coeur*, which means "heart." One can take it back to the Latin, *cor*, which translates as "heart" or "soul." To be courageous is to "take heart," to be or do something "with all your mind" or "soulfully." Understood as such, it is easy to see how courage is the quality of spirit enabling humans to face the future bravely and to act valiantly.

Standing alone for a year against Hitler's blitzkrieg, which conquered Europe in less than a year, Winston Churchill rallied the British at their darkest moment. After the war, he said, "Never flinch, never weary, never despair. No matter how bleak the forecast, courage would carry us forward, for courage is the essential virtue because it guaranteed all the others."[1]

From the same time period, there is no better example of courage than the life and tragic death of Dietrich Bonhoeffer. The Nazis executed Bonhoeffer on April 9, 1945, only a few days before the Allies liberated the prison camp at Flossenbuerg, Germany, where he was incarcerated. A brilliant young theologian, musician, and man of international culture, Bonhoeffer had been a pastor in Barcelona and lecturer in Berlin before spending the academic year 1930–1931 (the year after the collapse of Wall Street) in study at Union Theological Seminary in New York City. After a couple of years in London, he moved back to his native Germany to lead an underground theological seminary. He returned to the United States in the summer of 1939, and his American friends pleaded with him to stay and teach at the seminary. Instead, Bonhoeffer felt called to return to Germany to work with his people to resist the evil that was spreading across Europe.

He became involved in a plot to kill Hitler and, when the plot was uncovered, Bonhoeffer and others were arrested and detained. Payne Best, an English officer imprisoned with him, shared this final scene of Bonhoeffer: "the door opened and two evil-looking men in civilian clothes came in and said, 'Prisoner Bonhoeffer, get ready to come with us.' Those words 'come with us'—for all prisoners they had come to mean one thing only—the scaffold."[2]

Was Bonhoeffer virtuous or stupid? He could have remained safely in New York City and written many more books. Clearly, in one sense he failed: the plot to kill Hitler was unsuccessful. Hitler's frightening competence and total absence of character led to the execution not only of Bonhoeffer but also of six million Jews and too many others. Even though the plot failed and he was executed, Bonhoeffer was a man of courage, and this courage shaped his character. Comparing Hitler and Bonhoeffer presents a stark contrast of character. Bonhoeffer's actions were courageous—virtuous—because they aimed at the greater good.

5-2 The Anatomy of Courage

Some would argue that courage is the most comprehensive virtue of all virtues. At the beginning of his magisterial study on courage, Paul Tillich observes that "few concepts are as useful for the analysis of the human situation. Courage is an ethical reality, but it is rooted in the whole breadth of human existence and ultimately in the structure of being itself."[3]

Another fascinating study, *The Anatomy of Courage,* by World War I British medical officer Lord Moran concludes: "Courage is a moral quality; it is not a gift of nature like an aptitude for games. It is a cold choice. . . . Courage is will power."[4] Five important features of courage, uncovered in the penetrating quotation from Lord Moran, determine whether servant leadership occurs. Because courage is a moral quality, it is ethical—that is, it is virtue. Second, and very important, courage is learned. Third, courage has to do with will. Fourth, courage is motivational. Finally, courage is power; that is, there is energy in courage. We can explore each of these five features in order to understand how people learn to "take heart."

For something to be courageous, virtue must be there. Courage always brings to bear a moral quality. We have already seen that virtue aims at the good and that the good is what introduces the moral quality. With this understanding, we are able to be more careful about what actions we describe as courageous. Is a daredevil stunt "courageous"? It is not, by this definition, which says courage is virtue. A daredevil stunt may be stunning, unbelievable, or just plain dangerous, but that does not make it courageous. The daredevil certainly has guts. Courage must have a moral quality.

Courage does not have to be daring. It does not even have to be difficult or involve heroic effort or unusual strength. To be sure, in the ancient world as well as our contemporary era, there are appropriate links between the idea of courage and the battlefield. Courage suggests struggle and requires action and endurance. All of these ideas of courage continue to be present when courage is understood as virtue. The foe is not a known enemy but, rather, anything that prevents or corrodes the good. Courage is everyone's "fight" for the good life, and the good life has to be understood as the virtuous life.

Hence, we can see the basic difference between having courage and having guts. Courage has to do with heart—with virtue. The other, guts, has to do with pure willfulness. There is no moral quality. Scott Sullivan, WorldCom's CFO, certainly had guts to misrepresent earnings by treating operating expenses as capital expenses, but there is no courage in evidence.

Second, courage is learned. Like character, of which it is a part, courage is not a gift of nature. As part of character, it must also be taught. One has courage because one learns it. This is true for all the virtues. As far back as Aristotle, it can be shown that "all the moral virtues have to be learned and practiced, and they become virtues only through action, for 'we become just by doing just acts, temperate by doing temperate acts, brave by doing brave acts.'"[5]

That courage can be taught gives it a democratic aspect—that is, anybody can become courageous. It is not reserved for the smart, the strong, or the select, nor is it limited to the heroic. No one is simply lucky because he or she has courage. Every human being can learn courage. Simply put, courage is learning and supporting what is right and good. It is the good or the right that will define the moral quality, which makes the choosing of it courageous. And every choice of right or good is an act of courage. It is a virtuous move, contributing to the development of character.

WorldCom's Cynthia Cooper and her colleagues were credited with uncovering the evidence that Scott Sullivan had misrepresented earnings. This action was not war, but courage was called for in their decision and action. There were risks and, appropriately, there were fears to be conquered. They risked their jobs. With limited power, these middle managers challenged the unethical conduct of WorldCom's senior financial officer and its auditors. They were courageous because their choice had a moral quality to it. They were virtuous.

To speak of choice introduces the third feature of courage—the will. In fact, it could be said that courage concerns what people "will be" or "will do." Here it might be objected that the Bonhoeffer story, then, is not one of courage, because Bonhoeffer had no choice whether to be hanged. This is true, but, once the plot was uncovered and he was imprisoned, one can say Bonhoeffer's hanging became his destiny. Clearly, Bonhoeffer made a choice when he decided to return to Germany to free his country from tyranny. That was his choice. Bonhoeffer did not choose his death, but his choice, like all choices, had consequences and it was a choice for which he paid the ultimate price.

It is in the act of choosing that the notion of will is central to understanding courage. Once again, the Latin word behind will is instructive; "will" translates as *voluntas*. Our English word *voluntary* comes from this

Latin root. *Voluntas* also can be translated as "desire, attitude, purpose, and aim." This range of words gives breadth to courage.

We can see how Bonhoeffer was a man of courage, even though he could not alter his tragic destiny. Bonhoeffer's choice to return to Germany and become involved in a plot to eliminate Hitler was an act of courage. It would not have been courage *only if* it had succeeded. It was an act of courage—a choice with a moral quality—because Bonhoeffer chose the good. Although he was uneasy with taking another person's life—even Hitler—Bonhoeffer saw no other option to eradicate the evil that Hitler incarnated and enacted.

A corporate application of this ideal is captured in Lubrizol's *Ethical and Legal Conduct Guidelines,* which illustrates the voluntary nature of courage and the price that is often paid to act with courage: "do what is right even when it is likely to cost us more than we want to pay and more than we think is fair. It occasionally requires us to stand up and be counted, to fight for our beliefs, to demonstrate the courage of our convictions. Because social, economic and political pressures may make it difficult for us to do the right thing, integrity embodies the idea of moral courage and is considered a fundamental measure of character."[6]

This is a contemporary rendition of Heraclitus' words "character is destiny." If we have character, we act with courage. That is our destiny. But destiny is not predestination. To act courageously means to choose our attitude, our purpose, and our aim. But it does not mean we can dictate or control how our choice will play out.

The fourth feature of courage is its motivational aspect. Motivation is a key concept in the contemporary business world. It is also one of the key features of the modern study of psychology, and it is a core issue in human development. For example, a widely used text in psychology states, "Motivation is the general term for all the processes involved in starting, directing, and maintaining physical and psychological activities."[7] However, this does not yet mean we are talking about courage. It might mean that nothing more than being hungry moved one to eat. This is exactly what motivation does: it moves us.

Another word hiding in *motivation* is the word *motive*. Motivation is having the motive that moves us. Again, psychology says, basically, "All organisms move toward some stimuli and activities and away from others, as directed by their appetites and aversions."[8] The idea that some things motivate us by attracting us—by causing us to want them—and that some things move us to avoid them gets us closer to understanding how courage is motivational.

To understand the motivational component of courage, it is necessary to remember what makes courage a virtue—namely, the right or the good. It is the good that attracts us or causes us to desire it that motivates us to act courageously. If one has not learned to value doing the right thing or being a good person, one has no motivation to become a person of courage. Sometimes the motivator is a drive—a driving force. Thus, we can say that courage is driven by the desire to do the right thing or to choose the good thing. Or motivation can be seen as an incentive. An incentive lures instead of drives. Lubrizol's *Guidelines* demonstrates that there may be competing incentives. If we aim to do the good, that is one incentive. But there may be other social, economic, or political pressures offering incentives contrary to choosing the good or the right thing. The decision to act courageously—to act ethically—is often difficult or complex, because there are competing incentives.

Indeed, this is the key to understanding how otherwise good people make unethical choices. They have no will to resist; they lack resolve to chart the course of virtue. They may be driven by something other than the good. Or there are compelling incentives not to do the right thing. The central question of the recent Enron, WorldCom, and Tyco corporate scandals is "Why did the controls not work?" What motivated the auditors, the audit chair, the compensation committee, the board, and the analysts? Why did these otherwise ethical people not choose to fulfill their oversight responsibility? In many cases, board members did not benefit and in fact, were hurt by misstated earnings, which reduced their wealth, along with that of other shareholders, so why were they asleep at the switch?

The will to do good is closely linked to the last feature of courage—namely, energy. Courage demands energy. Motivation may be the drive, or incentive, for choosing the path of courage—the virtuous way. But one needs the energy to will it and then pull it off. The key word here is *power*—there has to be power for the will to be motivated to choose. Energy is power. Finally, courage is an act, not merely an intention.

Science tells us that there are two kinds of energy: potential and kinetic. Potential energy is stored energy, there to be tapped when needed. A good example of this is a car battery, ready to power an engine when the key turns. Potential energy can be positional. When the ram of a pile driver is raised, ready to strike, that is potential energy, always ready to be released. This kind of potential energy in courage is easily seen in a person who already has developed character, who already is a virtuous person. The energy for courageous action—or any of the other virtues—is ever ready to be released into any life situation. The person is like a virtuous battery; the energy for courage is already there. The younger person—or the less developed person in terms of character—obviously has much less (or no) potential energy for actions of courage.

Probably every one of us could name people with this kind of potential energy. In September 2002, Hank Paulson, CEO of Goldman, Sachs Group, had the courage to speak the truth. A self-described reserved person who kept his distance from reporters, Paulson chose the National Press Club in Washington as a forum to state that, in the course of his business career, he had never known business leadership to be less reputable.[9] Even though Paulson believed that the Enrons and WorldComs are the exception and not the rule, it took courage for him to say to his peers that the scrutiny under which business finds itself is well deserved.

The opposite of potential energy is kinetic energy—the energy of motion. Motion creates energy. It is not already available. When applied to courage, this means that courage is created. This fits very well for the person who is learning to be virtuous. As we have seen, no one starts out life as virtuous, as a person of character. Often there are incentives to develop courage. The incentive to be good may be rewarded with one being told one is a "good person." The move to achieve this creates the kinetic energy of courage. It is not yet a habit, but it is the first act, which can be repeated to form a habit. Hence, character is learned, and this learning process develops the kinetic energy of courage by the very motion of learning.

5-3 Developing Courage

Extreme behaviors such as Bonhoeffer's courage of selflessness or WorldCom leaders' cowardice in accepting responsibility for self-serving behavior clearly reveal the presence or absence of virtue, yet most of us conduct ourselves somewhere between these two extremes. Perhaps most of us fail to exercise courage to do good more often than exhibit the cowardice of self-serving conduct. We might give more of our heart to personal success than to the success of others.

The concept of Level 5 leaders captures the subtle difference between leaders who focus on personal success and leaders who focus on the success of others. A Level 5 leader has all the abilities of leaders at the other four levels, but leaders do not necessarily move through each level sequentially.

> Level 1: *highly capable individual*—A person who uses talents, knowledge, skills, and a work ethic to make a contribution.

Level 2: *contributing team member*—A person who works effectively with others to achieve a group objective.

Level 3: *competent manager*—A person who organizes people and resources to achieve a goal.

Level 4: *effective leader*—A person who creates a high-performance team that has a common vision.

Level 5: *Level 5 executive*—A person who lifts a company from good to great through a seemingly contradictory blend of personal humility and professional will.[10]

The primary difference between Level 5 and the other levels is humility and will—humility in the sense that Level 5 leaders credit success to other people and good fortune, will in the sense that Level 5 leaders are driven to build a stronger company independent of personal gain for themselves.

The Fortune 500 list has included 1,435 companies since 1965, and only 11 companies have averaged 6.9 times return over the general stock market for 15 years. For perspective, Jack Welch outperformed the stock market 2.81 times during his reign at General Electric from 1986 to 2000. The common denominator of the 11 companies was Level 5 leaders, people who possessed remarkable will to credit others for corporate success and the courage to take full responsibility for poor results.[11]

Colman Mockler, CEO of Gillette, displayed this unusual blend of will and humility. He was reserved and gracious during three colossal takeover attempts, twice by Ronald Perelman and once by Coniston Partners. Those who underestimated Mockler's gentle nature as a weakness lost to him. During one proxy battle, Mockler and other senior leaders contacted thousands of investors personally to win their votes. He dug in for a fight to build a greater company, rather than pocket millions by selling his own shares. If an investor had accepted Perelman's offer of a 44 percent premium over Mockler's offer and invested these funds in the stock market for 10 years, he or she would have made 64 percent less than the investor who had stuck with Mockler.[12]

It is often easiest to understand how something develops by seeing what is avoided or overcome by its development. What is avoided or overcome by courage is a degree of cowardice. Cowardice involves concern for self-preservation, personal gain, and recognition. We all know what a coward is, but uncovering the features of cowardice reveals that it actually is a complex concept. Let us look at three components of cowardice and then see how developing courage leads to the formation of character.

The first aspect of cowardice is ignorance. Simply not knowing leads many people into the cowardice of what can be called "ignoring" (notice the relationship of *ignorance* and *ignoring*). *Ignorance* is not necessarily a passive word. Actually, ignorance can be quite active in forming people. It can be said that ignorance "mal-forms" people into cowardice. A mal-formed person is a badly formed person. Ignorance makes it difficult, if not impossible, to know how to be or what to do. The longer one is ignorant, the more deforming the experience is.

Corporate boards and senior leaders may well be ignorant of the financial benefit of Level 5 leadership, since only a fraction of 1 percent of all leaders in charge have this characteristic. In contrast, many egocentric leaders populate boards and senior executive positions, which explains why so few companies can make the leap from good to great.[13]

In the face of ignorance, the development of courage really does require learning. At the basic level, the development of courage means learning about virtue—courage being one aspect of the virtuous life. Courage is first among the virtues for good reason; it underlies every other virtue.

The second aspect of cowardice is fear. Fear intimidates or even debilitates. Fear constricts or even shuts one down. Because of fear, we are unable to be what we could be. Fear disempowers our will to act with courage. Unlike ignorance, fear is not an intellectual deficit. It can be linked to not knowing, but fear has an emotional component. The essence of fear is that it has a specific object, or focus. We might be afraid to let a customer know about a defect in our company's product for fear of losing an account. We know it is wrong, but we fear speaking out. Fear mutes our voice and makes us a coward.

In confronting fear, the development of courage requires learning, but a different kind of learning than that which overcomes ignorance. We can develop courage and cope with fear in four different ways: facing it, analyzing it, attacking it, and enduring it.[14] Learning to face fear is itself a first act of courage, a movement of our will (kinetic energy). As we saw, courage is learned first as a specific act. For example, what does one do when one's boss is a tyrant, pitting people against each other as she threatens to lay off anybody who dares challenge her authority? The first act can be as simple as turning to face fear.

Analyzing fear is another intentional step. Sometimes analysis reveals that there actually is nothing to fear. Some companies have established ethics hot lines, which allow an employee to seek help, risk-free, on how to respond to a perceived problem of ethics. For instance, an employee might be convinced that a supervisor has failed to address a blatant problem of sexual harassment. The truth might be that the supervisor has worked with the firm's counsel to initiate a discreet investigation, which has uncovered conflicting views of "he said, she said." Since information is incomplete and conflicting, authorities do not know if they are to resolve a case of harassment or false accusation. The problem is not lack of action, as the employee thinks; the company is trying to be fair to those involved in the face of unclear facts.

We all know that not all fears are illusions. Some fears are legitimate and justified. If fear is real, we learn what is appropriate to fear and what is not. Attacking fear is yet another step. To attack the fear is to deal with it. Level 5 leaders accept full responsibility when things go wrong.[15] This decisive step requires even more courage to develop. It calls for a number of the features of courage; at the least, it calls for motivation and for power—indeed, for will power. Attacking fears does not always mean eradicating them. Some fears may be eliminated. Others might only be minimized, yet other fears we might deal with only by putting them in their proper perspective.

To right a wrong does not necessarily require dramatically falling on a sword. To this end, Harvard ethicist Joseph Badaracco, Jr., cautions against whistleblowing as a virtuous act, especially if there is no power to affect the problem. The unaffected injustice will continue even as the whistleblower is fired. Badaracco offers "quiet leadership" as an alternative, whereby the leader requires courage to right a wrong but explores ways to work within the system and to engage others collaboratively to achieve a "virtuous" outcome.[16]

Finally, fear can be endured. In some instances, fear will not go away, nor will attacking it make it any less frightening. Suffering the fear might be our only option. Suffering might be something we fear, and always will, but we can learn to endure. Learning to endure is itself a form of courage. In the corporate world, there is no assurance that, in challenging a person with more power than us, our story will have a happy ending. We might fail to gain support to rid the company of the "tyrant" and lose our job.

The last aspect of cowardice is anxiety. Unlike fear, anxiety has no specific object. Possibly Lee Iacocca's rise and fall from grace at Chrysler was in part due to the anxiety of losing his spot as ringleader. He lifted Chrysler from a government bailout to a stock that rose 2.9 times higher than the general market. Then attention appeared to be what he desired: he starred in over 80 commercials, considered running for president of the United States, made TV appearances on shows such as the *Today Show* and *Larry King Live,* and wrote a book that sold 7 million copies worldwide. If anxiety for attention was his motive, the consequence was a stock that fell 31 percent below the market during this part of his leadership of Chrysler. He delayed retirement so many times that the joke became that the very word *Iacocca* stood for "I Am Chairman Of Chrysler Corporations Always." After he retired, he demanded stock options and a private jet. He aligned with Kirk Kerkorian to make a failed hostile bid for Chrysler.[17]

Whereas our character always stays with us, power and fame are fleeting. Leaders rent their positions, but influence can cause a leader to think the job is for life. Anxiety is a general uneasiness that we might say makes us afraid. Leaders whose identity is defined by their job are afraid of losing their position. What they do is how they define who they are. This kind of anxiety can be disconcerting, stressful, or even immobilizing. We are not quite sure where to look, what to do, or how to go. Iacocca might have had a general anxiety about losing his position of influence. Other people with far less power and fortune worry if their company will be sufficiently profitable to avoid layoffs.

Again, facing anxiety requires learning, but a subtler learning than for either ignorance or fear. It is more difficult precisely because there are no specifics. What is at stake is our sense of who we are. The development of courage occurs in taking the steps to be grounded and centered in life. This obviously is a huge endeavor—literally a lifetime's work. And it is why it is a work of courage.

Recall in the quotation from Tillich in the section "The Anatomy of Courage" that courage is both an ethical reality and a part of the fabric of being human. We are uneasy that we might suffer. We are anxious that we will die. And because anxiety is pervasive, there is not one thing to learn to be or to do that will fix it. Most of us would like to control our anxiety.

However, anxiety is not an issue of having control but, rather, an issue of being off-center. In business, our center can be off by focusing too much on personal ambition and gain and too little on building a stronger corporation. It is not without reason that employees anxious about losing their job want to manage this fear. We cannot control the events of corporate downsizing, but we can control our response to it. We can work hard doing what is right for the company, rather than playing office politics, and we can focus on serving others even when others are self-serving. Approaching anxiety in this fashion invites us to live from our center. Another word for *center* is *heart* (remember that this is the core meaning of *courage*). Our heart—our center—is treating others in a way that is authentic. It is our place of connection to the self, to others, and to the world. It is the place of meaning and purpose. Often we do not know this deeper self, or we are out of touch with it, and this can cause anxiety. We would prefer that, if we could just learn enough, then we would be in control.

Winston Churchill
The prime minister of Great Britain during World War II,
Churchill was an exemplar of courage and leadership.
Source: Library of Congress, Prints and Photographs Division, LC-USZ62-110528.

The development of courage is the process of learning to live from our center, rather than learning to control our life. To live from the center will integrate our life. Integrity rests at the center of our conduct at work, with family and friends, and in the community. How we live a centered life becomes even clearer as we learn to develop all the virtues that contribute to the formation of our character and that act as a compass to guide the conduct of a servant leader.

5-4 Courage Action

When everything is said and done, courage is really courage only when it becomes an action. Before that, courage is an idea, a concept, a principle, or a virtue. Courage is something we might hope to have or even intend to be. But until we act—until *courage* becomes a verb—it is not real. In the language of business, the issue is one of execution. *Courage* remains a noun if it continues to be merely a plan, an intention, or a hope. What do we do to be courageous?

It is not clear how Level 5 leaders develop the courage to be humble and responsible. It is clear that Level 5 leadership is out of reach for people who focus on personal ambition over something that is bigger than them and that will outlive them. Minus the will to serve others, professional success is ultimately measured by fame, fortune, and power. In contrast, Level 5 leaders measure success by what they build, create, and contribute. The paradox is that the personal ambition that drives people to become successful is at odds with the humility required of Level 5 leaders.

How do Level 5 leaders develop the courage to put aside concerns for personal gain to build strong corporations? They choose to put the interests of others in front of their comfort and develop an iron will to stay focused on this purpose. Darwin Smith, the leader of Kimberly Clark, hit his stride after a successful battle with cancer. Colman Mockler of Gillette was disciplined in applying his religious values to corporate life in a way that he put the company's needs before his own. In World War II, Joe Cullman was forever changed by a last-minute order that took him off a ship that was sunk and would have surely killed him. He concluded that the next 60 years of life were a gift. Cancer, religion, and fate, among other issues, do not offer a guidebook to developing courage.[18] However, we can learn through stories and examples of Level 5 leaders. In a myriad of contexts, these leaders demonstrate courage. If we want to act with courage, we need to be aware and pay attention to the meaning of courage. And if we are ignorant, we need to learn.

A former president of a hospital tells a story about her former boss, who was regional CEO of a large health care system. She called her boss to let him know a young mother had died on the operating table due to an unintentional error by the medical staff. Her boss immediately jumped in the car to meet with the family. He told the family how sorry he was for the loss of their loved one and that he owed them the truth. He informed the family that death was caused by a medical error. The family sued the hospital and won their case.

Time passed and the former president got a phone call that someone had died on the operating table due to an unintentional error by medical staff. She immediately met with the family and told them how sorry she was for their loss and that she owed them the truth. She informed the family that the death had been caused by medical error. In her case, she became friends with the family and they did not sue the hospital.

Building courage among leaders is enhanced by stories such as that of a hospital president's learning people are owed the truth independent of legal counsel to never admit fault. Of course, there are other means to begin to act with courage. The end, such as building strong, responsible corporations, is usually focused. But the means are varied. Long ago, Aristotle said, "The exercise of the virtues is concerned with means."[19] He added that "virtue also is in our own power" and that "where it is in our power to act it is also in our power not to act."[20] Thus, there is usually more than one way to begin to act with courage. And we must begin, although it is always in our power not to act. And not to act guarantees its own outcome.

One act of courage is just that: one act. It is not yet a habit. Nor is it yet part of our character, so to act with courage requires that we repeat the beginning with many more acts. Repetition is habit-forming. Occasionally we will fail, but failure is part of the human fabric. The key is to begin again.

As we repeat acts of courage, we begin to accumulate some important experience. With experience comes the opportunity to reflect on what is happening. What can we learn from reflecting? Finally, are there ways to adapt our actions of courage to grow, deepen, and broaden? Reflecting, learning, and adapting are significant ingredients in the courage formation of our character.

Over a sufficient period of time with sufficient experience, courage comes to be part of our character. This means we become more likely in any context to act ethically with courage. As it becomes part of our character, it becomes more habitual. We do not have to *intend* it as yet another act. To have courage as part of our character is to be in a place where we intentionally live courage without needing to think about it, choose it, and act on it in every instance. People who do so are the people who often emerge as heroes—the Mother Teresa, Gandhi, Martin Luther King, Jr.

Every leader may or may not be a hero. But every leader needs to have courage and to act courageously. The good news is that courage can be learned; indeed, if we have it, we have learned it somewhere along the way. And if courage is part of our character, then we can trust ourselves to choose the good in any situation. That is encouraging.

Chapter Quiz

1. Which does not characterize cowardice?
   a. fear
   b. peer group pressure
   c. ignorance
   d. anxiety
2. Courage is never understood as an ethical issue. T or F
3. The word "will" comes from the Latin word *voluntas,* which means voluntary. T or F
4. Using Collin's hierarchy, match each level with the associated leadership description.
   1. Level 1   a. competent manager
   2. Level 2   b. highly capable individual
   3. Level 3   c. effective leader
   4. Level 4   d. contributing team member
5. Level 5 executives are a paradoxical combination of will and humility. T or F
6. Which of the following is not a kind of energy?
   a. potential
   b. delayed
   c. kinetic
   d. all of the above
7. Which of following characteristics of courage is true?
   a. innate
   b. learned
   c. accidental
   d. natural
8. Using the definition of courage in this chapter, which one of these is the person of courage?
   a. stuntman
   b. mountain climber
   c. race car driver
   d. whistle blower
9. Learning courage to cope with fear moves through four steps. When coping with fear, how would you sequence courage?
   1. Step 1   a. facing fear
   2. Step 2   b. enduring fear
   3. Step 3   c. analyzing fear
   4. Step 4   d. attacking fear
10. Which of the following is not a part of developing courage as a habit?
   a. act of courage
   b. reflection
   c. discipline
   d. luck

Note: You can find the correct answers to these questions by taking the quiz and then submitting your answers in the Online Edition. The program will automatically score your submission. If you miss a question, the program will provide the correct answer, a rationale for the answer, and the section number in the chapter where the topic is discussed.

Questions for Thought

1. Consider a time when you were not courageous and explain why this was the case.
2. To what degree did ignorance, fear, or anxiety influence your conduct early in your childhood? Do you have a recent experience?
3. How have you learned to be courageous?
4. Was there ever a situation in which you wanted to be courageous but did not have the power to do what you thought was right?
5. Courage is not the same as control. Describe an experience in which you acted courageously, even though you could not control what was happening.
6. Describe an experience in which fear blocked your ability to act courageously.
7. Describe an experience in which you were so anxious that being courageous was difficult.
8. Clearly, Bonhoeffer had time to reflect on his courageous action to return to Germany. Describe a time when your own action of courage enabled you to reflect upon it.
9. Consider a time when you were courageous and/or cowardly. What did you learn from this experience?
10. Can you think of an experience in which you were courageous and that led to an adaptation or a change? How did you adapt or change?

Web Exercises

In 1984, a gas leak from a Union Carbide plant killed thousands of people in Bhopal, India. Visit the Union Carbide site at http://www.bhopal.com and read about Union Carbide's responses to the incident. In what ways did the company's leaders show courage? In what ways did they fail? What can every industry learn from this case? How does this compare to the way the Chernobyl disaster (http://www.un.org/ha/chernobyl) was handled by the Soviet Union?

In 2004, Merck announced that it was taking its drug Vioxx off the market following reports that it caused an increased risk of heart attack and stroke. Visit Merck's site at http://www.merck.com/newsroom/vioxx_withdrawal and read their statement about this issue. Are there aspects of courage in the company's actions? Or was it motivated by other factors?

Case

Kickbacks

Walter's company has experienced major changes in the last few years, resulting in employees working long hours, being concerned about their jobs, and usually feeling tired from hard work. In this environment, some employees think they are invisible.

As the engineering manager, Walter's responsibilities include building budgets for tooling and labor for a manufacturing plant. As tool-room supervisor, Jason reports to Walter. He is responsible for ordering appropriate tooling from vendors. Walter approves expenditures, but not necessarily the vendors.

Vendors called Walter to inquire how they could earn a greater share of the business. He assumed the best vendors offered the ideal combination of performance and low price. However, he was unaware that a single vendor secured most contracts. That Christmas, Walter received New York steaks, grade "A" Angus beef, special delivery to his home. There was no name on the package, and Walter presumed it was from a friend. A few days later, Walter received a call at work from the vendor, inquiring about his present and asking if it was to his satisfaction. Walter was shocked and furious, at first, but then became inquisitive. He wondered how the vendor got his address to give him a gift.

Walter wanted to collect more information on this vendor before talking to the tool-room supervisor, whom he trusted. He contacted the Purchasing Department to see the distribution of orders awarded to vendors in the past year. He was stunned to read that the vendor in question had been awarded $2 million in business, while six others shared approximately $1 million. He asked the purchasing manger how this had happened. The manager replied, "The vendor was the cheapest and you approved the transactions." Although Walter agreed that he had approved these purchases, how did the vendor always offer the lowest price? With the assistance of the purchasing manager, Walter learned that the vendor in question always submitted the last bid.

Walter met with Jason and the purchasing clerk. During a tense and difficult discussion, Jason admitted that he owned stock in the vendor's company and had received gifts of significant value. He confessed that he told the vendor about the price they needed to bid. He defended his actions by pointing to the vendor's quality and delivery performance. He had sought the lowest price, as Walter had asked.

Corporate ethical guidelines gave Walter the authority to terminate Jason. Instead, he suspended him for three days without pay. In an effort to restore confidence in the purchasing department, the clerk was also given a written warning. Walter concluded that the supervisor and purchasing clerk were good, responsible human beings who acted irresponsibly by seeking personal gain.

Walter reflected on the fact that everyone in this incident had a choice to make, including himself. He rationalized that the continuous struggle to meet daily pressures to perform resulted in his lack of follow-through. Looking back, Walter realized he should have been more involved in the purchasing process.

Questions for Discussion

1. Did the punishment fit the crime?
2. Are kickbacks the exception and treated accordingly or are rigorous internal controls necessary?
3. How does a leader balance control and empowerment?

Endnotes

1. Jon Meacham, *Franklin and Winston* (New York: Random House, 2003), 367.
2. Dietrich Bonhoeffer, *Letters and Papers from Prison,* ed. Eberhard Bethge, trans. Reginald H. Fuller (New York: Macmillan, 1966), 14.
3. Paul Tillich, *The Courage To Be* (New Haven: Yale University Press, 1968), 1.
4. Charles McMoran Wilson Moran, *The Anatomy of Courage* (Boston: Houghton Mifflin, 1967), 61.
5. Samuel Enoch Stumpf, *Socrates to Sartre: A History of Philosophy* (New York: McGraw-Hill, 1966), 110.
6. *Ethical and Legal Conduct Guidelines* (Wickliffe, OH, The Lubrizol Corporation, April, 2002), 6.
7. Richard Gerig and Philip Zimbardo, *Psycholoy and Life,* 16th ed. (New York: Pearson Education, 2001), 364.
8. Ibid.
9. John Cassidy, "The Greed Cycle," *The New Yorker,* September 23, 2002, 64–77.
10. Jim Collins, *Good to Great: Why Some Companies Make the Leap . . . and Others Don't* (San Francisco: Harper Business, 2001), 20.
11. Ibid., 3.
12. Ibid., 23.
13. Ibid., 27.
14. Tillich, 36.
15. Collins, 35.
16. Joseph L. Badaracco, Jr., *Leading Quietly: An Unorthodox Guide to Doing Things the Right Way* (Boston: Harvard Business School Press, 2002), 971–72.
17. Collins, 132.
18. Ibid., 37.
19. Aristotle, "Nichomachean Ethics," *The Basic Works of Aristotle,* ed. Richard McKeon (New York: Random House, 1941), 971–972.
20. Ibid., p. 972.

πίστις

Faith

6

Outline

6-1 Faith (Trust, Ultimate Concern)

Over 85 million Americans trust the capital markets to invest in directly and additional millions invest indirectly through 401K plans. Millions of shareholders trust management to build their wealth to fund their homes, their kids' orthodontia work and college education, and their retirement. This gives even more punch to a corporate board entrusting a CFO with certain duties. In one sense, the board is saying nothing more than "keep the faith." Trust, or faith, always transcends the individual. It invests leaders in something or someone outside themselves. It is the guiding principle of servant leadership.

In 2002, the Conference Board created a Blue-Ribbon Commission on Public Trust and Private Enterprise, which made the following recommendations to resolve matters of trust—specifically, "corporate abuses that breach the compact of corporate capitalism."[1]

1. *Management should expense stock options. The New Yorker* reported that, if S&P 500 companies had expensed options between 1995 and 2000, profits would have grown at 6 percent annually rather than the 9 percent annually that was reported.[2]
2. *Boards provide compensation oversight.* Foxes often do not look out for the chicken coop; boards, rather than management, should drive executive compensation.
3. *Directors and senior leaders should own stocks for extended holding periods.* Let those who lead the company stay in the game, so that long-term shareholder and executive interests are aligned.
4. *Shareholders should approve the resetting of option prices.* Require disclosure about resetting option agreements, rather than letting management make new arrangements behind closed doors.
5. *Employment agreements and equity dilution should be disclosed.* When the number of shareholders is increased through management options, then the supply of stock is divided among more owners, thereby decreasing its value.
6. *Executives should give adequate advance notice of stock sales.* The Conference Board wants shareholders to be informed whether stocks are being sold for estate-planning reasons or whether the rats are leaving a sinking ship.

These Conference Board recommendations shed light on fiduciary issues that a servant leader must take seriously. PriceWaterhouseCoopers offers three guiding principles to resolve these issues, so that trust in financial information is restored:

1. *Transparency.* Rather than manage earnings to meet analyst expectations, all those involved in financial reporting must agree to be forthright in communicating openly with those affected by corporate performance.
2. *Accountability.* Responsible cultures have the following characteristics: management provides relevant, reliable information, which serves shareholder interests; boards ensure that they and management fulfill their obligations; independent auditors ensure objective, independent evaluations; analysts produce accurate, unbiased research; and investors and other stakeholders hold themselves accountable for their decisions.
3. *Integrity.* Public trust is dependent on people with integrity, since a culture built on transparency and accountability cannot happen without individuals committed to these values. Ultimately, actions more than rules demonstrate the integrity necessary to earn the trust of society and the capital markets.[3]

Conference Board and PriceWaterhouseCoopers proposals identify ways that boards and senior leaders can fulfill their fiduciary responsibilities to investors. Recall that fiduciary simply comes from the Latin word for "faith," *fiducia.* Thus, likely without knowing it, corporate leaders, boards, legislators, and regulators must fulfill their obligation to "keep faith." Another way of thinking about *fiduciary* responsibilities is to shift to its synonym, trust. When we say we trust somebody or something, we can say that faith is trust in action.

Servant leadership is a model of leadership that cannot occur if those served lack trust, or faith, in those who hold power. Robert Greenleaf, founder of the servant leadership model, "speaks of the absolute necessity of trust, a form of love in which people are free of rejection."[4] Greenleaf adds, "The servant always accepts and empathizes, never rejects. The servant as leader always empathizes, always accepts the person, but sometimes refuses to accept some of the person's effort or performance as good enough."[5] This distinction between accepting the person and not accepting the effort or performance is important. The distinction can work where there is a relationship of trust. Keeping the relationship intact because of trust enables the leader to bring about change to enhance the effort or boost the performance.

People who have earned our trust and with whom we have faith are responsible servant leaders. Responsible servant leaders think, speak, and act as if they were accountable to everyone affected by their thoughts and actions. People cannot be servant leaders if they are irresponsible in fulfilling their obligations. The pursuit of responsible conduct is not an option; it is an ethical requirement to be pursued throughout life. In fact, our society has been strongest when the most able among us took on more responsibility rather than devoted themselves to leisurely pursuits.[6]

We are purposely using here the language of responsibility rather than reaction. A reaction can be reflexive—done without thought, without rational consideration. It is for good reason we talk about chemical reactions rather than responses. When we touch a hot stove, we react. Responsibility language is rooted in the Latin *respondeo*, meaning to "reply" or "answer." Responding and responsibility require thinking about a situation. They take different things into account. There may be time for pondering, for weighing options, even for consultation. To be responsible involves considering the impact of our decisions on others and remembering that responsible behavior must continue to happen if we are to earn and keep the trust of others. It is an ongoing process of investing; otherwise, we "lose" faith. As with all the virtues, faith is never a given; it is always chosen.

6-2 In What Do Leaders Trust?

Karl Eller was the CEO of Circle K when the company was in financial trouble in 1989 and 1990. Eller proposed a leveraged buyout to fix the firm's financial mess. A powerful member of the board rejected Eller's plan and undercut confidence in his leadership with other board members. Eller concluded the right thing to do was to submit his resignation. Shortly after he resigned, Circle K declared bankruptcy. Eller owned 20 percent of the company, so his shares became worthless. Without a job, income, and assets, Eller was broke.

Lawyers and bankers urged Eller to declare personal bankruptcy, but he refused. Eller figured that he had contributed to his financial problems and that he should contribute to the solution. He planned to pay back what he had borrowed. Instead of seeking bankruptcy protection, Eller fully disclosed all facts to those he owed. Eller believed that integrity demanded transparency so that he could repay the faith and capital that others had placed in him.[7]

In similar circumstances, we would understand and expect leaders to put faith in a competent bankruptcy attorney to protect their economic value, rather than put faith in virtue to protect their character. Eller's choice was surprising precisely because he put faith in justice and compassion over the protection of his economic interests.

It is not without good reason that most leaders put their faith in factors such as career advancement, economic security, power and status, a spouse, or other concerns. Most of us do not mind doing a good turn for a neighbor, but most of us put our faith in our interests first. The unusual nature of Eller's story is that he lived out his convictions. Faced with similar circumstances, most of us would protect our self-interest. However, looking out for our interests necessitates that we trust others, according to Robert Shaw: "We cannot survive without others. Thus, we trust because we have no choice but to depend on other people. How many of us can produce our own food and water? Cure ourselves when we are sick? Build a protective shelter? In each case, we must rely on the good will and ability of others if we are to survive." We will not trust everyone, but we have to trust many people to survive.[8]

We might accept the idea that most people want to do the right thing; they want to fulfill their obligations to others and demonstrate competence. However, even if we accept this idea, we can readily see that people differ in what they believe should be their obligations and in how dedicated they are to fulfilling them. For example, most agree we are obligated to serve our families, friends, and immediate co-workers, but we might differ widely on how well we do in fulfilling these obligations. If we believe in serving those we know, what about those we do not know, such as stakeholders with whom we have limited contact—suppliers, joint ventures, or global communities in which our firm operates? Most leaders want to do the right thing, but the most responsible servant leaders go beyond this and develop an ability to see the range of available choices; they can pursue a result that achieves the greatest possible good for the most people over a long period of time.

How is faith formed, so that we might expect an adult who becomes a manager or even a CFO to exercise fiduciary responsibility? It would be impossible to give a detailed account of trust formation, although it is imperative to remember that faith/trust is always relational; it is always trust in something or someone. Furthermore, we all have faith, or trust, in something. Our trust might be in the divine, the desire to be independently wealthy, personal success and associated status and power, professional growth and career advancement, our spouse, or ourselves. Our character emerges from the choices of whom, what, when, where, why, and how we believe. Trust shapes our motives, our motives define our character, and character directs our actions, defining who we become.

Trust formation always happens in a context, or culture. Within the context of business, a reasonable assumption is that few corporations strive to conduct unethical acts, just as few actively seek ways to build a better society. In light of shareholder demands to meet quarterly earnings, it is not without reason that leaders trust the following:

1. Short-term earnings over long-term competitive advantage
2. Personal achievement linked to quarterly results, rather than the building of a stronger corporation and community based on long-term strategies
3. The avoidance of legal liability, rather than a focus on what good can be done

A focus on short-term earnings, personal achievement, and legal compliance reveal, sometimes unwittingly, a leader's faith. In a hurry-up culture, where success is measured by profitability and where the threat of layoffs due to inadequate performance hang in the air, how does a leader promote trust?

In a business world full of uncertainly, leaders' concerns or faith influences how they approach their responsibilities. We expect and need leaders to outline strategies for growth, innovation, and profitability. We expect and need leaders to build a culture of integrity. We might also expect and need leaders to build and restore trust.

6-3 Building and Restoring Trust

C.S. Lewis created an image of hell, which was made up of abandoned homes. He borrowed the image portrayed by Dante's inferno. Lewis' version of hell illustrates our ultimate choice of isolation over community. Imagine a traveler who arrives in hell. Immediately, he or she would be confused, wondering why hell is full of homes without people. Lewis tells us why this is the case:

> The trouble is that they're so quarrelsome. As soon as anyone arrives he settles on some street. Before he's been there twenty-four hours he quarrels with his neighbor. Before the week is over he's quarreled so badly that he decides to move. Very likely he finds the next street empty cause all the people there have quarreled with their neighbors and moved. So he settles in. If by any chance the street is full, he goes further. But even if he stays, it makes no odds. He's sure to have another quarrel pretty soon and then he'll move on again. Finally, he moves right to the edge of town and builds a new house. You see, it's easy here. You've only got to think a home and there it is. That's how the town keeps growing.[9]

If only we could think about a new job and new co-workers and "there they are." Isolating ourselves from people, through quarrels and other means, is always an effective (but often negative) move. Although we might not be able to "move to the edge of town," mentally and physically we can ignore co-workers who have faults that drive us nuts. But isolating ourselves and ignoring people, is finally to choose hell. It may seem like this is the way to solve our problems; however, it tragically puts us squarely in the midst of an unsolvable problem—hell.

While teaching psychology at the University of Nebraska in the early 1950s, Don Clifton concluded that his discipline focused almost entirely on what was wrong with people. With good reason, the "quarrelsome" nature of people dominated the field of psychological research.

Clifton's grandson, Tom Rath, conducted research that revealed the number one reason people left their job is that they did not feel appreciated. Sixty-five percent of the people he studied had not received any recognition in the previous year. In most instances, Clifton and Rath concluded that we are more likely to engage people and engender trust by focusing on strengths, rather than focusing on weaknesses or poor performance.[10]

Surely there is room for trust to grow in any company intent on developing leadership and enhancing productivity. As trust develops and deepens, it moves in the direction of mutuality. At this stage, it seems that faith/trust now feels like a given; trust has been earned or achieved. We do not think about it or worry about it. In the best sense of the word, we count on it. It does not ever mean that trust cannot be broken, but we are "trusting" it will not.

But what happens if trust is broken or if trust is never formed in the first place? First, we note that faith that is mal-formed is mistrust. Many people are formed by family and their culture to mistrust instead of trust. Go into any room full of people and do not be surprised when you learn half of them may approach life with a basic sense of mistrust. A leader who mistrusts is one who is wary of taking someone at his or her word. Wariness is a form of mistrust. That person is hesitant to believe we mean what we say. Mistrust is the core experience of the person who feels the world is out to get him or her. Our culture is full of phrases expressing this experience of basic mistrust. For example, "look out for number one" implies either that there will not be enough or that some scoundrel will beat us to the punch. Mistrust breeds suspicion, sarcasm, and cynicism because of the worldview to which it is linked.

Consider the quotation "Deep within all of us is an image or picture of reality, whether consciously articulated or not, which more than

If you build it . . . , they will come. The film *Field of Dreams* contains a perfect example of faith in second chances.
Source: AP/Wide World Photos

anything else shapes how we live."[11] We see reality from one of three possible perspectives: most people can be trusted, most people are out to get us, or most people are indifferent. Are we more likely to bring an attorney or a handshake to a business relationship? We can personalize whether we are suspicious or trusting by considering how many people we trust. Our answer might reveal how trust influences our relationships with others. Similarly, corporate cultures can be described along a continuum of low to high trust.

We can change our reality by changing our ideas and behavior. It seems clear that viewing reality differently and acting differently can change corporate culture. This is just where faith comes in. A person whose basic experience is one of mistrust can learn to trust, and this will make a big difference in life. As we saw earlier, initial acts prompt the process of character formation. To develop faith as a virtue requires these beginning acts of trust.

Trusting others in a corporate or community setting is more than a "feel good" exercise, because corporations and communities that lack trust do not work well. Trust and good faith nurture and enhance relationships. Trust is the currency of reciprocity. "A society that relies on generalized reciprocity is more efficient than a distrustful society, for the same reason that money is more efficient than barter. Honesty and trust lubricate the inevitable frictions of social life."[12] It is easy to understand how important generalized reciprocity is to sustaining a good business over time. Honesty and trust offer another way to express faith. If one cannot trust one's boss or fellow worker, the atmosphere in the business is strained. What might be a mood of openness and engagement and a helping attitude in a healthy business become tainted by suspicion, wariness, and aloofness in a business climate of mistrust. An entrepreneurial culture that "trusts" people to respond to customer needs and to adapt to external change is built on competence and discipline in place of inefficient bureaucracy. A slow-moving bureaucratic enterprise built on distrust will often fail to adapt to shifting customer preferences and market forces.

The role that trust, faith, honesty, and reciprocity play in corporate servant leadership becomes apparent during a performance evaluation. Responsible people want feedback about their performance and want to be accountable to people who are impacted by their conduct. Responsible managers want to provide people with whom they work with an honest evaluation about their performance. A climate of trust that produces sound results is often built on three pillars:

1. Mutual trust—a relationship built on goodwill and mutual support
2. Shared goals—a relationship built on a shared vision, or future direction
3. Mutual faith in ability—a relationship built on mutual respect and trust in each other's competence

When working relationships are strained, a combination of these three pillars is lacking. When these three qualities are present, trust and faith are high. Unfortunately, performance evaluations are least effective when they are needed the most—when there are problems with trust, shared goals, or mutual faith. In contrast, formal performance evaluations are needed the least when the three pillars of trust are present.

In personal and corporate lives where mistrust is the basic experience, it is normal to feel on guard—to sense life out of balance or off-center. The activity of mistrusting—lacking faith—is energy draining. One cannot build healthy or productive relationships on mistrust. Corporations and communities cannot be formed on bad faith. Mistrust is isolating, alienating, and enervating. One might ask, is this any way to spend one's life?

Trust impacts even rocket scientists. A Columbia Accident Investigation Board report concluded that the space shuttle disaster was not due to a lack of technology or ability but, rather, from NASA's culture. Investigators concluded that the death of the seven-member crew had been caused by a culture that minimized the risk of the malfunction and censored dissent about the problem with the shuttle's wing. The report presented

NASA with a sober conclusion—unless organizational weaknesses are resolved, these factors could contribute to another disaster.[13]

The NASA case illustrates that lack of trust can trump ability. Those involved were literally rocket scientists, professionals who were brilliant in their fields. It also illustrates that mistrust is a choice. Once more, this suggests that faith/trust is not simply a given. It is a matter of choice; changes can be made. Bad characters can develop virtue and become good characters. In the business world, many performance issues have much to do with trust. The good news is that corporate cultures characterized by distrust can be altered.

Not surprisingly, it is far faster and easier to change a corporate strategy than it is to change corporate culture. Culture change often requires leadership change at multiple levels, which critics of NASA have proposed. Tools such as the Balanced Score Card can help focus a change in process, which leads to behavior change. Changing processes is difficult but possible, and it is easier than changing the collective values that define a corporate culture.

The NASA case illustrates that competence does not overcome lack of trust. On the other hand, lack of ability can also lead to lack of trust. "We have no clue," admitted one FirstEnergy engineer whose computers failed to explain why the Midwest, the Northeast, and Canada lost electrical power in August 2003. The best scenario held that the utility company was a victim of circumstances it could neither understand nor prevent. The worst scenario was that the firm's maintenance of power lines was inadequate and it had failed to alert other grid users about the pending trouble. Although there is no evidence of corruption, it appears that Ohio's utility companies, its regulators, and its political leaders have "no clue" about what happened or how it could have been prevented.[14] These incompetencies give us no reason to trust them.

Finally, beyond a basic principle of transparency and integrity is a trickery ground to balance competing trusts issues. Consider a friend who seeks your advice about investing in a company in which you are involved. Your friend plans to invest a significant percentage in a company that you know is involved in merger discussions. You know that the value of your friend's shares will be worth far less after the merger. If you break confidence, you run the risk of violating insider-trading laws. If you say nothing, your friend will be poorer. This poses a core question.

In what should we put our faith, confidence, or friendship? The dilemma is made clear with the well-known phrase, "a rock and a hard place." The rock is earning trust by maintaining confidentiality and the hard place is transparency to inform those who are impacted. Although most business issues can and should be transparent, confidentiality must also be honored in cases such as intellectual property, mergers, acquisitions, and a wide range of personnel matters. A breech of confidence can be illegal and can violate trust.

6-4 A Leader's Faith in Building a Stronger Company

Kenneth Lay instilled trust during most of his tenure as CEO of Enron, yet people's faith was lost in his leadership when he used his competence to acquire $246.7 million in salary and stock options, even though his company went bankrupt.[15] If business leaders should, at least in part, spend their professional lives fulfilling fiduciary responsibility through character and competence, then few would know that Darwin Smith would be the poster boy.

Darwin Smith was a servant leader who earned and kept the trust of board members and employees alike. He was shy, awkward, and largely unknown, even among business leaders and academics. Smith became chief executive officer of Kimberly Clark in 1971. At the time, Kimberly Clark had lost 36 percent of its market value, compared with the S&P 500 for the previous 20 years. During the next 20 years, with Smith as Kimberly Clark's CEO, the company outperformed the S&P 500 by 4.1 times, far exceeding the performance of companies such as Procter and Gamble, Coca-Cola, and General Electric.[16]

In addition to being a leader who created value, Smith was a person of virtue. As a young man, he worked at International Harvester during the day to pay his way through Indiana University at night. One day he lost a finger on the job, yet he still attended classes that night and returned to work the next day. Two months after accepting the CEO position at Kimberly Clark, he was diagnosed with nose and throat cancer and was given one year to live. He informed Kimberly Clark's board he had no intention of dying. His first year as CEO included a weekly commute from Wisconsin to Houston for radiation therapy. And he lived for another 25 years.[17]

Darwin Smith possessed a mix of humility and will. Although Smith outperformed more high-profile leaders, such as Jack Welch, he credited Kimberly Clark's colleagues for its success. This humility was matched by unusual determination to lead a firm even while recovering from cancer. Smith accepted the burden of leadership without complaint and without desire to bring attention to himself. He exercised fiduciary responsibility that earned the faith of others through his ability to add value and to do so with virtue.

One of Kimberly Clark's competitors was Scott Paper, led for 19 months by Al "Chainsaw" Dunlap. If Smith defined the qualities of a servant leader, Dunlap was the antithesis. The disparity can be seen in the following two quotes. Dunlap stated, "The Scott story will go down in the annals of American business history as one of the most successful, quickest turnarounds ever." Smith stated after his retirement, "I never stopped trying to become qualified for the job." A dollar invested in Kimberly Clark in 1971 would have earned a shareholder $39.87 in 1991.[18] The SEC fined Dunlap for misrepresenting earnings. Dunlap's faith was in expecting recognition for what was in his eyes, unequaled leadership ability. Dunlap did create short-term value but later was exposed as a leader who destroyed value for the long term. Dunlap lost the faith of everyone else, including the SEC. Character, more than charisma, defines leaders of companies who are the best at creating shareholder wealth. Leaders who are best at enhancing shareholder wealth are self-confident, not self-centered.

As we have already seen, the Latin words for "faith," primarily *fiducia*, ease us from virtue into the realm of value. *Fiduciary* means trustworthy and faithful. Faith—trustworthiness—is one aspect of character. Less able leaders than Smith look in the mirror to admire their achievements and look out the window to blame poor performance on external events. Smith looked in the mirror to accept total responsibility for the conduct of his company, credited success to others, and looked out the window to best position Kimberly Clark to adapt to external circumstances.

6-5 Conclusion

Servant leaders are clear about their obligations and whether these obligations have, in fact, been fulfilled. Utility companies and their regulators have an obligation to consumers and to other utility companies with whom they share grids to transmit electricity. Governing boards, independent auditors, board audit/compensation committees, analysts, regulators, and shareholders all have oversight obligations to ensure that stakeholders can have faith in those with fiduciary responsibility.

We differ widely in whether we think and act out of a clear sense of purpose. Faith also involves a deeper question: how do we search for meaning or purpose? Sharon Daloz Parks worked with MBA students enrolled in a prestigious business school. She wanted to link faith/trust with questions about meaning. She notes, "When I told a cynical colleague that I was interested in the *meaning-making* of M.B.A. students as a way of understanding their ethics, he was intrigued. If I had said I was interested in their *faith*, he might have found it odd or inappropriate in a culturally plural, professional setting, or he might have simply concluded that ethics and faith or religion go together—all important, but somewhat marginal in the 'real world.'"[19]

Parks helps us see that a person's faith is uncovered by looking at how he or she finds purpose in life. In fact, how we find purpose is revealed by two simple questions. First, the more philosophical question asks, "to what do we devote our life?" As our culture presents it, people have a multitude of things to which they might devote their life. Sometimes we discover our object of devotion was not worth it—or was not worth all that we put into it. Success might be one such object. It is worthy, but maybe not the ultimate object of servant leadership. In 1914, Harvard's President Lowell spoke to the question of success and worthiness.

> The world is full of people who have attained what they wanted and are neither happy nor satisfied. Mere competence or even excellence, in a chosen field of endeavor is an insufficient basis for success, for they do not take into account questions of worth, value and merit. True success does not consist in doing what we set forth to do, what we had hoped to do, nor even in doing what we have struggled to do; but in doing something that is worth doing.[20]

The second question that asks about purpose is more economical: how has our life been spent? Unlike time or money, life is not a commodity. Life is our activity, the way we choose to spend our time. For our life to make sense, to have meaning, it requires a center, or focus. Put this way, we can always ask President Lowell's question: what is worth doing? Lowell warns that, without virtue, competence and the success it can bring will be found wanting. Lowell's question can be answered many ways. Aristotle stated that happiness is the exercise of vital powers along lines of excellence. The servant leader seeks to put competence into the service of a worthwhile purpose and to do it with character.

Chapter Quiz

Chapter Quiz

1. Which of the following is *not* one of the principles Price Waterhouse identifies to ensure trust in financial information?
   a. accountability
   b. transparency
   c. power
   d. integrity

2. The Latin word *fidicuia* means trust. T or F

3. Which of the following is *not* one of the three pillars of effective performance evaluation?
   a. mutual trust
   b. mutual friendship
   c. mutual faith in ability
   d. mutual shared goals

4. Which of the following does *not* characterize a business climate of mistrust?
   a. reciprocity
   b. suspicion
   c. wariness
   d. aloofness

5. This chapter argues that conduct should be an issue of responsibility and not reaction. T or F

6. It is equally challenging to change corporate strategy and corporate culture. T or F

7. Competence and ability are insufficient to overcome a lack of trust. T or F

8. People develop faith and trust apart from and independent of any context or culture. T or F

9. Match the corporate board recommended action with the way trust is restored.

Corporate Board Recommended Actions	Restore Trust
1. Expense stock options.	a. Align shareholder and management interests.
2. Have board compensation oversight.	b. Shareholders learn if sale is for estate planning or a sinking ship.
3. Have directors/seniors hold stock long term.	c. Decrease profitability.
4. Shareholders approve resetting option prices and equity dilution.	d. Reduce excessive executive compensation.
5. Executives give advance notice of stock sales.	e. Disclose executive compensation changes.

10. What percent of workers received no recognition in the last year?
    a. 20 percent
    b. 65 percent
    c. 48 percent
    d. everyone

Note: You can find the correct answers to these questions by taking the quiz and then submitting your answers in the Online Edition. The program will automatically score your submission. If you miss a question, the program will provide the correct answer, a rationale for the answer, and the section number in the chapter where the topic is discussed.

Questions for Thought

1. Likely all humans and all corporations have multiple faiths. In what or in whom do you have faith, or trust?
2. How does adversity test what you trust?
3. Do you basically trust or distrust people? Explain.
4. If someone basically mistrusts people, how does that person honor fiduciary responsibility?
5. Think about a trusting relationship you have. Explore and explain how it came to be.
6. When trust is broken, what are various ways to restore it?
7. Explain how courage and trust interact.
8. Comment on how the relative competence of a leader affects the degree to which people trust that leader.
9. How is trust/faith an issue in transactions such as the selling and purchasing of products, investments in stocks and bonds, and employee relations?
10. In situations in which businesses form long-term strategic partnerships, where and how does trust come into play?

Web Exercises

The Great Place to Work website (http://www.greatplacetowork.com/index.php) lists companies that rate highly among employees on trust and faith issues. Take a look at some of the companies listed. How do they compare with one another? By what means do they promote a corporate atmosphere of faith?

Patagonia, Inc., is often listed as a high-trust organization and a company that employees believe in. Visit the company's "About Us" website at http://www.patagonia.com/about/main_about_us.shtml and look at the mission statements and materials on what makes Patagonia work the way it does. What aspects especially promote faith in the company, its leaders, and its culture?

Case

Building Trust

It is not uncommon for the person who commits fraud to be a very nice neighbor. Who among us has never committed fraud in the sense of doing something that benefited us at the expense of others? Take something as common as expense reports. How might opportunity, pressure, and rationalization lead us to commit fraud on business expenses?

Tom, an MBA student, and Frank, a middle manager, enjoyed a wonderful meal that included appetizers, lobster, dessert, and some expensive wine. The dinner cost well over $200. Frank nonchalantly stated that they needed a third person to sign the back of the receipt to bring the average cost per person down. Tom agreed, and they found a friend to sign the receipt.

Because Tom viewed himself as a good person, he found it difficult to admit fudging on a travel report at the very time he was completing an assignment for his ethics class. Tom did not report to Frank, but Frank had more positional authority. Frank stated, "Man, that ethics class you're taking has really messed with your mind." He made this comment after overhearing Tom asking for guidance on how to handle a dinner expense that was higher than the travel policy. How did Tom find himself in this situation? Easy: opportunity, rationalization, and pressure.

Opportunity. Finding a third person to sign the receipt was easy, and no one would be the wiser. There would be no problem getting reimbursed.

Rationalization. They had worked two straight 12-hour days away from home prior to a long flight, and it was midnight before they had a chance to eat dinner. The company owed it to them, right? Furthermore, they reasoned that they didn't get paid for traveling on their own time.

Pressure. Frank encouraged Tom to cheat and made fun of him for worrying about "doing the right thing." Although Tom didn't report directly to Frank, Frank had more power than Tom, and Tom didn't want to offend him.

Tom decided not to submit the receipt for reimbursement.

Questions for Discussion

1. In what did Tom and Frank put their faith?

2. How does faith reveal our ultimate concern?

3. Identify a time when opportunity, rationalization, and pressure contributed to your doing the wrong thing.

4. What can organizations do to reduce the effect of the fraud triangle?

5. What can individuals do to reduce the effect of the fraud triangle?

Endnotes

1. The Conference Board Commission on Public Trust and Private Enterprise, "Research Report," January 2003.

2. John Cassidy, "The Greed Cycle," *The New Yorker,* September 23, 2002, 64–77.

3. Samuel DiPiazza and Robert Eccles, "Building Public Trust: The Future of Corporate Reporting," *PricewaterhouseCoopers,* July 18, 2002.

4. Shann R. Ferch, "Servant-Leadership, Forgiveness, and Social Justice," in *Practicing Servant Leadership: Succeeding Through Trust, Bravery, and Forgiveness,* eds. Larry C. Spears and Michele Lawrence (San Francisco: Jossey-Bass, 2004), 235.

5. Ibid.

6. Bill Thrall, Bruce McNicol, and Ken McElrath, *The Ascent of a Leader* (San Francisco: Jossey-Bass, 1999), 123–24.

7. Ibid., 71.

8. Ibid., 44.

9. Ibid., 45.

10. Tom Rath and Donald Clifton, *How Full Is Your Bucket?* (New York: Gallup Press, 2004).

11. Marcus J. Borg, *Jesus: A New Vision: Spirit, Culture, and the Life of Discipleship* (San Francisco: HarperSan Francisco, 1991), 99–100.

12. Robert D. Putnam, *Bowling Alone: The Collapse and Revival of American Community* (New York: Touchstone Books, 2000), 135.

13. Editorial, "The Hard Lessons of Columbia," *The Plain Dealer,* August 27, 2003, sec. B8.

14. Douglas Clifton, "No Clue," *The Plain Dealer,* September 7, 2003, sec. H2.

15. Cassidy, 70.

16. Jim Collins, *Good to Great: Why Some Companies Make the Leap and Others Don't,* (San Francisco: Harper Business, 2001), 17.

17. Ibid., 18.

18. Ibid., 19.

19. Sharon Daloz Parks, *Big Questions Worthy Dreams: Mentoring Young Adults in Their Search for Meaning, Purpose, and Faith* (San Francisco: Jossey-Bass, 2000), 15.

20. Peter J. Gomes, *The Good Life: Truths That Last in Times of Need* (San Francisco: HarperCollins, 2002), 125.

δικαιοσύνη

Justice

Outline

7-1 Justice (Fair, Equal, Right)

Jurors watched a video of dancing women, half-naked male models, and Jimmy Buffett singing "Margaritaville" at a $2 million birthday party that Dennis Kozlowski, former CEO of Tyco International, threw for his wife on the Italian island of Sardinia in June 2001. Jurors only saw 21 minutes of the 4-hour tape—presiding State Supreme Court Justice Michael Obus believed scenes such as men dressed as Roman soldiers carrying Kozlowski's wife over their heads would prejudice the jury against the defendants and were not relevant to whether they had committed crimes. Kozlowski had estimated to the party planner that he would pay half of the $2 million party costs and Tyco would pay for the rest. Kozlowski was reported to have said, "It's going to be a fun week. Eating, drinking, whatever. All the things we're best known for." Defense lawyer Austin Campriello allowed that the party was held as a birthday celebration but that Tyco business was conducted, too. Prosecutors accused Kozlowski and his CFO, Mark Swartz, of stealing $170 million from Tyco by taking and failing to disclose unauthorized compensation and bonuses and forgiving loans to themselves. Prosecutors also charged that the defendants had made another $430 million on Tyco stock by lying about the corporation's financial health from 1995 to 2002.[1]

The party that Kozlowski threw for his wife is a symbol of a much larger issue about executive compensation, corporate largesse and justice. A powerful image of justice is captured by media pictures of Enron's CFO, Andrew Fastow, handcuffed and being led to jail and much later agreeing to a plea bargain for a 10-year jail sentence. However, justice is not limited to whether an act is lawful. Issues such as executive compensation also raise questions about what is fair, even if no criminal conduct is present. In 1980, the average pay for American CEOs who led the nation's largest companies was about 40 times the average wage of a production worker. In 1990, it was about 85 times. Today it is thought to be about 400 times. Whereas profits and share prices fell in 2002, the average compensation for American CEOs rose 6 percent.[2] Leading a corporation takes incredible ability and fortitude to look out for the interests of customers, employees, shareholders, and the communities in which the company operates. Because the talent pool of senior leaders is in short supply, executive compensation is high, yet even corporate boards appropriately are asking if greed rather than competence is guiding corporate strategies.

Executive compensation introduces the notion of corporate responsibility into the discussion of justice. The words *responsibility, responsive,* and *respond* are rooted in the Latin *spondeo,* which means "to promise." To respond means to promise again, not the first time. It means to renew a relationship, not to begin one. Justice is about being responsible as an individual or as a corporation. Justice is central to responsible conduct because it is the crossroad of the religious, the political and the legal. Indeed, in all times justice is seen comprehensively as a religious and philosophical duty, a political goal and a legal guarantee.

The legal guarantee is etched on the Supreme Court building itself: "equal justice under law." Lady Justice herself, typically portrayed holding scales, guarantees this equal justice. For good reason, Lady Justice is often portrayed as blindfolded. Otherwise, it would be too easy to prejudge people based on race, religion, or wealth. Without judicial blindness, the poor and marginalized in society usually would not have a chance.

Because of these court associations, it is easiest first to link justice and law. Typically, we link them in reverse order by saying, "Law and justice." Somehow we are tempted to assume that the law determines what is just. In fact, it is the opposite: justice establishes the law. The relationship between justice and law becomes very clear when we look at the primary Latin word for "law"—namely, *ius*. In Latin, the *i* at the beginning of words becomes *j* when translated into English; thus, the Latin *ius* is our English word *just*. Hence, by definition what is just is law.

The normal meanings of *ius*, "law, rule, code, and sanctioned by law," square with this definition. All these uses of the idea of law should take one right to the heart of justice. This definition means that law is always just, which one expects always to be true. But it is also easy for most Americans to remember times in our country when a particular law was deemed unjust. More to the point, cultural understanding shifted a meaning of justice and new legislation had to follow. Civil rights legislation is one example.

The idea of legislation brings us to the other Latin word for "law"— namely, *lex* and the genitive, *legis*. Clearly, our English words *legislation* and *legislator* come from this Latin word. *Lex* means "law, rule, statute, and principle." Congress and the judicial system work hand in hand to determine issues of justice and to establish laws enacting this justice. Not surprisingly, this world of justice involves a couple of the virtues. The world of justice is called "jurisprudence." It combines "juris" (*ius, iuris* = "law") and "prudence" (*prudentia*).

Therefore, "justice and law" affirms that justice precedes law. Laws are made upon determination of what is just. But justice is still more than this precept. It is also political and religious/philosophical. These two arenas of society necessarily have a great deal to say about what is just. Then laws are passed to enforce justice. To consider both political and philosophical arenas helps one see that justice is always first a virtue.

Besides *law,* two other terms for "justice" help one understand what constitutes justice. The first term is *fair.* Justice is concerned with what is fair. This may be our first-learned word for justice. How many times have we witnessed children playing? A conflict arises and one child screeches, "It just isn't fair!" Or most parents can recall those days when one of their children counters a suggestion with the retort, "That's not fair!" In fact, how many times do adults see someone else's fame, fortune, good luck, or good looks and complain about life's unfairness? Legitimately, when they hear of insider information with respect to stock deals, disaffected stockholders lament, "That's just not fair."

Once more, the Latin background is revealing. The Latin word for "fair" is *aequus,* which obviously comes across as equal. Thus, fairness is rooted in equality, impartiality, and evenness. Fairness does not always mean that every person gets the same—the same money, the same amount of food, and so on. An easy way to see this is the assumption that people will play a game fairly. That means each player plays "by the rules." There are winners and losers, but a game can be played fairly.

Again, games and life work best if every person is given a chance, maybe even an equal chance; that is only fair. However, what each makes of his or her chance is up to him or her. Some make more out of their chances than others, and that is only fair. With respect to compensation, it is usually held to be fair for some to earn more money than others. Some have more experience, more talent, and more ability. Sometimes seniority makes a difference. To determine what is fair is always to determine justice.

This last example points to obvious ways in which fairness has been denied or overlooked. Favoritism always slights fairness. Many children first experience the unfairness of life at the hands of favoritism at school. Even more pernicious than favoritism is prejudice. By definition, prejudice dims or even destroys someone's chance. Prejudice is both a personal and a corporate cancer that eradicates the pretense of fairness. Finally, one can point to fraud as a malignancy that is both illegal and immoral.

All of these potential dark sides of fairness can be seen in countless examples of justice or fairness issues in corporate life, and they are easy to list: age, race, and sex discrimination; equal opportunity and affirmative action; prohibition of bribes; the honoring of intellectual property; the fair treatment of laid-off workers; corporate responsibility for paying its fair share of taxes; and environmental responsibility, to name just a few.

Besides law and fairness, a third term helping us understand justice as virtue is *right*. Once again, it is easy to connect "rights" to laws. Today people impetuously claim their "rights." Some can remember people claiming that it was their right to decide whether they wanted to wear a seat belt. Some still claim it is their right not to wear a motorcycle helmet.

Whether or not there are "divine rights" may be a question, but there is no question that Americans and most of the rest of the world think there are "human rights." As school kids, Americans are taught about the Bill of Rights, the initial 10 amendments to the Constitution, ratified in 1791, two years after Congress convened in New York City to pass this bill. The First Amendment to the Constitution says, for example, that there should be "no law respecting an establishment of religion, or prohibiting the exercise thereof." It goes on to talk about freedom of speech and the press. To the original 10 amendments have been added 17 more. For instance, in 1865 the anti-slavery bill was passed, and the Fifteenth Amendment prohibited people from being barred from voting based on race. The infamous Eighteenth Amendment, which instituted the prohibition of liquor, required the Twenty-First Amendment to repeal it.

The point in this brief historical lesson is to demonstrate how the idea of "human rights" has evolved. The belief that it was "right" to hold another person in slavery changed in the nineteenth century. Clearly, as American views about rights changed, so did the idea of justice. Once more, we see that laws were passed to codify this evolving sense of "what is right."

Behind our English word *right* is the Latin word *rectus*. In addition to "right," *rectus* means "correct, proper, guide, and rule." *Rectus* comes from the Latin verb *rego*, which carries the meaning of "guiding, ruling, and controlling." Within this context, it is easy to see what is at stake when people talk about human rights or civil rights. It is also clear why issues such as abortion and capital punishment are still being debated; "is it right" to take someone's life?

Questions revolving around rights demonstrate how justice often is a legal issue; it has to do with law. But the law is usually an expression of a larger philosophical, religious, or political discussion. Not all discussions at these levels—philosophical, religious, and political—wind up with legislative action. Those discussions may, however, significantly influence institutional guidelines, rules, and regulations.

7-2 Impact of Justice (Law, Equal, Right) on Leadership

Executive compensation is a recent example of justice's impact on business. *The New Yorker* cited a 2001 *Financial Times* article entitled "Barons of Bankruptcy." It reported that, from 1999 to 2001, officers and directors from bankrupt companies received $3.3 billion in salary, bonuses, and stock options. The most impressive barons were Global Crossing's Gary Winnick ($512.4 million) and Enron's Kenneth Lay ($246.7 million).[3]

Justice is so important that the late Harvard philosopher and ethicist John Rawls, in his widely acclaimed book *The Theory of Justice,* noted on the initial page that "justice is the first virtue of social institutions."[4] A business is a social institution and thereby must attend to the issue of justice. Paul Volker stated that firms such as Enron and WorldCom broke the foundation on which capitalism is built: "investors entrust their assets to management while boards of directors oversee management so that the potential for conflict of interest between owners and managers is policed."[5] Volker was quoted in *The New Yorker:* "Traditional norms didn't exist. You had this whole culture where the only sign of worth was how much money you made."[6] Of course, Volker was right, but Kenneth Lay and his fellow barons of bankruptcy are only the latest to violate the centuries-old idea of social contract.

Since stocks were first offered in 1814, the capital markets have helped cure disease, fund university and hospital endowments, and promote unprecedented global economic growth. In 1890, Alfred Marshall, a British economist, stated, "It is a strong proof of the marvelous growth in recent times of a spirit of honesty and uprightness in commercial matters, that the leading officers of great public companies yield as little as they do to the vast temptation to fraud which lie in their way."[7] In 1929, the stock market crashed, in part due to insider trading, stock price manipulation, and the diversion of corporate funds for personal use. The resultant cries of injustice led to the Securities Act of 1933, which imposed financial disclosure requirements and prohibited insider trading and stock price manipulation. In 1934, the Securities and Exchange Commission was set up to enforce these new regulations.[8]

The assumption of capitalism is that greed, if checked wisely with a mix of regulation, market forces, and moral restraint, can promote just economic growth. By analogy, in his writing from within the Shantung Compound—a Japanese internment camp in China during World War II—Langdon Gilkey clarified the difficulty of achieving this goal. For a period of time, he worked in the camp's kitchen. There he confronted the challenge of proportioning food in a fair way. Although prisoners were not starved, they did not get all the food they wanted. Gilkey used this experience to reveal something deeper about human nature. He observed that, "when there is plenty to eat . . . the size of the portion is irrelevant, since one can always get more. But when there is less than enough, all servings must be exactly equal. . . . If we guessed wrong either way, there was always trouble."[9] Gilkey moaned about the difficulty of dividing food into 800 equal parts.

Gilkey philosophized on the relation of justice to self-interest. When faced with complaints of unequal portions, Gilkey lamented to a colleague, "My God, Bertram, the root of the demand for equal treatment . . . is not the outraged sense of justice for the other fellow. It is the frustrated desire to get for yourself all that is coming to you. Self-interest, of course, is *also* the root of our desire to get *more* than our neighbor—and that is one reason, isn't it, that life is so damned complicated!"[10] Not surprisingly, this predicament is not limited to internment camps.

Analogously, colleagues are outraged when they fail to get the compensation, promotions, professional awards, or other forms of recognition they want—or if others receive what they believe is unfair recognition. Gilkey agreed with Adam Smith, who stated that justice rests more on self-interest than on virtue. In other words, our sense of injustice is not driven as much by concern for our neighbor as it is by our desire to get our fair share—or more. One reason life is so complicated is because virtue and value are so complicated.

Milton Friedman disciples Michael Jensen and William Meckling accept Gilkey's assumption that self-interest rules, although they assert that competition will resolve most problems. About 30 years ago, they proposed the notion of principles and agents, which speaks to the problem of a principle (a shareholder) hiring an agent (an executive) to do a job. Hiring a contractor to renovate a home, a teacher to educate a student, an elected official to govern, or a CEO to manage shareholder interests presents the same problem—those who are hired may not take their responsibility to the principle seriously. Jensen and Meckling recommended we treat the CEO like a plumber and reward him or her for acting in the best interest of the principle—stockholders.

In the 1960s and 1970s, executives (agents) were rewarded more for the size of the firm they ran than for enhancing shareholder (principle) wealth. The bigger the firm, the bigger the paycheck to the executive, which contributed to CEOs building far-flung enterprises rather than focusing on profitability. In the 1980s, nearly half of all major public corporations received a takeover offer through a leveraged buyout (LBO). An

LBO was to ensure that executives (agents) served shareholders (principles) by increasing share price. Instead, LBOs destroyed investor and shareholder wealth and contributed to unhealthy corporate debt levels.

According to *The New Yorker,* if S&P 500 companies had expensed options between 1995 and 2000, profits would have grown at 6 percent annually, rather than the 9 percent annually that was reported. In other words, by not revealing the true impact of executive compensation on stock price, companies inflated their earnings. In 1980, stock options were offered to less than one-third of all public company CEOs. In 1994, stock options were offered to 70 percent of the CEOs and represented about 50 percent of their compensation. Of the top 200 CEOs in 1997, 92 received options valued at $31 million, on average. In 1997, U.S. President Bill Clinton viewed this trend as unjust and limited tax deductions for executive salaries, so that the government would not subsidize highly paid executives. Since tax laws did not expense options as regular compensation, corporations had further incentive to compensate agents with less salary and more options, an unintended consequence of Clinton's legislation.[11]

Justice is further complicated by what Gilkey implied is the "lawyer within" us, our infinite capacity to rationalize our behavior as being moral, when, in fact, our behavior is self-serving.[12] "Chainsaw" Dunlap wrote in his book *Mean Business* that "the most important person in any company is the shareholder. I'm not talking here about Wall Street fat cats. Working people and retired men and women have entrusted us with their 401Ks and pension plans for their children's tuition and their own long-term security. If we're not concerned about them every step of the way, they're screwed."[13]

Gilkey also warned against legalism, which he defined as judging others and ourselves by inflexible and sometimes trite "do's and don'ts": "the intense difficulty that each of us has in being truly humane to our fellows, and the infinitely subtle ways in which we are able to avoid facing up to this difficulty" is the way Gilkey describes human nature after experiencing a particularly troubling incident.[14] Insightfully, Gilkey concluded "that rarely does self-interest display itself frankly as selfishness. More often it hides behind the very moral idealism it is denying in action; a legal, moral, or even religious argument is likely to be given for what is at base a selfish action."[15]

Gilkey's conclusion again should caution us against simply assuming that a law automatically determines justice. Rather, laws are always a means to do what is right. But everyone knows that having a law does not guarantee that people will obey the law. Quite simply, to know the right does not ensure that the right will be done. Former New Hampshire Sen-

Martin Luther King, Jr.
King gave his life to create a just America.
Source: Library of Congress, Prints and Photographs Division, LC-USZ62-111164.

ator Warren Rudman speaks precisely from this truth. He observes, for example, that even in a post–Enron world preexisting laws were sufficient to indict that kind of corporate fraud. Furthermore, he suggested that legislation, such as Sarbanes-Oxley, had more to do with grandstanding than with justice.[16]

7-3 I'm Just; It's the Other Guy You Can't Trust

The trouble with justice is that it is often in the eye of the beholder. Of course, when evidence of fraud or corruption is beyond any doubt, the issues are clear. However, even if the facts reveal that a crime has indeed been committed, it is difficult to gain agreement about the penalty. Some might come down hard on justice, whereas others emphasize compassion.

Usually, we want a just workplace, but we discover that it is easier to discuss it than to put it into practice. For example, everyone is for equal opportunity (EO), but affirmative action (AA) is trickier. EO can be thought of as a practical application of Martin Luther King's speech to treat people by the content of their character and not the color of their skin. AA is the price for EO, since sometimes one group is harmed to serve another group that has been disadvantaged historically. The idea of pay for performance is sound, but can we clearly define performance and/or reward people with money alone? It is easy to be against sexual harassment, but often hard to know who is guilty of it.

The trouble with justice is that we all claim to be just and moral. Immorality is difficult to see in oneself. As Gilkey noted, "The moral disguise usually deceives even the self who has donned it. For no one is more surprised and outraged than that self when someone else questions the validity of his moral concern."[17] When someone else's morality is questioned, we are only too eager to stand on principle. We may not bear malice, but neither are we eager to extend grace. "It's the principle of the thing" is a discussion stopper.

Gilkey discovered that the meager existence found in a Japanese internment camp was an excellent place to see how people responded to difficult moral choices. He concluded that a marginal existence did not necessarily change people's character for the better or worse, but it did increase the "emotional voltage" of their relationships with each other. An internment camp tests our character far more than suburban life, but it may only be a matter of degree. The difference may only be what we are asked to share. In both the camp and suburbia, the real question may be very simple: do we value moral excellence more than our comfort and security? The following story, told by Gilkey, about the plea to three families to help resolve the overcrowding of living conditions in the camp offers interesting insights into this question.

Gilkey was in charge of housing in the badly overcrowded camp, so when carpenters added dorm rooms by fixing two buildings in disrepair there was much hope that the overcrowding would be relieved. The plan was to add teenage dorms, which would create more space for families with small children. In turn, some families who currently had teenagers living with them would give up space. In the name of overall justice, Gilkey asked three families to move their teenagers to the dorms.

The Whites had been pillars of their prior community. Mr. White was an Ivy League graduate, intelligent, sophisticated, and handsome. Mrs. White was capable, respectable, civic-minded, elegant, and gracious. She responded to Gilkey's request to send her two boys to the dormitory with a polite, caring acknowledgment of the problem and a promise to spend the night praying and discussing with her husband how to be as helpful as possible.

Gilkey thanked her and returned the next day to her warm smile and gracious determination to do the right thing. The Whites had concluded that their 16-year-old was vulnerable to peer pressure, caught colds often, and ate too little, all of which required that the family watch out for him. Their younger teenager could not go, since it became clear that the Whites' first moral responsibility was to keep a home for the boys. Mrs. White had found a clear moral principle to support what she had planned to do all along.

Gilkey knocked on the door of the Pickering family and was greeted by Mr. Pickering, a tall, nervous man with a fierce temper. Predictably, in response to the request to move his 19-year-old daughter to the dorm, Mr. Pickering lost control and ordered Gilkey off his property. He slammed the door in Gilkey's face and screamed that overcrowding was not his problem. He then cracked the door only to threaten Gilkey with a lawsuit after the war. Gilkey mused about which court would have jurisdiction over the case of an Englishman against an American interred in a Japanese camp in China.

Gilkey then visited the Schmidt family, who had two teenage girls. Mr. Schmidt was an American missionary who expressed love with a smile and friendliness. He did not get angry, curse, or threaten anyone and was about to help the situation, but not at his own expense. When Gilkey asked him to move his daughters to free up part of his property to assist those more crowded than he was, he smiled, but less authentically than usual. He informed Gilkey that he wrote many sermons for others, so for the sake of the missionaries, he needed a little extra space and quiet to think and write out sermons.

Clearly, Gilkey and the Housing Committee had turned down a dead-end street. The committee had no recourse but to go to the Japanese for help. The Japanese sent for these families, asked them their side of the story, and then promptly ordered each to evacuate one of their two rooms. To Gilkey's amazement, the families agreed submissively, doing as they were told.[18] Force rather than an appeal to fairness and rationality was needed for justice to be done. When impartial reason was most needed and when the stakes were high, impartial reason was often missing in action. Gilkey's experience in the internment camp led him to conclude that we are reasonable and moral primarily when it serves our interests. We find rational and moral reasons to justify what we have already decided to do. Again, what Gilkey learned in camp about human nature surely has parallels in life outside the camp—life as every one of us is living it at work and in the home.

Leadership expert Warren Bennis believes that business must study what philosophers and experts on moral development have to say about human nature if we are to promote authentic, or "just," leadership. The process of becoming a fully integrated and authentic leader is simultaneously the same process of becoming a fully integrated and authentic human being. The goal of the servant leader is difficult to achieve. Bennis offers an example of a leader who is authentic—Bill George. Bennis sees Bill George as a corporate paradigm of justice. George, former CEO of Medtronic, drove a sense of purpose through his corporation to the extent that 87 percent of the employees stated they aligned their personal values with the values of the company. Bennis credits George with creating an organization that aligned people with its mission while adapting to its environment.[19]

Realistically, few have the discipline and ability to develop fully the character and competence of George, yet any servant leader can make a big difference in the life of a corporation and community. Furthermore, we are all well served if more leaders simply make progress in the development of their competence and character.

This chapter introduced, defined, and exemplified the virtue of justice. Justice rests at the heart of corporate responsibility. Business ethics issues are largely questions about justice at three levels. At the global level, justice issues include the obligations of the developed world to address poverty in the developing world, to balance environmental preservation and economic growth, and to balance the economic growth of globalization with culture and worker dislocation. At the corporate level, justice issues include whether corporations should expand their mission beyond shareholder wealth, consumer protection, fair competition, and environmental responsibility. At the individual level, justice issues often include human resource issues: affirmative action/equal opportunity, executive compensation, layoffs, sexual harassment, and so on. Chapter 8 will address the role of leadership in promoting corporate responsibility and citizenship.

Chapter Quiz

1. Kozolowski's story is limited to a legal issue. T or F
2. Which of following elements is not at the crossroads of justice?
   a. religion
   b. aesthetics
   c. legal
   d. political
3. Which of the following terms is not used to describe justice?
   a. fair
   b. acceptable
   c. equal
   d. right
4. Justice and self-interest are synonyms. T or F
5. Clearly, compensation is a justice issue in so far as people expect to be paid fairly. Although profits and share price fell in 2002, the average compensation for American CEOs rose or fell at what rate?
   a. −6 percent
   b. 6 percent
   c. 20 percent
   d. 35 percent
6. Rationalization is a typical way to excuse or explain one's actions. T or F
7. Justice by definition involves fairness and equality. Which of the following has not been used in the pursuit of affirmative action and justice?
   a. race
   b. gender
   c. seniority
   d. age
8. It is irrelevant whether business leaders know anything about moral development and human nature if they are to become "just" leaders, according to Warren Bennis. T or F
9. Ethical leadership deals with the issue of justice at the individual, corporate, and global levels. T or F
10. *Juris* and *prudentia* are two Latin "virtue" words that are combined in the law. T or F

Note: You can find the correct answers to these questions by taking the quiz and then submitting your answers in the Online Edition. The program will automatically score your submission. If you miss a question, the program will provide the correct answer, a rationale for the answer, and the section number in the chapter where the topic is discussed.

Questions for Thought

1. Recall the first experience in which you were left feeling "this is not fair." Describe why you did not think the result was fair.
2. If you believe that justice is more than simply what any individual thinks it is, then how do you or any individual establish what justice is?
3. Our common language, "law and justice," is intentionally reversed in this chapter, arguing instead that justice precedes law. Why is this the case?
4. Do *fairness* and *equality* mean the same thing? Why or why not? Think about the justice issues of equal opportunity and affirmative action. Is one about fairness and the other about equality?
5. When you begin to focus on justice issues, it is not unusual to become aware of other issues asking for attention. As an example, EO/AA is dealing with a justice issue, but it also raises issues about compassion. How do you see this connection?
6. In a corporate setting, how is a performance evaluation a justice issue?
7. Among issues such as market rates for leadership talent, should corporate boards also deal with executive compensation as a justice issue?
8. Identify and comment on the ways that justice is an issue when companies are laying off people.

Web Exercises

Workplace Fairness (http://www.workplacefairness.org) is a website dedicated to providing up-to-the minute information on equitable workplace solutions. At their site on discrimination (http://www.workplacefairness.org/sc/discrimination.php), the site's authors provide information about racial, sexual, age, and other kinds of discrimination. Do any of the statistics surprise you? What about the companies that have been found guilty of discrimination? How can you personally work towards a more fair workplace or school environment?

Affirmative action is a controversial topic. Visit these two sites, one pro and one con, and think about your position on it.

Pro: http://www.affirmativeaction.org
Con: http://www.cir-usa.org/mission_new.html

Would your position change if you were running a small business? A large corporation? A university?

Cutting Corners

A picture that embodied justice captured Enron's former CEO, Jeffrey Skilling, being escorted in handcuffs by federal marshals up the courthouse steps. Finally, people thought, a poster boy for corporate greed was getting what he deserved. His crime was outrageous, but was it any more illegal than speeding or unethical than plagiarism? Are we all guilty of cutting corners, with the only difference being degree?

David Callahan asserts in a book, *Cheating Culture,* that we have become a nation of cheaters—evading taxes, stealing supplies from employers. Callahan states that we are liberal with claims on resumes and readily copy music without concern for intellectual property. Do we cheat more today than in the past or report it more? Callahan claims we cheat more than in the past. He defines cheating as breaking rules to get ahead academically, professionally, or financially. Some forms of cheating are against the law, while others are not. In both cases, perpetrators view themselves as honest and ethical.

Callahan is concerned that the more we have to gain, the more tempted we are to cheat. Since chances are they will not be caught, since people at the top cheat, and since the system is rigged so that the honest are suckers, why choose character? In other words, the only way to get ahead is to cheat.[1]

Wendy Fishman, Howard Gardner, and others interviewed recent college science, theatre, and journalism graduates who had achieved early success in their careers. He gave them ethical dilemmas to resolve and interviewed them about their values. The conclusion of the study was that the only ethic in the workforce was economic (value) with no counter force (virtue). Common conflicts included the following:

1. *Pressure from above.* Although journalists did not want to interview families in grief, editors required reporters to include distressed people as part of the story.
2. *Pressure from peers.* If scientists wanted to run another trial to ensure a study's reliability and validity, peer researchers often pressured each other to publish results as is.
3. *Ambition.* The desire to get ahead led theatre majors to perform for a production underwritten by Phillip Morris even though their politics were strongly opposed to cigarette companies.[2]

None of these examples rise to the level of Jeffery Skilling's fraud crimes. These young professionals will not share a cell with Skilling, but corner-cutting for professional success defines their character. If parents teach us what is right when we are young, sometimes the workplace teaches that cutting corners is needed to succeed. Almost everyone who participated in Gardner's study understood right from wrong, but concluded that people have to do whatever is necessary to get ahead. They wish others would be ethical, but they can't afford to be so in every case.

Because no one starts out to be a cheater, never mind a crook, what choice do you have when others cut corners?

Questions for Discussion

1. How is cheating an issue of justice?
2. Will students who cheat in college cheat in the workplace?
3. If you cut corners no worse than others do, how does this shape your character?
4. If you choose character over cheating, what price will you pay?

Footnotes

1. David Callahan, *The Cheating Culture: Why More Americans Are Doing Wrong to Get Ahead* (New York: Harcourt, 2004).
2. Wendy Fishman, Becca Solomon, Deborah Greenspan, and Howard Gardner, *Making Good: How Young People Cope with Moral Dilemmas at Work* (Cambridge, MA: Harvard University, 2004) 168.

Endnotes

1. Samuel Maull, "Jury Sees Birthday Bash Video in Trail of Ex-CEO," *The Plain Dealer,* October 29, 2003, sec. C1, 3.
2. *The Economist,* "Where's the Stick?" October 11, 2003, 13.
3. John Cassidy, "The Greed Cycle," *The New Yorker,* September 23, 2002, 64.
4. John Rawls, *A Theory of Justice* (Cambridge, MA: Belknap Press, 1973), 3.
5. The Conference Board Commission on Public Trust and Private Enterprise, http://www.conferenceboard.org/.
6. Cassidy, 64.
7. Ibid., 66.
8. Ibid., 64.
9. Langdon Gilkey, *Shantung Compound: The Story of Men and Women under Pressure* (New York: Harper & Row, 1966), 134.
10. Ibid., 135–136.
11. Cassidy, 70.
12. Gilkey, 112.
13. Collins, 28.
14. Gilkey, 111.
15. Ibid., 112.
16. Warren Rudman, "Business Ethics," Baldwin-Wallace College Berea, OH: October 14, 2002.
17. Gilkey, 112.
18. Ibid., 85–89.
19. Warren Bennis, "Being Intensely Attentive," http://pwcglobal.com.

άρχηγέτης

Chapter

Leadership and Corporate Responsibility

8

Outline

8-1 Value, Virtue, and Corporate Responsibility

Krispy Kreme was a Wall Street favorite, as its stock traded as high as $50 per share. In November 2004, the stock traded at $9.64, almost exactly the price it traded during its initial public offering in April 2000. CEO Scott Livengood attributed its financial trouble to the low-carbohydrate diet trend. Analysts attributed the financial trouble to the Securities and Exchange Commission investigation into accounting for franchise purchase buybacks and the price paid for these franchises. The company also departed from standard practice to answer questions when analysts were instructed to submit inquiries in writing.[1]

Krispy Kreme readily makes donations to the communities in which it operates. However, in a Sarbanes-Oxley world, even a sniff of misstated earnings sends a stock into the tank and often results in senior leaders' losing their jobs. Today's financial markets punish firms even for a hint of an integrity issue.

General Electric (GE) executives reported to CEO Jeff Immelt that social responsibility mattered to GE employees, to a limited but growing number of investors, to European customers in particular, and to nongovernment organizations (NGOs), whose power to influence business practices is growing. GE executives uncovered a survey that ranked GE in the top five among U.S. companies for its leadership, its focus on quality, and its investment value but seventy-second in social responsibility.

Immelt appointed Bob Corocran to be GE's first corporate citizenship vice president. Under Corocran's leadership, GE has completed 3,100 audits since 2002 to ensure that suppliers comply with labor, environmental, health, and safety standards. Corocran said, "Think about your neighbors. If they obey the law, if they pay their taxes, if they don't park a Winnebago on the street, are they just compliant? Now what about the neighbor who organizes the block party? Or the one who picks the kids up after school? That's a good neighbor. And that's what we mean when we say we want to be a good company. The question of how much better we have to be to be recognized as a good company, we don't know. It is more today than it was five years ago."

Immelt allows that reputation is good for business and supports GE's desire to sell more wind power and energy-efficient locomotives. Accordingly, GE audits supply chains to ensure they are not linked to sweatshops and grants domestic partner benefits. The company cannot afford the reputation risk of being seen as anything other than a good company.

The complexity of applying virtue to economic decisions is illustrated by whether GE should sell oil and gas equipment, hydropower, and medical equipment to Iran. U.S. firms are legally prohibited from conducting business in Iran, since the country has financed the terrorist organization Hezbollah, which has attempted to develop nuclear weapons and has possibly supported terrorists to kill U.S. soldiers in Iraq. Although GE cannot invest in Iran, its foreign-owned subsidiaries can. Frank Gaffney, a former Reagan Defense Department administrator, wants to pressure pension funds to divest investments in firms such as GE for conducting business in Iran. In 2003, GE's board defeated a New York City police officers' and fire fighters' pension fund proposal to review reputation and financial risks attributed to its Iranian investments. The old GE would have permanently closed off debate after defeating a proposal like this. Immelt's new GE wants to be held to a higher standard of virtue, so in the future it is open to reviewing Iranian subsidiary investments risks. How GE will navigate ethical dilemmas like its Iranian investments will be closely watched by corporate America.[2]

A half-dozen years ago, concern for a wider range of stakeholders such as those outlined by GE would have been considered unconventional. Today, ethical hell is trying to appear ethical without the culture to back up the claim. A transparent world will expose imposters. Martha Stewart went to jail; Enron ruined reputations and ended careers. Corporate responsibility has become nondiscretionary due to concern of regulatory backlash, media attention, and activist NGOs.

However, character comes from within, not out of fear that watchdogs are looking. There are plenty of corporate leaders who know this and will build cultures that embed, not impose, character. There are plenty of corporate leaders whose ethics are relative and sooner or later, sometimes years later, unjust conduct is exposed. Given the Darwinian nature of business, our faith should increase when justice is served, and we should invest in businesses in which character defines their culture.[3]

8-2 Materialism Trumps Meaning

The power of the U.S. economic system is unmatched, but along with this strength is concern that U.S. culture is dominated by materialism, commercialism, and consumerism. However, materialism is not the cause for a lack of meaning but the disease of people starved for a larger vision for commerce.[4] Struggling with materialism and meaning is not a new phenomenon. Authors from Plato to contemporary business writers have written about the human struggle to balance the quest for material well-being with a sense of meaning.

Plato believed that to seek the good—virtue—is the ultimate purpose of leadership; otherwise, all other knowledge is worthless. Beyond providing goods needed for a comfortable life, Thomas Aquinas wanted leaders to be teachers of virtue and caretakers of human needs. He believed that leaders should aim for continual improvement for themselves and those they serve by cultivating and exhibiting high moral standards.

Machiavelli was cynical about virtue, since he believed that humans are governed by greed and desire, are easily offended, are quick to fault on obligations, and are disloyal without regret. He viewed vice as an advantage over virtue, although he thought it useful to appear to be virtuous. Rather than have the good be above all other pursuits, he thought power, order, and stability justified the means to coddle or crush people. Even Plato recognized that knowledge of the good is the most abstract and difficult knowledge to master. Socrates candidly shared with friends that he was not able readily to define the good.[5]

In the 1850s, Chief Seattle demonstrated Thomas Aquinas' call to pursue high moral standards in his eloquent response to the U.S. government inquiry to sell tribal lands:

> The President in Washington sends word that he wishes to buy our land. But how can you buy or sell sky? The land? The idea is strange to us. If we do not own the freshness of the air and the sparkle of the water, how can you buy them?
>
> Every part of this earth is sacred to my people. Every shining pine needle, every sandy shore, every mist in the dark woods, every meadow, every humming insect. All are holy in the memory and experience of people.
>
> We know the sap which courses through the trees as we know the blood that flows through our veins. We are part of the earth and it is part of us. The perfumed flowers are our sisters. The bear, the deer, the great eagle, these are our brothers. The rocky crests, the juices in the meadow, the body heat of the pony, and man, all belong to the same family.
>
> The shining water that moves in the streams and rivers is not just water, but the blood of our ancestors. If we sell you our land, you must remember that it is sacred. Each ghostly reflection in the clear waters of the lakes tells of events and memories in the life of my people. The water's murmur is the voice of my father's father.
>
> The rivers are our brothers. They quench our thirst. They carry our canoes and feed our children. So you must give to the river the kindness you would give any brother.

If we sell you our land, remember that the air is precious to us, that the air shares its spirit with all the life it supports. The wind that gave our grandfather his first breath also receives his last sigh. The wind also gives our children the spirit of life. So if we sell you our land, you must keep it apart and sacred, as a place where man can go to taste the wind that is sweetened by the meadow flowers.

Will you teach your children what we have taught our children? That the earth is our mother? What befalls the earth befalls all the sons of the earth.

This we know: the earth does not belong to man, man belongs to the earth. All things are connected like the blood that unites us all. Man did not weave the web of life, he is merely a strand in it. Whatever he does to the web, he does to himself.

One thing we know: our god is also your god. The earth is precious to him and to harm the earth is to heap contempt on its creator.

Your destiny is a mystery to us. What will happen when the buffalo are all slaughtered? The wild horses tamed? What will happen when the secret corners of the forest are heavy with the scent of many men and the view of the ripe hills is blotted by talking wires? Where will the thicket be? Gone! Where will the eagle be? Gone! And what is it to say goodbye to the swift pony and the hunt? The end of living and the beginning of survival.

When the last Red Man has vanished with his wilderness and his memory is only the shadow of a cloud moving across the prairie, will these shores and forests still be here? Will there be any spirit of my people left?

We love this earth as a newborn loves its mother's heartbeat. So, if we sell you our land, love it as we have loved it. Care for it as we have cared for it. Hold in your mind the memory of the land as it is when you receive it. Preserve the land for all children and love it, as God loves us all.

As we are part of the land, you too are part of the land. This earth is precious to us. It is also precious to you. One thing we know: there is only one God. No man, be he Red Man or White Man, can be apart. We are brothers after all.[6]

Soon after Chief Seattle's plea for brotherhood in 1868, Walt Whitman lamented the prosperity that came from "beating up the wilderness into fertile farms," not long after the U.S. Civil War. Despite unprecedented materialistic advancement, he concluded that society was "crude, superstitious, and rotten. Moral conscience, the backbone of the state and man, was entirely lacking or seriously enfeebled or ungrown. Never was

Chief Seattle
Chief Seattle's plea for tolerant leadership
was an eloquent testimony to his
character.

Source: Library of Congress, Prints and Photographs
Division, LC-USZ62-100492.

there, perhaps, more hollowness at heart than at present, and here in the
United States."[7]

Mintzberg concluded that not since the 1920s has there been an era
that gave more praise to self-interest and greed than today. Companies
claim that shareholder wealth lifts all boats, but the evidence reveals that
only the rich ships got the lift. CEOs behave as if only they have contributed to wealth creation. We would be skeptical about the creation of a
society without selfishness, yet a society that lauds selfishness can only
result in cynicism and corruption. Social decisions have economic consequences, but economic decisions also have social consequences. Our society is out of balance, favoring economic over social needs. We need both
but are controlled by only one.

On February 4, 2002, *Fortune* magazine's list of the 100 best companies to work for did not include a name that was familiar to most people
until number 15 (Cisco Systems). About 50 percent of the firms had revenue below $650 million, and most were below $250 million. None were

listed on the New York Stock Exchange and only three were listed on AMEX.[8] For over 2,000 years, civilization has struggled to balance value and virtue. Although contemporary life is full of problems, we can lose sight of all the progress that has occurred in the past 100 years. The following 10 advancements illustrate human benefits made possible by the U.S. political and economic system:

1. American life expectancy increased from 47 to 77 years of age in the past century.
2. In 1952, polio killed 3,300 Americans; this disease, along with others, has been largely eradicated.
3. Americans' greatest public health problems are due to unlimited supplies of affordable food.
4. Americans have twice the purchasing power their parents had in 1960.
5. The widening income gap disappears if wages for immigration are controlled while keeping in mind that immigration wages benefit immigrants compared with what they earn in their native country.
6. The claim that household incomes are only moderately higher than 25 years ago does not take into account that fewer people live in each household. When this factor is controlled, middle-class income is 50 percent higher today.
7. Since 1970, the number of cars has increased by 68 percent and the number of miles driven by more than that, but smog has declined by a third and traffic fatalities have declined from 52,627 to 42,815.
8. In 1953, Americans spent limited money on a cleaner environment or medical advancements (for instance, $5.2 billion a year on artificial knees, which were not available a generation ago).
9. The incidence of heart disease, stroke, and cancer, adjusted for population growth, has declined.
10. America soon will be the first society in which most adults are college graduates.[9]

Market-driven economies represent our contemporary ethos, since our sky has long been blotted by "talking wires" and wireless. The preeminent question raised by corporate responsibility is whether the profit sector has an obligation to serve its shareholders and its stakeholders. However, the term *corporate responsibility* has no widely accepted definition, so how can we achieve a fuzzy objective? This chapter examines the corporate responsibility debate, the triple bottom line, and questions that can evaluate ways for corporations to pursue responsible conduct.

8-3 Corporate Responsibility Challenges

8-3a Motives (Intentions) versus Results (Consequences)

Aaron Feuerstein, president of Malden Mills, became the poster boy for corporate responsibility when he continued to pay employees even after his mill had burned down. Malden Mills received support from banks and vendors to dig out of bankruptcy. The company treated employees as an asset, not an expense. They valued their employees and recognized the quality of their employee's work.[10] Feuerstein's motives defined virtue and earned national praise. However, Malden Mills struggled to work out of bankruptcy, protected from creditors and vendors at their expense. Is it wise or possible to create a competitive advantage for a New England textile firm when off-shore competitors can produce less expensive products?

Bill Gates' motives were called into question by the U.S. Justice Department for Microsoft's use of market power and coercion to protect its monopoly. The same person who used ruthless business practices simultaneously established the Bill & Melinda Gates Foundation in order to spend $200 million of its $24 billion in assets to treat AIDS, malaria, and other diseases.[11] Gates is admired for his competence but, unlike Feuerstein, many people question his motives and the business practices that created his wealth.

If value is added without virtue, has the corporation been responsible? If virtue is present but value has not been added, has the corporation been irresponsible? Self-serving conduct can result in a public good, even though we prefer that virtue guide good results.

8-3b Do Well by Doing Good—Sustainability

Sustainability requires that corporations worry about how they make money, not just how much they make. Consumers and employees are increasingly expecting corporations to fill needs formerly left to government and to better align shareholder and stakeholder interests. Today corporate citizenship means employee health and safety, sustainability, equal opportunity/global diversity, and philanthropic contributions in the communities where the firm does business. Approximately 60 percent of managers believe these activities promote good will and support business goals. In the future, many leaders expect citizenship will need a global focus that can be measured and that is integrated into corporate decision making. Globalization is pulling corporations into a broader set of responsibilities, which most leaders accept is a trend that cannot be ignored, but they are not yet clear on how to respond. Wise leaders realize that they must withstand increased scrutiny in an intensified regulatory climate that demands transparency on financial, societal, and environmental performance. Critics and supporters differ on whether or how to embrace corporate citizenship, but the idea of sustainable economic development has become part of conventional business thinking. In 2003, 66 percent of companies sampled used their websites to promote their responsible conduct. The motive for these efforts may not be selflessness, but they are motivated because they fear unwanted media or regulator attention. However, corporate citizenship supporters ask whether motivation should matter if the consequence is a better society.

A CEO cannot publicly rebuke corporate responsibility, because, if nothing else, it has become a cost of doing business. However, citizenship is rarely incorporated into strategic decisions, so critics fear that more companies will do as Enron did—disingenuous image making.[12]

8-3c Mission Creep or Corporate Citizenship?

The corporate citizenship fault line rests on whether companies have obligations beyond profit maximization, a point on which there is no agreement. Regardless of the importance a corporation gives each stakeholder, the firm must balance the desires of customers, owners, and employees.

Customers breathe life into a corporation in the form of revenue. Customers want good value for the money they spend on products and services. In addition to economic value, customers want noneconomic benefits, such as service, ease of doing business, integrity, and warranties.

Corporations need to attract capital for purposes of investments and sometimes for operations. Shareholders want corporations to offer economic value as measured by a return on their investment. In addition to economic value, shareholders want responsible financial disclosures that are honest, accurate, and timely, in addition to effective investor relationships supported by sound corporate governance.

Corporations must attract talented people capable of satisfying customers and shareholders. In turn, employees want economic value in terms of fair wages and benefits for their labor. Employees also want noneconomic values, such as meaningful work, security, good working relationships, and a sense of teamwork.

Critics challenge adding citizenship to the traditional mission of creating owner wealth, since profitability is what corporations do best. The profit sector is ill-suited to contribute to a "greater good" that cannot be defined with any rigor and that wastes resources. Corporations provide employees with a paycheck, so they can be socially responsible. The argument would be that CEOs are inept social workers and should stay focused on making profits without lying, cheating, or stealing. Besides, the "invisible hand" of the marketplace provides positive social benefits (employment, a tax base, valuable products, and so on), even though business is motivated by self-interest.

Some might agree with this conclusion, but not with the analysis. Business leaders are ill-prepared to prioritize or solve social problems, so corporate contributions are wasted at best or make the problem worse through corrupt practices. As multinational power expands, corporations can threaten to pull out of their social responsibilities and can exert unhealthy influence over governments. Social problems are the responsibility of the public sector and corporations should not be trusted to perform public works.

8-3d Every Good Deed Goes Punished

Cynicism rules when companies such as Enron are selected for "most admired" awards. Enron's acts of financial fraud discredited all companies. Executive compensation, in particular, is viewed as unfair at best, obscene at worse, especially when leaders demand performance from employees but are paid handsomely despite destroying shareholder wealth. Many employees view unprecedented executive compensation as unjust, especially when employees are laid off or find their benefits cut.

Skeptics attack corporate responsibility on its face, since doing the right thing for the wrong reason raises suspicion. They are cynical about business motives, charging corporate citizenship is a public relations scam to cover up the ways that companies dislocate local cultures, treat workers, and abuse the environment. In an era of instant communication, stories of child labor, pollution of water supplies, and corporate malfeasance are broadcast around the world, with severe bottom line consequences. We can consider Nike, McDonald's, and Ford in their battle against charges of corporate irresponsibility.

An MIT graduate student used the word *sweatshop* as his ID when he tried to order shoes from Nike. The company refused to accept the order, since the word was "inappropriate slang." The student agreed to use a different ID but asked for a picture of the 10-year-old Vietnamese girls who had made his shoes. His email was sent around the planet and took on a life of its own after the media picked it up. Nike responded effectively, but defensively, to charges of worker exploitation in its corporate responsibility report. Fair or not, a case such as Nike's contributes to a view that the only reason a company such as Microsoft donates computers for schools is so they can advertise to youth.

McDonald's placed fourteenth in *Financial Times*/PriceWaterhouse-Coopers' 2000 and 2001 surveys of the world's most respected companies for their environmental performance. However, to some, McDonald's is the poster company for the destruction of local business and culture, for the promotion of unhealthy food, and for the bad treatment of workers. Like Nike's, its corporate responsibility reports did little to combat the Golden Arches as a symbol of the problems associated with global capitalism.

The Ford auto company was hammered from business and environmental supporters when it reduced greenhouse emissions goals and gas mileage goals due to earnings problems. The editorial page of the *Wall Street Journal* challenged William Ford, the auto company's CEO, to stop listening to environmentalists desires since the firm made an honest profit by selling consumers the cars they want. The Sierra Club stated that Ford's action was wrong for the company, for consumers, and for the environment.[13]

8-3e The Business Case for Corporate Responsibility

Whether corporate motives are driven by virtue or vice, companies must meet social and environmental goals, in addition to financial goals. Ironically, the more a business focuses on the bottom line at the exclusion of factors such as quality of leadership, corporate citizenship, and environmental responsibility, the more the business is at risk. Civil rights legislation prohibits discrimination. Environmental laws and regulations prohibit or limit pollution. Consumer protection legislation prohibits or limits product defects, false advertising, monopolistic behavior, and the like. Corporate governance and securities law prohibits fraud, in addition to holding management accountable for shareholder fiduciary responsibility.

All corporations have a fiduciary responsibility to create shareholder wealth. Increasingly, they must also commit to a social bottom line (fair employment and consumer protection) and an environmental bottom line (to limit or prevent pollution). Although the concept of a "triple bottom line" (planet, people, and profit) can be another management fad, the risks need to be managed, even if the concept is not embraced. In a post-Enron world, firms such as Krispy Kreme have learned that reputation impacts financial result.

Although corporate responsibility has become a mainstream issue, what responsibility looks like to different stakeholders and how one measures success remain elusive. In 2000, the International Chamber of Commerce identified more than 40 codes of conduct to govern global business. The notion that one set of standard measures will fit an incredibly diverse range of corporations seems unlikely. Chiquita Brands International is focused on responsible farming in the tropics and, accordingly, has formed a partnership with Rainforest Alliance to inspect operations for responsible land use. Key Bank in Cleveland, Ohio, supports financial education in the inner city.

Most studies reveal a positive correlation between corporate social responsibility and the corporation's reputation, its ability to attract talent, and increased sales to environmentally conscious consumers, yet the studies fall short of demonstrating that responsible corporate behavior improves financial performance. An Australian sustainability index indicates there is no such thing as a sustainable company today. Therefore, this index does not measure which firms are angels but focuses on which firms are the best devils and show promise of sustainability. If a clear relationship between responsible corporate behavior and financial performance could be proven, even the devils would get on board.[14]

8-4 Adding Value and the Balanced Scorecard

There is growing interest in using a variation of the Balanced Scorecard (BSC) to put into practice the idea of a triple bottom line—finance, social, and environmental. Its purpose is not to act as a corporate social justice tool, but it does take into account the consequences of corporate action on customers, employees, vendors, regulators, and the communities in which the firm operates, in addition to shareholders.

The BSC is an execution tool that measures whether a corporation has been competent in satisfying its stakeholders. The tool can enhance feedback to lead change, set targets, and align business units, functions, and people.

8-4a What Is the Balanced Scorecard?

The BSC asks the question "How will the corporation measure success?" If the corporation were successful in achieving its intentions, what would it look like to its customers, shareholders, employees, and other stakeholders? What processes and learning must take place to meet subjective and objective stakeholder desires? The BSC is not a foolproof tool, but it raises the right questions, and, when applied well, it can create a competitive advantage in a socially responsible way (see Figure 8-1).

A detailed account of the BSC is beyond the purpose of this book, but what follows are examples of how it works. First, the corporation creates a vision that outlines its competitive advantage. Then the following questions are asked:

Figure 8-1
The Balanced Scorecard
Source: Adapted from Kaplan and Norton.[15]

1. If our vision were successful, what would we look like to
   a. Our customers?
   b. Our shareholders?
   c. Our employees?
2. To satisfy our stakeholders, at what processes must we excel?
3. To satisfy our stakeholders, what must we learn and how must we change?

The intention of the BSC is to drive performance, so that the corporation adds value to customers, shareholders, and employees. To do so requires the corporation to link processes and organizational learning to stakeholder satisfaction.

8-4b Adding Customer Value

Southwest Airlines defined its business by customer need, not product, by providing air travel at the cost of ground transportation. The company built the business on the notion that people need transportation and that, if Southwest could provide this service at the cost of travel on a car or bus, it would grow beyond the airline industry.

Consider what most people value when they fly on a plane—on-time delivery, baggage handling, and price. Consider the types of values that many airlines emphasize to passengers, such as frequent flyer programs.

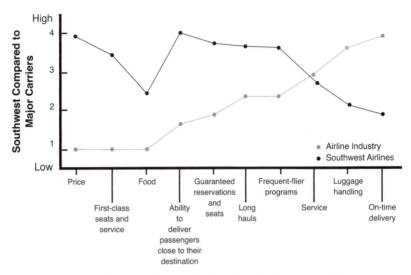

Figure 8-2
Southwest Airline Industry Value Curve
Source: Adapted from Trombetta.[16]

Southwest Airlines emphasizes benefits sought by most travelers at a lower price than most competitors. Competitors emphasize benefits that customers may want but for which they are not willing to pay. Customers will fly Southwest because of its benefits of on-time delivery, baggage handling, and price, since they are willing to trade off on benefits such as better food. Traditional airlines invest in customer benefits, such as food, that reduce their margins and funds available for shareholders and employees or for reinvestment into the company (see Figure 8-2).

To achieve the vision of providing air transportation at the cost of ground transportation, how must Southwest look to its customer? Customers want safety, on-time delivery, baggage handling, and low fares. These could be measured by accidents and near misses, variance between stated and actual arrival time, and number of lost bags. The rigor of measurements ensures that the company delivers on its promise.

8-4c Adding Shareholder Value

To achieve its vision, what must the company look like to its shareholders? Shareholders want return on their investment, growth, profitability, asset utilization, and the like. Shareholders might also be interested in corporate governance reform. Appropriate financial measures could be selected to evaluate financial performance, and qualitative measures could include increasing the number of independent directors or expensing options.

8-4d Adding Employee Value

To achieve its vision, what must the company look like to its employees? Employees want wages, benefits, job security, and meaningful work. Direct measures, such as wage and benefit rates relative to the industry and limits on layoffs, could evaluate employee satisfaction. Indirect measures, such as attrition rates relative to the industry and productivity rates, such as the number of employees divided by total revenue, offer an indication of whether employees are satisfied and productive.

8-4e Adding Value through Improved Processes

To achieve the corporation's vision to satisfy customers, shareholders, and employees, at what processes must it excel? The purpose of reviewing process change is to link tightly operational excellence to service to stakeholders. For example, Scott Technology bought Figgie International, which sold equipment to municipal fire departments. Scott's strategic goals included customer satisfaction and revenue growth. One of the processes used to achieve this goal was to meet with fire chiefs to learn about equipment that helped them fight fires. Fire chiefs told an interdisciplinary leadership team from Scott about an infrared helmet that enabled firefighters to see through smoke, to help them determine whether there were people inside burning buildings needing to be rescued. However, the light was attached to the helmet, so firefighters had to risk their safety, for instance, by removing their helmet and mask to shine the light under a bed to locate a child. Scott officials used this insight to design an infrared light that would be attached to firefighters' shoulders using Velcro and an extension wire. The light pointed in the direction firefighters were looking. However, they could keep their helmet and mask in place and pull the light off their shoulder if they needed to rescue someone hidden in a closet or under a bed. Scott's process led to a dominating market share for a product it had not produced up to that point. The process was that a multidisciplinary team met and listened to customers—in this case, fire chiefs—and then designed a product to serve their needs—to rescue people. In turn, Scott was rewarded financially by increasing its customers' satisfaction.[17]

Success measures should be selected to fit customer needs, wants, and values. Examples of common process measures include delivery time, R&D, time spent prospecting calls, safety processes, weight and scrap units rejected, bids with revised drawings, new accounts opened, and job-related injuries.

8-4f Adding Value through Organizational Learning

To achieve customer and shareholder goals, how can an adaptive culture be developed? What organizational and employee competencies must be developed? The purpose of evaluating learning and growth objectives is to identify the performance drivers necessary to achieve customer and shareholder goals. These performance drivers are likely to include employees' competencies, the organizational structure, technology and information, and the creation of a climate for action.

Parker Hannifin, a company that is a world leader in motion and control technology, earns $6 billion in revenue annually and employs nearly 50,000 people in 44 countries. Parker is organized into largely independent strategic business units that serve different markets. In order for the firm to strike a balance between serving distinct markets while supporting corporate objectives, Parker integrated the BSC into all of its operations around the planet to communicate goals and results and to allocate and leverage resources.[18]

In order to be effective, organizational learning objectives should be linked to customer and shareholder objectives. Common learning success measures include employee productivity (profits divided by number of employees), satisfaction (indirect measures, such as retention or turnover rates, or qualitative measures, such as employee satisfaction surveys or open meetings), the number of people trained in the use of the BSC, and new product development revenue divided by R&D expenditures.

8-5 Integrating Competitive Advantage and the Triple Bottom Line

The question of what is a fitting response to what is happening in a market economy is worth debating. An example of how a BSC can achieve a triple bottom line may be an inadequate view of social responsibility for some and admirable for others. At least it fits the standard of a better devil rather than unleashed individual profitability at the expense of stakeholders.

The BSC is tailored to fit the unique mission and vision of each company. In turn, it can take into account the unique way each corporation can integrate profitability, social responsibility, and sustainability as illustrated by the following example of an industrial furnace company three-part vision:

1. Increase the life of industrial furnaces, so customers can achieve their productivity goals. Furnaces are repaired while customers continue to operate, so the manufacturer does not lose productivity time.
2. Achieve revenue and profitability through global growth and continuous internal operational improvements built on the firm's core competencies.
3. Offer a superior service that increases worker safety and reduces toxic emissions while forming partnerships with the local communities in which the company operates.

Planks one and two of the vision statement focus on strategic business goals, and plank three of the vision statement focuses on worker safety, the environment, and local community goals. The following BSC application integrates financial, sustainability, and social goals.

8-5a Customer Satisfaction

1. Repeat business and revenue growth is an indirect customer satisfaction measure.
2. A customer relationship system meets with customers on a systematic basis to identify their business, environmental, and worker safety concerns.
3. The percentage of sales coming from international markets indicates whether global growth is occurring.
   - Customer satisfaction, revenue growth, environmental concerns, and worker safety are integrated.

8-5b Shareholder Satisfaction

1. Reduce overhead as a percentage of total expenses to improve operating margins.
2. Improve cash flow by reducing accounts receivable.
3. Reduce debt levels by refinancing loans to take advantage of lower interest rates.
   - These are traditional financial or profitability measures.

8-5c Process Improvements

1. Integrate the customer relationship system into operations, so that customer needs and process are linked.

2. Operations measure the variance between the budget and actual expenditures to control overhead.

3. The safety and environmental system is linked to services provided to customers as measured by reduced accident rates and reduced toxic emissions.

   • Execution is difficult to achieve unless process measures are linked closely with customer and financial objectives.

8-5d Learning and Growth

1. Create a global leadership program to build international expertise of senior executives to better understand the needs of customers and local business.

2. Train all employees in safety and environmental processes.

3. Create a sense of team by participating in a "green day" in the community in which the corporation operates.

   • Execution also must include learning, since corporations never have all the skills needed to execute a perfect triple bottom line.

Of course, more objectives and more precise measures could be included. For example, regulators such as the Environmental Protection Agency could be added and the success measure could be to reduce the environmental impact of pollutants. The key point of this example is the integration of business and citizenship into strategic decision making.

8-6 Balanced Scorecard and Sustainability

In practice, the relationship between the BSC and sustainability is mixed. Some firms drop the use of the BSC altogether because of the discipline it requires. Some firms fail to update metrics to fit new realities because of a comfort with old metrics. Some firms implement a BSC with no attempt to align corporate objectives with environmental responsibility.

These mixed results raise a healthy skepticism about the tool as a magic bullet, yet what do we have to put in its place? The good news is that corporations such as Shell have successfully integrated environmental concerns, social issues, and financial objectives into the firm's strategic intent using a scorecard. The main advantage of the BSC is the discussion it can foster among managers about strategic issues. Of course, this assumes that the managers involved will raise concerns about environmental and social issues. The problem is more about the misuse of the tool than its potential benefit, since corporations have successfully integrated sustainability and social concerns throughout their enterprise. Whether the BSC will help firms depends on leaders' ability to understand how corporate responsibility can enhance or at least not distract from the creation of a competitive advantage. The answer might also require a simpler version of the BSC, although the risk of a simple approach is a failure to take into account the complexity of balancing the triple bottom line. The bottom line is that we have no choice but to enter the fray of all the problems associated with defining, gaining agreement, and measuring issues associated with justice if we are to take this classical virtue seriously.[19]

8-6a Balanced Scorecard Limits and Benefits

There are always problems in data availability, reliability, and validity. The benefit of gathering data not available might exceed its costs. Reliability is whether the same results would occur over time. For instance, are costs and revenues defined consistently? Validity concerns whether we are measuring what we think we are measuring. Customers might report they are satisfied but, in reality, not know what they want or not want to share their real concerns.

The BSC is not a cure-all for availability, reliability, and validity issues, but it does keep the firm's ignorance in full view. Subjective and objective data are used to manage reliability and validity issues. For example, customer satisfaction is measured by objective data, such as actual customer buyer behavior, and subjective data, such as focus group results and complaints that reveal consumer perceptions and feelings.

The BSC relies on leading indicators and lagging indicators. Leading indicators drive or forecast performance by changing processes and learning. In other words, how will strategic goals be reached? Lagging indicators measure outcomes or track past performance, such as customer satisfaction or profitability. In other words, what are the firm's strategic goals?

The goal of the BSC is profitability through stakeholder satisfaction. Shareholder wealth is the end and stakeholder satisfaction is the means. The BSC is an enlightened self-interest tool in that owners understand their wealth creation is dependent on stakeholder satisfaction. When executed well, the BSC illustrates what it means to be competent and responsible in business by achieving profitability through stakeholder satisfaction.

8-7 Asking the Right Questions

Theologian H. Richard Niebuhr outlines a classical ethical way to determine corporate responsibility as defined by Aristotle's proposal that "every art and every inquiry and similarly every action and pursuit, is thought to aim at some good".

1. What is the goal?   (teleology)
2. What is the law?   (deontology)
3. What is happening?
4. What is the fitting response?   (responsibility)

Question one views character-based leadership as creation and achievement goals. Question two views character-based leadership as discovering what is already there (law or rule) and then obeying it. Question three represents the way Niebuhr determines ethical action. This view is more contextual than the other two. It is guided by a corollary, follow-up question: "what is the fitting response to what is happening?"[20]

8-7a What Is the Goal?

An important and challenging goal is to answer the question "Which stakeholders are served by the business and how would each measure success?" Even if a company embraces corporate responsibility, tools such as the BSC illustrate that defining success is less than clear. Philosophical and practical issues aside, today's business climate requires that corporations serve stakeholders; otherwise, they risk unwanted media and regulator attention or an inability to attract customers and employees. Even if a company rejects corporate responsibility, it dare not say so. Maybe there is less of a debate about the need for corporations to serve stakeholders, but the dilemma is how this can be achieved.

8-7b What Is the Law?

This question assumes that a law or moral principle exists and that our charge is to discover the rule to govern our conduct. The process is discovery, not creation. Once the rule is discovered, the duty is for leaders to obey.

Corporate legal compliance depends on the rule of law. Moral laws depend on virtue. Laws that guide commerce include consumer protection, fair employment, worker safety, and prohibition against fraud and environmental irresponsibility. Moral laws of our family, community, and nation also regulate our actions. Some legal and moral laws we accept and some we reject. Increasingly, employees are expected to accept a corporate culture to be accountable for performance, to add value (competence) with virtue (character).

8-7c What Is the Fitting Response to What Is Happening?

Corporate scandals make headlines precisely because they are unusual and outrageous and distort responsible corporation action, yet ethical leadership is less spectacular than unethical lapses in that leaders of character and competence build corporations and communities in a way that is slow and steady. Ethical leadership is built on the excellent execution of a clear strategy through extraordinary teamwork whereby people feel connected to something larger than themselves.

Sometimes adversity gets in the way of our goals, yet adversity, whether individually or in groups, defines our character. What is possible to us in the situation in which we find ourselves? Events such as the American Civil War led to the abolition of slavery, the Great Depression led to the New Deal, and international politics led the United States to enter two twentieth-century world wars despite isolation desires. Often we must learn to respond to circumstances rather than pursue an ideal.

Corporate responsibility is an elusive concept. The questions raised by Neibuhr help us struggle with ethical issues that defy simple answers or clear responses. These questions help us to see how we understand ourselves and what it means to be responsible.

8-8 Conclusion

Competence matters. The well-intentioned incompetent can do as much harm as those who lack virtue. An ethical family business owner can mean well in placing inept relatives in vital positions. A caring owner who makes a great neighbor can fail to create a competitive advantage and be ignorant of the firm's financial health. Good intention minus competence can drive a corporation off the cliff.

Competitive advantage matters. There is a Darwinian quality about competence in that individuals and corporations must adapt to market changes with innovation or perish. Prosperity is not an assurance that ethical conduct will occur, but companies that are able to compete effectively are positioned well to provide fair value to customers, adequate returns to shareholders, and decent working conditions to employees.

Adding value matters. Corporate performance must add value to shareholders, which is difficult to do if stakeholders are not also satisfied. Whether society assigns corporations with narrow or broad responsibilities, a company cannot be successful if one of its key stake-holders pulls its support of revenue (customers), funding (shareholders), or talent (employees).

Corporate responsibility matters. Is society best served by corporate profit maximization or alignment of shareholders and stakeholders? This debate is complicated, since some distrust corporate motives. In addition, companies that want to be responsible do so without clear guidelines of what corporate citizenship looks like. The BSC provides a tool to enhance shareholder wealth through stakeholder satisfaction that is relevant to each corporation's unique circumstances. It offers a more rigorous meas-urement of whether value has been added to stakeholders than do more conceptual stakeholder models.

Competent and servant leadership matters. Competent servant lead-ership is about change that makes life better for stakeholders. The impor-tance of servant leadership to promoting strategic thinking and behavior that integrates competitive advantage and social responsibility cannot be emphasized too much. It is very difficult to meet the expectations of cus-tomers, shareholders, and employees simultaneously, never mind adding other stakeholders, such as vendors, regulators, and environmentalists. Competent leaders will increasingly have to be extraordinary strategists capable of creating a competitive advantage that responds to constant change and be skilled at building relationships, teams, and talent. Leader-ship competence has and will continue to be central to building profitable and responsible corporations.

Chapter Quiz

1. Which of the following philosophers believed that leaders should be teachers of virtue and caretakers of human needs?
   a. Plato
   b. Aquinas
   c. Aristotle
   d. Kant
2. According to *Fortune's* "100 Best Companies to Work For," what percentage of NYSE-listed companies was listed?
   a. 0 percent
   b. 15 percent
   c. 30 percent
   d. 75 percent

3. The corporate citizenship fault line rests on which of the following?
   a. whether companies have obligations beyond profit
   b. whether companies have the right to seek profits
   c. whether companies' profits are a privilege
   d. whether companies can maximize profits

4. The chapter provided examples of companies that are experiencing charges of corporate social irresponsibility. All of the following companies were mentioned *except*
   a. Nike.
   b. Malden Mills.
   c. McDonald's.
   d. Ford.

5. Which of the following does *not* belong in the "triple bottom line"?
   a. social
   b. political
   c. financial
   d. environmental

6. There is a positive correlation between corporate social responsibility and all of the following *except*
   a. reputation.
   b. financial performance.
   c. recruiting power.
   d. increased sales to socially-conscious consumers.

7. Which of the following is not true about the Balanced Sorecard?
   a. It is a corporate social justice tool.
   b. It asks how the corporation will measure success.
   c. It takes consequences of corporate actions into account.
   d. It considers how much stakeholders have been satisfied.

8. Which of the following is *not* a measure of added value to employees?
   a. attrition rates
   b. productivity rates
   c. asset utilization
   d. benefit rates

9. Whether the BSC will help firms depends on which of the following?
   a. the level of discussions it fosters
   b. the level of reasonability it directs
   c. the extent to which leaders understand how to use the BSC
   d. the extent to which employees carry out the goals of the BSC

10. Theologian Richard Niebuhr poses all of the following questions to determine social responsibility *except*
   a. What is the goal?
   b. What is the law?
   c. What is the fitting response?
   d. What is the industry norm?

Note: You can find the correct answers to these questions by taking the quiz and then submitting your answers in the Online Edition. The program will automatically score your submission. If you miss a question, the program will provide the correct answer, a rationale for the answer, and the section number in the chapter where the topic is discussed.

Questions for Thought

1. Clearly, there is a relationship between *moral* and *morale*. How do you see this relationship and how would you explain it?
2. Corporate responsibility is always a call to action. Can you recall a time when not acting was irresponsible on your part?
3. How would you compare Chief Seattle's bottom line with a corporation of your choice?
4. Describe how the Balanced Scorecard is a very focused and flexible tool to help a corporation be responsible.
5. What is the goal of a corporation?
6. Explain how laws, policies, and culture shape corporate responsibility.
7. Can corporate responsibility change? If so, how?
8. Who monitors corporate responsibility and how do they evaluate it?
9. Why is building a responsible culture a slow process?
10. How does adversity test, strengthen, or weaken corporate responsibility?

Web Exercises

Visit Target's Community Giving website at http://target.com/target_group/community_giving/index.jhtml. What kind of programs does Target help promote? How does it encourage business leaders to participate in its programs and foster a sense of corporate responsibility?

Now visit http://www.globalexchange.org and take a look at their coverage of Nike's (http://www.globalexchange.org/campaigns/sweatshops/nike/index.html) practices of using low-paid labor for manufacturing. What does the ongoing battle over this kind of labor indicate about Nike's corporate goals in regard to social responsibility? What kind of image does it project to consumers?

Endnotes

1. Melanie Warner, "Krispy Kreme Tumbles into the Red," *The New York Times,* November 23, 2004, sec. C1.
2. Marc Gunther, "Money and Moals at GE," *Fortune,* November 15, 2004, 176, 5p, 7c.
3. George Anderson, "Lights, Camera, Ethics," Ethical Corporation, January 11, 2005, http://www.ethicalcorp.com/.
4. Jacob Needleman, *The American Soul: Rediscovering the Wisdom of the Founders* (New York: TarcherPutnam, 2002), 6
5. Charles Manz and Christopher Neck, *Mastering Self Leadership: Empowering Yourself for Personal Excellence,* 3rd ed. (Upper Saddle River, NJ: Shriberg, Shriberg, and Lloyd, 2003), 231–236.
6. Betty Sue Flowers, ed., *The Power of Myth* (New York: Doubleday, 1988).
7. Needleman, 317–18.
8. Henry Mintzberg, *Managers Not MBAs: A Hard Look at the Soft Practice of Managing and Management Development* (San Francisco: Barrett-Koehler, 2004), 153.
9. Will George, "The Good News Isn't Sinking In," *The Plain Dealer,* January 10, 2004, sec. B 9.
10. Art Boulay. "Malden Mills: A Study in Leadership," http://www.opi-inc.com/malden.htm, 1996.
11. "Bill and Melinda Gates Foundation Announces $200 Million Grant to Accelerate Research on 'Grand Challenges' in Global Health; Grants to Help Overcome Scientific Roadblocks in AIDS, Malaria, Other Diseases," http://www.gatesfoundation.org/globalhealth/announcement/ announce-030126.htm.
12. Sophia Muirhead, "Corporate Citizenship in the New Century: Accountability, Transparency and Global Stakeholder Engagement," *The Conference Board 2,* no. 16 (2002).
13. A.J. Vogel, "Does it Pay to Be Good?" http://www.cfodirect.com/ (2003).
14. Andy Gilliam and Marc Newson, "Sustainability: Quest for the Best Devils." PriceWaterhouseCoopers http://www.pwcglobal.com (2003).
15. Robert Kaplan and David Norton, *Balanced Scorecard* (Cambridge, MA: Harvard Business School, 1996).
16. Ralph Trombetta, "Value Innovation," Baldwin-Wallace College, Berea, OH: February 21, 2003.
17. Mark Kirk, "Leadership Competence, Character and Power," Baldwin-Wallace College. Berea, OH: October 28, 2002.
18. Trombetta.
19. Francesco Zingales and Kai Hockerts, "Balanced Scorecard and Sustainability: Examples from Literature and Practice, *INSEAD,* http://knowledge.insead.edu/index.cfm (2003).
20. H. Richard Neibuhr, *The Responsible Self: An Essay in Christian Moral Philosophy* (New York: Harper & Row, 1963).

σοφία

Prudence

Outline

9-1 Prudence (Wisdom, Responsibility, Foresight, Common Sense)

9-1a Prudent Leadership

John Adams felt the burden of leadership when he was appointed as United States ambassador to France. His awareness that his leadership abilities would determine whether his new nation would win its freedom led him to comment, "I cannot but wish I were better qualified."[1] Although the admiring Benjamin Rush hated to lose his friend to the service of his country, Rush's confidence in Adams was captured in this passage:

> I am aware that your abilities and firmness are much wanted at the Court of France, and after all that has been said of the advantages of dressing, powdering, and bowing well as necessary accomplishments for an ambassador, I maintain that knowledge and integrity with a common share of prudence will outweigh them all. . . . I am willing to risk the safety of our country upon this single proposition, that you will effectually baffle and deceive them all by being perfectly honest.[2]

Whereas Rush had confidence in John Adams' prudence, Adams' wife, Abigail, was less sanguine as to whether prudence would trump power as she reflected on human nature, political power, and the good of society:

> I am more and more convinced that man is a dangerous creature, and that power whether vested in many or few is ever grasping. The great fish swallow up the small and he, who is most strenuous for the rights of the people, when vested with power, is as eager after prerogatives of government. You tell me of degrees of perfection to which human nature is capable of arriving, and I believe it, but at the same time lament that our admiration should arise from the scarcity of the instances.[3]

Benjamin Rush thought John Adams' prudence would be more valuable to the ambassador than his knowledge of French culture. Abigail Adams was cautious about the ability of most leaders to handle power with wisdom. Mr. Rush and Mrs. Adams understood that the desired end of leadership included justice and compassion, and that prudence was the means to that end. This chapter defines prudence, provides examples of prudent behavior, and describes four common imprudent behaviors that confront us all—ignorance, neglect, denial, and willfulness.

9-1b The Ant and the Grasshopper

In a field one summer's day, a grasshopper was hopping about, chirping, and singing to its heart's content. An ant passed by, bearing along with great toil an ear of corn he was taking to the nest.

"Why not come and chat with me," said the grasshopper, "instead of toiling and moiling in that way?" "I am helping to lay up food for the winter," said the ant, "and recommend you to do the same." "Why bother about winter?" said the grasshopper. "We have got plenty of food at present." But the ant went on its way and continued its toil. When the winter came the grasshopper had no food and found itself dying of hunger, while the ants were daily distributing corn and grain from the stores they had collected in the summer. Then the grasshopper saw the truth: It is best to prepare for the days of necessity.[4]

This Aesop fable is a child's introduction to prudence. At a certain age, the child "gets it" and the child's ethical education has been furthered. The

Abigail Adams
John Adams was counseled by his wife, Abigail, to remain prudent in his role as a leader of the new United States.
Source: Library of Congress, Prints and Photographs Division, LC-USZ62-10016.

moral of the story is contained in its last line: preparation for the future necessities. But there are additional lessons learned on the way to the punch line. For example, the fable affirms there are seasons in life—the plenty of summer and the scarcity of winter. The seasons become metaphorical ways of describing every person's life. There are times of health and sickness. Life has its ups and downs. When one is young, so much seems possible—that is, so much seems possible unless one grows up in a frighteningly abusive context or is stuck in a situation of grinding poverty. The way we experience our fate in life often shapes and, then, reflects how we view reality (threatening? neutral? supportive?).

We also learn that work seems necessary to get ahead in life and that those who do not work do not eat. Even if reality is experienced as supportive, life is not simply handed to us on a platter. It is not without reason that we talk about "making a living." To live takes effort. To live well, to live meaningfully, requires prudent effort. It is prudent to work, to give effort, in preparation for the winter seasons when literally it is not possible to produce the food of life.

Whatever else is true, Aesop's fable underscores the importance of being prudent in life. Not to be prudent is to live shortsightedly—to give no thought for the morrow. Prudence is always a story of human choices. And imprudence is inattention to the consequences of one's actions. Prudence says that how we live matters. Imprudence naïvely says it does not matter. The fable establishes the context for understanding why prudence is a virtue.

Like the fist three virtues (courage, faith, and justice), prudence is also a virtue because it aims at the good. As we saw in Chapter 1, *prudence* comes from *prudens* and *prudentitia*, words that translate in suggestive ways. *Prudentitia* means "sensible, reasonable foresight, skill, and common sense." Yet another Latin word for prudence is *cautus,* which obviously gives us the word caution. The sum of these words is an excellent description of a competent, successful business leader—a prudent leader. Perhaps the best synonym for *prudence* is *wisdom.* This idea of prudence as wisdom will play an important role in Chapter 13, where we conclude our discussion about effective leadership by talking about the worth and worthiness of life.

A seventh-century monastic sage noted, "When we draw water from a well, it can happen that we inadvertently also bring up a frog. When we acquire virtues we can sometimes find ourselves involved with the vices, which are imperceptibly interwoven with them. What we mean is this. Gluttony can be caught up with hospitality . . . malice with prudence."[5] This monastic sage, John Climacus, rightly understood that life is usually lived without the clear distinction of white and non-white. Rather, the color of normal life is gray. Life is complex; it is mixed.

We are often betwixt and between, and the right choice is not obvious or clear. Furthermore, Climacus showed that even if we make a prudent choice—pursue the virtuous action—the action may generate troubling ripple effects. In much of life and business, not choosing is not an option. The only option is how, in a given situation, we choose to act. Every business leader knows that even a prudent economic decision may have unpleasant human consequences. In fact, the study of economics is the study of trade-offs—on the one hand and then the other. We must continue to remind ourselves, however, that *prudence* is not primarily an economic or fiduciary word but, rather, comes from the vocabulary of virtue.

A monk from the fourth century underscored that prudence is a virtue because it is aimed at the good. Evagrius Ponticus revealed how prudence works in making a virtuous decision. He said, "Those things which are good or evil according as they are used well or ill are the objects making up virtue or vice. Prudence is the virtue that employs these objects for the one or the other."[6] An important aspect of prudence is its role as a means to an end. In this sense, prudence is not the goal—it is the means to the goal. Put in the language of Aristotle, the goal of human life is to be good. Prudence assists us in getting there. Put in business language, the goal is to be successful; prudence assists us in getting there.

As the head of the New York Stock Exchange (NYSE), Dick Grasso was highly popular. His leadership was at its zenith after the September 11 attacks on the Twin Towers in New York City's Wall Street area. He chose to sleep in his office rather than go home, as he guided Manhattan's financial district back from that horror. Between September 11 and September 17, Grasso helped financial markets fulfill their purpose by preparing to trade again. With a massive American flag as a backdrop, New York's Senator Hillary Clinton and Governor George Pataki joined Mr. Grasso in ringing the bell that reopened the market for business. The press lauded him as the "president of capitalism." His rise from being a young floor trader, making about $80 a week, to providing leadership for the New York Stock Exchange was seen as another classic story of success American-style.

Opinions about Mr. Grasso, however, started to change when Exchange members learned that he had accepted a $5 million bonus for his efforts following the horror of September 11. When this bonus was added to his 2001 salary, his income for the year totaled $30 million, nearly equaling the net income of the entire Exchange. In late August 2003, the board disclosed that Mr. Grasso was set to earn a retirement package worth $139.5 million and, in early September, it was reported that he was entitled to an additional $48 million.

According to transcripts, in an unusual move for a floor trader, Patrick Collins stated that brokers thought Mr. Grasso's pay and retirement package must be a typographical error, since the numbers were so shockingly huge. Collins' question to the Exchange Board was a prudent one: "You men held very important jobs. Did you ever make this amount of money?" A host of critics, including the president of the California Public Employees Retirement System and California's treasurer, called for Grasso's resignation. Officials in New York, North Carolina, and Iowa soon joined them.[7]

In response to a growing intensity of criticism about his pay—which was joined in by some NYSE directors—Grasso offered to forgo $48 million of deferred compensation. When board member Carl McCall phoned Grasso to inform him the board had voted to accept his resignation, Grasso responded by stating he had offered to forgo his compensation and had not offered to resign unless voted to do so by the board. McCall told Grasso, "Well, the board has voted you out, Dick."[8]

Grasso's performance had earned him the respect of traders on the floor, the NYSE board, and well-regarded political leaders, such as former New York Mayor Rudolph Giuliani. However, Grasso's compensation became a lightning rod to a broader set of concerns about corporate governance, self-regulation, and financial disclosure. Performance and compensation are both issues of prudence, but they are not the same issue. Insiders in the investment community and on the trading floor questioned the prudence of Grasso's accepting the compensation. They did not question the legality of the situation. The issue of legalities is a justice issue; prudence deals with issues in a different way than justice.

Even though Grasso's compensation had been approved originally by the board, and even though seven members of the new board did not vote to ask for his resignation, his constituency expected him to choose wisely. Certainly, the accolades in recognition of his excellent performance impacted his choice, but the issue that faced Grasso, and that we all face, involves balancing what we have with what we can have. When looked at as a choice, prudence is an issue of will—intentionality balanced with skill in managing our lives.

To understand prudence as an issue of will, let us go back more than 30 years to when Rollo May offered a trenchant insight into Freud's influence on our world and his effect on our idea of the human will. May said Freud believed that we "are determined by unconscious urges, anxieties, fears, and the endless host of bodily drives and instinctual forces. In describing how 'wish' and 'drive' moves us rather than 'will,' Freud formulated a new image of man."[9] May concluded that Freud's work carried "an unavoidable undermining of will and decision and an undercutting of the individual's sense of responsibility. The image that emerged was of man as determined—not driving any more, but driven."[10] The person who is or feels driven is the one without choices, bereft of the freedom to choose, and, hence, the one who is no longer a responder but, rather, a reactor. In this view, human will is lost and humans become determined and, perhaps, predestined.

Since Freud's work was so influential, it is essential that we recover and reestablish the human will. Only in this way will prudence again have a role to play in human decision making. To talk about character and to affirm that humans can develop character presuppose that we have a will. Humans do have choices, and humans are responsible, in part at least, for their choices; we are not predestined. The human will can be defined simply: it is "our capacity to choose and direct our behavior, and self-esteem, which is the respect and value with which we view ourselves."[11]

Human will most often manifests itself as intentionality. Incorporated in the word *intentionality* is the idea of "tending" and indeed "tendency." Rollo May also used the idea of "stretching."[12] Intentionality is our way of stretching between what is and what will be, or could be. Simply put, human will is our capacity to choose which way to stretch—to develop the direction of our tendencies. Character, then, would be these defined tendencies (chosen rather than determined).

Let us go back to the furor over Grasso's compensation. In moral terms, Grasso and the board had a choice between prudence and imprudence. Not surprisingly, the board comprised thoughtful leaders who had earned excellent reputations for their abilities and integrity. Unquestionably, those involved were not "bad" people. Rather, the question is whether Grasso made a "bad" choice and to what degree the board fulfilled its oversight responsibilities. In sharp contrast to Enron executives and Arthur Andersen auditors shredding documents, Grasso's actions were not illegal.

The question in the case of Grasso and the NYSE board is whether their actions were prudent or wise. We can explore the gray area where the issue of prudence so often is decided by considering four determiners of behavior: ignorance, neglect, denial, and outright willfulness. Each of these can cause us to act imprudently.

9-2 Ignorance and Leadership

The most benign cause of imprudence is ignorance. It is easy to think of all those occasions when we chose badly, acted stupidly, or jumped without looking simply because we did not know. Even though we may shout, "But I didn't know," it usually does not matter. We still blew it; things still turned out poorly; and, finally, we are still culpable. The best antidote to ignorance is knowledge. Knowledge gives us the chance to make a prudent choice. We would all dearly love to avoid saying, "If I had only known!"

The 360-degree performance evaluation technique is a powerful tool to help leaders at every level gain knowledge about how their abilities are seen through the eyes of others. This tool is based on the assumption that, to some degree, others perceive us differently than we perceive ourselves. We might under- or overestimate our strengths and weaknesses when we compare our self-rating with the way others rate us. We might not realize that others see us as possessing effective leadership abilities. We might think of ourselves as being an effective communicator, whereas others may see us as being an effective speaker, but a poor listener.

A 360-degree performance evaluation involves a self-rating and feedback from several sources: the supervisor (above), peers (sideways), and subordinates (below). Perhaps those who participate in a well-designed 360-degree evaluation will learn about abilities that others appreciate and areas to improve more than they could have understood on their own. Without such a tool, our inability to see our abilities as others see them is understandable; nonetheless, we are still ignorant. We need to be aware of how we can improve our performance.

In the corporate world, prudence often directly links to the other virtues. As a leader, we may have to trust (faith) others to inform us about things that we need to know. We rightfully desire to know (hope) when appropriate. In fact, it is unfair (justice) if someone fails to inform us so that we might avoid acting ignorantly. Much reform around corporate governance and financial disclosure centers around questions of faith (fiduciary), hope (corporate strategy), and justice (fairness of executive compensation). Shareholders want faith that those who have oversight responsibility (a board, senior management, auditors, and regulators) will keep them informed about actions taken that impact the economic value of their investment.

9-3 Leadership Neglect and Imprudence

The second cause of imprudence is neglect. If ignorance opens us to risks of culpability, so much more so does neglect. Neglect turns us from the passive agent of ignorance into an active player. Neglect adds responsibility to the mix. Neglect does not "happen to us." There are many reasons for neglect, for neglecting to be or to do what would be prudent in any situation. We are often too busy, sometimes too tired. It is not unusual to be distracted or simply attracted to something more interesting, more pressing. Chronic neglect, however, is a form of carelessness. And careless leaders become dangerous.

All of these causes of neglect amount to nothing more than excuses for people. Many times these excuses become a rationale for leadership neglect. The key is to see neglect, however explained, as an expression of the human will. Neglect is simply the person saying, "I will not." For whatever reason, our choice is not what it should be or could have been; it simply is an imprudent choice. Although neglect is often not as malignant as ignorance, it is often still a "weaker" cause of imprudence than the other two causes, denial and willfulness. Typically, our neglect of something is rooted in a will weakened by busyness, carelessness, desire, and the like.

Prudence is a primary concern of Dr. Kazuo Inamori, founder and chairman emeritus of Kyocera Corporation. Inamori discussed how important it is that leaders not be tempted by personal achievement and wealth at the expense of developing their character. Inamori is a dedicated capitalist who believes that effective leaders should be rewarded for the genius they demonstrate in starting or growing a company, yet he is concerned that, in the past 20 years, the pay of U.S. CEOs has increased by a factor of 40, whereas the pay of workers has merely doubled. He concludes that this disparity corrupts otherwise ethical leaders. Although Inamori embraces the benefits of capitalism and believes that excellent performance should be well compensated, he is concerned that corporate leaders neglect character as they build wealth.[13] Examples are easy to find.

Even in cases such as WorldCom, in which executives were clearly wrong to treat operating expenses as capital expenses to overstate earnings, the question of neglect comes into question. In the case of those who face criminal fraud charges, there is no gray area for prudence—their conduct was criminal. But what about the majority group that was not involved in the fraud—board members, auditors, regulators, investment analysts, and employees? Did they "neglect" their oversight responsibility? In other words, although not corrupt, were those with fiduciary responsibility sleepy, incompetent, or irresponsible?

9-4 Leadership Denial and Imprudence

The third cause of imprudence, denial, is a more active concept than neglect, which tends over time to become passive. Denial is stronger in the sense that it takes more will to deny than simply to neglect. Indeed, denial introduces a willingness to act, whereas neglect is a bit like lack of will. Denial involves an active reshaping of the reality that is being denied.

Psychology Professor Daniel Kahneman won the 2002 Nobel Prize in economics for demonstrating that, although markets are usually efficient, investors often behave irrationally. The field of behavior finance demonstrates that investors take mental shortcuts that lead to systematic judgment errors, shortcuts that negatively impact their wealth creation. Typically, investors follow the herd, trade excessively, become anchored to ideas and estimates, hold on to losing investments, sell winners too quickly, and react too slowly to unexpected news. Investors stay glued to their assumptions, as they learned to do in the "I cannot be wrong" school of thought. These assumptions drive errors in judgment.

The main barrier to sound investing is overconfidence. Investors think they know more than they know and they act accordingly. During the 1990s, the equity market's bubble was about to burst after a prolonged increase in stock prices. At the start of the millennium, people who had heavily invested in stocks during the bubble knew stocks were overvalued, but they did not sell due to an exaggerated sense of their skill and an illusion of control. Often people take risks because they are deluded, not brave. The study of behavior finance concludes that people are overly optimistic, exaggerate their skills, and do things that harm rather than serve their own interests.[14]

9-5 Willful Imprudent Leadership

Finally, the most strident cause of imprudence is willfulness. This is the trickiest, because willfulness often is applauded as a necessary trait of the strong, effective leader. In this sense, willfulness presupposes the power to "pull something off." This is precisely the place where willfulness can cross the line from an admirable quality of leadership to the danger of imprudence. At this place the leader is tempted to be imprudent or act unwisely. Self-serving behavior is tempting simply because one can "pull it off."

Like denial, willfulness often involves a distortion of reality, usually motivated by self-interest. And usually, the smarter we are, the more creatively does our self-interest warp reality. And then it is only a matter of the next step "to get what we want." And what we want, not surprisingly, is exactly what we deserve anyway. Reality not withstanding, willfulness insists that we do deserve it—and we have the power to get it.

Among the four causes of imprudence, willfulness is the most aggressive use of our freedom to choose. But it is important to see all four—ignorance, neglect, denial, and willfulness—as choices, expressions of the human will. Only in this way can we assign responsibility to action. And with this comes the possibility of irresponsibility.

Using the language of virtue, business authors Ram Charan and Jerry Unseem explain why companies fail: "What undoes them is the familiar stuff of human folly: denial, hubris, ego, wishful thinking, poor communication, lax oversight, greed, deceit, and other Behind the Music plot conventions. It all adds up to a failure to execute. This is not an exhaustive list of corporate sins. But chances are your company is committing one of them right now."[15] Charan and Unseem state that common corporate prudence problems include managers' ignorance, neglect, denial, and willfulness behavior such as being unwilling to see evil, overdosing on risk, having dysfunctional boards, being softened by success, and being driven by acquisition lust.

In contrast, an example of a prudent, yet incredibly successful, life is that of Warren Buffett, chairman and CEO of Berkshire Hathaway. He still lives in the home in Omaha, Nebraska, that he bought for $31,500 and he receives the modest annual salary of $100,000. He acknowledges that his one extravagance is air travel, flying in a Gulfstream jet that he calls "The Indefensible."

Consistent with his prudent lifestyle, Buffett is also a prudent investor. If one had invested $10,000 in Berkshire shares in 1965, one would have earned $50 million in 1999, compared with a return of $500,000 for an investment in the S&P 500 indices over the same period. In the early 1960s, Donald Othmer, a chemical engineering professor at Polytechnic University, and his wife, a schoolteacher, invested $25,000, which had built their net worth to $750 million by the late 1990s, when they both died. Although Polytechnic University officials had no reason to expect that the couple would save them from bankruptcy with a $175 million gift, their surprise was tempered when they learned that the Othmers had been friends of Warren Buffett.[16] Prudence had paid off.

In June 1996, Buffett wrote a six-page booklet, entitled "An Owner's Manual," to explain Berkshire's economic principles to the company's shareholders. His business strategy is to search for undervalued companies with favorable growth potential, market share, and low price-to-earning ratios. Buffett will not invest unless he understands the company's business and its industry. He will not invest unless he is confident he can hold the stock for 10 years or more. He maintains that, when a good manager meets a bad industry, it is the industry that will leave with its reputation intact.

The manual reports that 99 percent of Buffett's wealth is in Berkshire shares, so he wins only when the owners win. If the owners lose, he does, too, although this is a rare occurrence. Annual returns have been about 25 percent for nearly 40 years. His prudence is revealed when he states that he needs only 1 percent of his stock to resolve his estate and tax obligations. The rest of his assets will be transferred to his wife and then, upon her death, to a family foundation.[17]

Buffett has avoided the public resentment often bestowed upon members of the mega-rich club. Perhaps his popularity is due to his prudence. He exhibits many concepts associated with prudence—he is honest, sensible, foresighted, skilled, and appropriately cautious. He has avoided much of the trappings and temptations of wealth with his frugal lifestyle, humble nature, and disciplined approach to buying and holding companies.

9-6 Conclusion

We end this discussion as we began, with a touching letter about prudence from a mother to her son, Abigail Adams to John Quincy. When invited to travel to France with his father, who would precede him as the nation's president, the younger Adams preferred to stay at home to prepare for his education at Harvard. The matriarch of the first American family to produce both a father and a son to lead the nation as president encouraged her son to accompany his father to France.

Abigail viewed her son's travel to France like a river that increased in volume the farther it flowed from its source. Thus, Abigail urged him to be courageous and prudent with the opportunities that awaited him:

> It will be expected of you, my son, that as you are favored with superior advantages under the instructive eye of a tender parent, that your improvements should bear some proportion to your advantages. These are the times in which a genius would wish to live. It is not in the still calm of life, or the repose of a pacific station, that great characters are formed. The habits of a vigorous mind are formed in contending with difficulties. Great necessities call out great virtues. When a mind is raised, and animated by scenes that engage the heart, then those qualities which would otherwise lay dormant, wake into life and form the character of the hero and the statesman.[18]

Chapter Quiz

1. Imprudence is which of the following?
   a. inattention to consequences
   b. inattention to motives
   c. lack of concern for others
   d. lack of good will
2. Prudence means all of the following *except*
   a. foresight.
   b. insight.
   c. caution.
   d. wisdom.
3. Which of the following philosophers believed that humans were determined and predestined?
   a. Aristotle
   b. Aquinas
   c. Freud
   d. Kant
4. Which of the following is the most benign cause of imprudence?
   a. ignorance
   b. willfulness
   c. neglect
   d. denial
5. A 360-degree evaluation involves feedback from all of the following sources *except*
   a. supervisors.
   b. peers.
   c. regulators.
   d. subordinates.
6. Which of the following turns an individual from the passive agent of ignorance into an active player?
   a. ignorance
   b. willfulness
   c. neglect
   d. denial
7. In the past 20 years, the pay of U.S. CEOs has increased by what factor?
   a. 2
   b. 10
   c. 40
   d. 50

8. The chapter argues that people often take risks because they are
    a. brave.
    b. daring.
    c. deluded.
    d. intrepid.
9. Which of the following causes of imprudence is the most aggressive use of the freedom to choose?
    a. ignorance
    b. willfulness
    c. neglect
    d. denial
10. Which of the following is *not* an example of how Warren Buffet is prudent?
    a. He still lives in his original home.
    b. He earns a salary of $100,000.
    c. He follows instinct to select companies in which to invest.
    d. He puts 99 percent of his wealth into one company, Berkshire Hathaway.

Note: You can find the correct answers to these questions by taking the quiz and then submitting your answers in the Online Edition. The program will automatically score your submission. If you miss a question, the program will provide the correct answer, a rationale for the answer, and the section number in the chapter where the topic is discussed.

Questions for Thought

1. What are the ways in which people are not prudent?
2. Identify a time when ignorance led you to be imprudent.
3. Identify a time when neglect led you to be imprudent.
4. Identify a time when denial led you to be imprudent.
5. Identify a time when willfulness led you to be imprudent.
6. Is prudence always a legal issue? Why or why not?
7. Consider the case of Dick Grasso's compensation. Where and how did this become a prudence issue?
8. Prudence calls for a combination of knowledge and experience. Describe how knowledge and experience develop prudence in a leader.
9. Consider the case of executive compensation. At what point has an executive made too much and is thereby considered imprudent?
10. Describe how prudence is seen as common sense.
11. Consider how prudence is a means rather than an end.

Web Exercises

The investment and insurance company The Prudential names itself for the virtue discussed in this chapter. Visit its website at http://www.prudential.com/index and see if its policies and statements of intent live up to this name. What advice does it give to investors at different stages of life? Is it indeed prudent?

Auction site eBay (http://ebay.com) announced an increase in its fees for sellers in early 2005. A number of vendors protested (http://www.petitiononline.com/ebayfee/petition.html) but others were unconcerned. Take a look at eBay's policies as well as this petition against the fees. Was it prudent of eBay to raise its fees? Could the notice of higher fees have been introduced in a more prudent way?

Case

Performance Problem

Randy, the CEO of a corporation, asked Richard to supervise Mary, even though she had performance problems and was a difficult person with whom to work. Mary was the first person to report to Richard. Over the course of a year, there were numerous performance problems, most of which Richard ignored and none of which were documented. Like many young and inexperienced managers, Richard avoided the problem. Mary filed a lawsuit against the company for being overlooked for promotions, which had nothing to do with Richard's department or quality of supervision.

Richard was called into Fiona's office; Fiona was the vice president for human resources. Richard considered Fiona a close colleague, but during this meeting she treated Richard as if he was a stranger. Fiona shut the door and gave Richard a directive to predate performance issues against Mary to demonstrate a year of problems. Fiona had already written the reports, but wanted Richard to sign and date the reports as if he was the author. Fiona looked at Richard and asked if he had any questions, but turned away and gave the impression of "Don't even think of asking a question." Fiona thanked him, opened the door signaling Richard to leave, and said nothing as he exited.

Richard returned to his office and did as asked. His rationalization was straightforward. He was not writing about anything that had not happened. He merely documented the incidents that had occurred. Therefore, the date shouldn't really matter. Mary claimed sexual discrimination, citing she was passed over for promotion because she was a woman. In fact, she was not at all qualified for the position and had performed poorly for a year. Given the frivolous nature of her suit, Richard concluded that he was doing the right thing. In fact, it later came out that Mary had filed the exact same lawsuit with her previous employer, so her history of frivolous lawsuits became the issue and Richard's forged documents never came up.

In hindsight, Richard had second thoughts. He now had a deeper understanding of his supervision responsibilities. He should have addressed the performance problems immediately and documented them fairly. Because he had failed to do this, he should have rejected the directive from Fiona and been prepared for the consequences of not fulfilling his supervision responsibilities. The question he was still not prepared to answer was, "Should I have spoken with someone about the human resource manager request?" Unfortunately, he was still uncertain as to whether he would have questioned Fiona's actions, even though he knew he should have.

Frankl's ideas about responding to adversity suggest that Richard's reaction to adversity determines his character. Richard's adversity does not compare to Frankl's survival of three years in a Nazi death camp. However, Richard concluded that he was in a "prison of sorts," enslaved by fear of losing his job. He wanted to survive more than to be at peace with himself, which would have come with knowing that he had acted with character.

Questions for Discussion

1. To what degree was the virtue *prudence* absent or present?
2. Prudence is a means rather than an end. How does prudence combine with other virtues in this case?
3. When asked to do something that is wrong, is it realistic to expect young managers to stand up to senior leaders having more experience and power?
4. How could you respond with both justice and prudence in a case like this so you avoid losing your job or your character?

Endnotes

1. David McCullough, *John Adams* (New York: Simon & Schuster, 2001), 167.
2. Ibid., 178.
3. Ibid., 101.
4. http://www.pacificnet.net/~johnr/cgilaesop/.
5. John Climacus, *The Ladder of Divine Ascent,* trans. Colm Luibheid and Norman Russel (Ramsey, NJ: Paulist Press, 1982), 237.
6. Evagrius Ponticus, *The Praktikos & Chapters on Prayer,* trans. John Eudes Bamberger (Kalamazoo, MI: Cistercian, 1978), 38.
7. Kate Kelly, Susanne Craig, and Ianthe Jeanne Dugan, "Closing Bell: Grasso Quits NYSE Amid Pay Furor—behind the Chief's Departure, a Profit Squeeze, Goverance Questions—Exhange at a Crossroads," *Wall Street Journal,* September 18, 2003, 1.
8. Suzanne Craig, Ianthe Jeanne Dugan, Kate Kelly, and Laurie Cohen, "As End Neared, Insiders Have Said," *Wall Street Journal,* September 26, 2003, 1.
9. Rollo May, *Love and Will* (New York: Norton, 1969), 182.
10. Ibid., 183.
11. Gerald G. May, *Addiction & Grace* (San Francisco: Harper & Row, 1988), 42.
12. Rollo May, 228–29.
13. Kazuo Inamori, "Leadership" (Cleveland, OH: Case Western Reserve University, October 2002).
14. Adam Levy, "Behavioral Finance Exploits Blunders Other Investors Make in the Market," *The Plain Dealer,* October 19, 2003, 1.
15. Ram Charan and Jerry Unseem, "Why Companies Fail," *Fortune,* May 27, 2002, 53.
16. "Brilliant Careers," http://www.salon.com/people/bc/1999/o8/31/buffett/.
17. Berkshire Hathaway, *Owner's Manual,* 1996, http://www.berkshirehathaway.com.
18. McCullough, 226.

σωφροσύνη

Chapter

Temperance

10

Outline

10-1 Temperance (Balance, Regulation)

Like prudence, the fifth virtue, temperance, is a means rather than an end. Prudence directs us to consider whether the greater good will result from action or inaction. *Temperance* means "moderation, balance, self-control; to regulate, manage, and temper." The focus of prudence is to consider the consequences of our actions. The focus of temperance, according to Thomas Aquinas, is to "govern the passions."[1] Temperance is often associated with discipline.

Temperance is the master of our urges and desires, so that we resist extreme behavior through self-governance and self-control. Temperance is the habit of Aristotle's mean between two extremes—indulgence and abstinence.

The concept of temperance does not have much currency in contemporary business circles. Although there is no need to rehabilitate the word itself, the concept and its intent are crucial. In this chapter, we apply the concept of temperance using examples of how discipline can guide servant leadership at both the individual and corporate levels.

10-2 Temperate Leadership

As we grow through childhood, most of us learn how to "temper" our actions and ourselves. We learn how to live temperately. To temper ourselves is an exercise of self-control. To control ourselves is to stay within bounds; perhaps self-control is to choose prudence. To be self-controlled is to live carefully—full of care—rather than carelessly.

Benjamin Franklin acknowledged the importance of this virtue when he said, "Temperance first, as it tends to procure the Coolness and Clearness of head, which is so necessary where constant Vigilance was to be kept up, and Guard maintained."[2] Doubtlessly, Franklin's emphasis on the cool, clear head of temperance reflects his experience. Without it, we often find ourselves too busy to have a purpose.

Temperance seeks to mitigate self-indulgence. Self-indulgence does not mean a willingness to be kind to oneself or to care for oneself, because kindness and self-care are usually both temperate and prudent. Rather, the self-indulgence of intemperance is usually linked to inordinate personal desires and a weak will.

The virtue of temperance addresses self-indulgence with balance. When life is balanced, there is less likelihood that self-indulgence will become a problem. If work and play are in balance, we avoid the extremes of workaholism and laziness, both of which are unhealthy forms of self-indulgence.

Balance means we have found the middle. To be lopsided for very long spells trouble. Having balance is different from multitasking, which is a kind of juggling. In the act of juggling, something is always up in the air. For the juggler, there can be no rest; to stop is to lose it. Juggling is constant motion. But nothing changes and no difference happens, unless someone throws in another ball, which only makes juggling more interesting and difficult. Given this image, it is no wonder that it becomes an apt metaphor for so many businesses and so much of contemporary life. In other words, the goal is not to multitask by juggling multiple balls but, rather, to create balance in our life.

In contrast, even though balancing may involve keeping multiple factors in play, these factors are weighted to give the right balance. Perhaps most important, balancing allows for rest and, appropriately, recreation. A balanced life encourages play and makes room for leisure. One can stop the movement and not lose it. In fact, the balanced life involves tempering activity and movement, so that life does not get out of whack. A life of temperance is a balanced life.

Another answer to self-indulgence is discipline. In a situation of abundance, it is difficult to be disciplined and to choose virtue, choose to be temperate. Even when we know that temperance is good for us, we often lack the will to follow through with our knowledge. Too easily, human nature leads us to rationalize our indulgences. Discipline is too easily put off until tomorrow, as *later* becomes a favorite word. Self-indulgence is almost always a "now" decision, a today experience.

Tempus, the Latin root, means "time, season, right time." To be virtuous is to be temperate—to do things in a timely fashion and in due season. This virtue is an ongoing engagement with the question concerning how we spend our time. And lurking behind this question is the core query "What are we living for?" Too often, we do not even stop to entertain this question until it is too late. It is especially important for all driven, pre-occupied, multitasking people to hear the counsel of author Mitch Albom's dying professor, Morrie Schwartz: "You have to be strong enough to say if the culture doesn't work, don't buy it."[3]

Morrie is not advising that we never buy the culture. Rather, he is advising, first, that we become aware and, second, that we pay attention. Temperance always requires these two As—awareness and attention. At a simple level, awareness is knowledge that each of us is "cultivated" by our particular culture. It is impossible to be human and not be cultured in some sense. Generally, our western culture is designed for us to "have it" and, if we do not have it, then to buy it. Temperance is the virtue asking, "Should we buy it?"

10-3 Balancing Work/Family/Community: The Struggle of Servant Leadership

Self-indulgence often entertains the desires we have that lead us to places that are not good for us or are not right. Self-indulgence normally does not involve legality, but avoiding it does involve morality—as all the virtues do, since they aim for the good. Hence, the key to understanding self-indulgence is to know our desires. For example, striving for success is not inherently a problem, as long as personal achievement has a clear purpose greater than comfort. If success is measured exclusively by compensation and status, then life will ultimately move out of balance.

For example, our busyness and personal achievement can come at the expense of our relationships with colleagues, family, friends, and the community. For example, it is not temperate to work so hard to buy a house that is 1,000 square feet larger than our current home if it costs us the relationship with our spouse. It is not temperate to work such long hours that we wake up to find that we do not really know our teenage son or daughter, who is about to go to college.

As we strive for success and a more comfortable life, we can learn that what we own begins to own us.[4] This is precisely the point at which balance becomes the issue—whether we are aware or not. Our desire to acquire and keep material things can cost us our relationships with our family, friends, and community. There is a sad place where we know we have it and discover we do not even want it.

Consider the business leader who takes a vacation to a secluded island. One day she watches a local fisherman, fishing happily but inefficiently. She explains to the fisherman how to finance a boat, increase production, and build a store to integrate the business from production to retail. As his profits rise, he can hire more staff. The fisherman asks why he would want to do this. The leader replies, "So you can retire comfortably on a beach, eat fruit, and spend time with your family." The fisherman replies, "Well, that is what I do now!"[5]

Maybe the world is a better place if we do not see it in either/or categories. Some of us appropriately choose the life of the fisherman. Others can build strong communities by becoming productive fishermen who create jobs, increase a tax base, and take care of the environment by not overfishing. This exemplifies the model of servant leadership—to be at work in the world to make it a better place, not only for oneself but for others as well. Whether we eat papaya on the beach or improve fishing production, servant leadership is focused on the question of what is worth doing. Personal wealth can be used to make life better for others or can distract us from what is worthy.

Stephen Spielberg's film *Schindler's List* revealed Oskar Schindler as first distracted from what was important and then focused on what was worthy. He was a shrewd businessman who profited during the Nazi occupation of Poland, even though he did not personally participate in the holocaust. As the evil of the death camps was revealed to him over time, Schindler's allegiance moved from his personal comfort to his efforts to save as many Jews as possible. He tempered his desire for wealth and comfort to use his influence and abilities to save lives.

In addition to balance and discipline, temperance also speaks to harmony, or being in rhythm. It is not always possible to hold all aspects of our life (work, family, friends, community, self) in perfect balance. There is a season when we might devote more energy to work, family, or community. These are times we can choose our seasons. But often circumstances dictate which arena receives our attention. Frequently, our seasons, our circumstances, are complex. It may not be convenient to support ailing parents at a particular time, but we know it is the right thing to do. We may not wish to spend more time at the office, but a new product launch that represents the future of the company depends on our efforts. Temperance asks how we can harmonize in the best sense all that is going on at a particular time. Rhythm always presents the possibility of modifying, or modulating, the motion of life and the business.

10-4 Individual Habits and Discipline

Disciplined leaders manage to balance the desires of stakeholders, which often compete. Corporations require a disciplined approach to balancing the needs of shareholders, customers, and employees, in addition to other constituents. At the individual level, the demands on leaders are best managed by an inner life that provides the moorings to balance all the relationships common to leadership. Just as corporations require a disciplined approach to executing strategy, leaders require a disciplined approach to executing a balanced life.

Balance is an ancient virtue. Aristotle tells us that temperance is finding the mean, the middle way between extremes. It is avoiding excess. This requires discipline, control, and good habits. It is easy to understand the risks of self-indulgence, but it is much harder to develop a temperate will. Individuals, their families, their corporations, and their communities all benefit when leaders are successful in developing character (temperance) and balancing their responsibilities. As we pointed out, the challenge of putting these ideals into action can be complex.

Theologian Martin Buber offered a partial answer when he proposed that we view our relationships with others along an it-thou continuum.[6] At one extreme, if we view people merely as an "it," we are considering others to be objects to be manipulated for our personal gain. An "it" orientation reduces people to the means to make our life more comfortable and to serve our urges. Contemporarily, one can think of Saddam Hussein as a person with an "it" orientation. At the other extreme, we can view others as a "thou"—we consider their welfare as central to our reason for being. This is the perspective of the servant leader. A "thou" orientation sees the "divine" in others, treats others with dignity and respect, and recognizes empathy as the root of ethical conduct. In this instance, think of Mother Teresa. Most of us operate somewhere between these two extremes, moving closer to "it" or closer to "thou," depending on the kind of day we are having. When we are at our best, we treat others as "thou." When we are at our worst, we treat others as "it."

The concept of emotional intelligence, the ability to work with people effectively, is a means, not an end. To be a virtue, it must point to the good. Emotional intelligence is to social genius what IQ scores are to intellectual genius. Emotional intelligence provides a framework for appreciating the reality that one needs more than "book smarts" to play and work well with others. People who have a high degree of emotional intelligence typically have strong family relationships, as well as an ability to form high-performance corporate and community teams.[7] Those with high emotional intelligence put Buber's "thou" concept into practice to resolve issues. In organizing a work team, leaders with strong emotional intelligence leverage the group's strengths and the differences of all the individuals, while minimizing the impact of team members who are too eager, too domineering or too uncaring. Without the "thou" dimension, social genius is nothing but a con artist—likeable and personable while picking our pocket.

The characteristics of those with high emotional intelligence represent the characteristics of temperance: the ability to delay gratification and to self-regulate. This is the kind of person who manifests self-awareness, self-management, social awareness, and social skills, as illustrated in Figure 10-1.[8]

Self-Awareness	Social Awareness
Accurate self-assessment of skill and emotion Self-confidence	Empathy and service orientation Awareness of organizational realities
Self-Management	Social Skills
Self-control Ingegrity Adaptable to change Initiative	Leading change Creation of shared vision and sense of team Communication and conflict resolution Relationship building

Figure 10-1
Elements of Emotional Intelligence

Emotional intelligence is not just soft fluff; rather, it represents a way to succeed in the marketplace. Usually, success is not simply a numbers game. To adapt to market forces, we must be open to learning from our mistakes and from other people. People with superior intellect sometimes find this lesson especially difficult to learn, since they are accustomed to being right and not needing advice from others.

Let us turn to the role that habits and discipline play in developing temperance. Conventional wisdom offers various views of why leaders fail: they lack leadership ability, they cannot foresee trouble coming their way, they fall asleep at the switch, they have limited resources, or they are corrupt. The reality, however, is different. Leaders who fail are often smart, accomplished, highly motivated, and honest. Sometimes these leaders have considered, and then dismissed the problems that led to their demise. More often, being unable to cope with change, misreading the competition, executing the wrong strategy, and clinging to inaccurate information while ignoring vital information are the real reasons for failure. In other words, smart, hard-working leaders can fail because they misperceive their corporation's circumstances, they mismanage information and control, and they persist in relying on unsuccessful habits.[9]

The best way out of a business debacle is to take a disciplined approach, learn from mistakes, and listen to others' advice. If Buber's concern for others is our guide and emotional intelligence reveals the needed

T a b l e   **10-1** Elements of a Disciplined Life

Inner Life	Outer Life	Corporate/Community Life
Exercise	Organized religion in a church, synagogue, mosque, temple/shrine	Community service
Meditation or prayer	Education	Corporate citizenship
Music	Family/friends	360-degree performance evaluations
Nature	Forum or small groups	Environmental concern
Reading	Book club	Volunteering as a tutor

skill set, then progress can be made in developing stronger personal, family, professional, and community relationships. The key is to understand that being human and being in business are both dynamic developmental processes. If either becomes static, stagnation is the result.

The goal is success in business and meaning in life. To achieve both goals necessitates paying attention to the means by which we reach these ends. And temperance is the means that can make all the difference. Of course, we will not achieve perfection. Furthermore, the habits that work for one person may not work for another. With these qualifications in mind, in order to develop character, we need to create disciplined inner, outer, and corporate/community means. Table 10-1 suggests some dependable means to a temperate life as a successful business leader.

If our inner life is expressed solely as a couch potato with a remote channel changer in one hand and snacks in the other, then we limit our ability to develop character. Maybe this is an extreme cliché for most people. More common unhealthy addictions include devoting endless time to activities such as shopping, decorating homes, lawn care, and TV sports. This is a caricature of the person who is too passive to be asking the earlier question of Morrie Schwartz: "Should I buy it?" In contrast, consider who we might become if, rather than spending hours watching TV, playing video games, or surfing the web, we reflected weekly on the following questions:

1. In what acts of compassion was I involved?
2. In what acts of social justice was I involved?
3. Did I reflect on my virtues?
4. Did I learn from my mistakes?

Compassion results in a private act to help someone else. Social justice involves public actions to correct a social wrong. Reflection and learning from mistakes is a requirement to developing a temperate life, a life in balance. The specific disciplines that people use to develop character are not as important as the fact that they find a way to do so.

How and where we bring balance to our lives is not important. That we do it is imperative. Some people reflect through exercise; some through nature. Some meditate or pray, and some read or listen to music. Whatever discipline we practice should put us in the place where we can ask our own question: "Should I buy it?" For most of us, this will be not an economical question, but will become a metaphorical question. The question will become more like "On what will I spend my life?" If the answer to this is only self-interest, there will be little development of virtue and character development.

The discipline is successful if it results in a reflection on compassion, justice, and learning from mistakes. Character development moves us toward the outer life, our relationships with other people and the communities in which we participate. Our relationships with other people reflect how we put Buber's it-thou concept into action. For many of us, our most intimate relationships involve family and friends. We also spend significant time in relationships at work or in recreation. Relationships include colleagues, collaborators, and even strangers. The outer life of relationships and the communities in which we participate should give us a second question: "Should we buy it?" Again, this is not simply an economical question; it leads to the communal query about how we should spend our resources—our time, talent, and treasure.

Wise leaders realize that they need trusted colleagues, board members, friends, and family to help them stay focused on corporate and personal priorities. In the final scene of the movie *Patton*, George C. Scott, playing the general, leads the American army into Rome to free its citizens from German occupation. When in Rome, he relies on Roman conventional wisdom that places trusted counselors next to the emperor to whisper in his ear that "glory is fleeting." Venture capitalists rely on a modern version of Roman wisdom directed at the leaders of the companies in which they invest. They remind leaders to wear a humility sweater. In other words, the status and financial wealth associated with leading a company can inhibit temperance.

The Young President's Organization (YPO) created a disciplined way for contemporary leaders to benefit from the age-old need for a trusted counselor, someone who could tell the emperor he had no clothes. Founded about 100 years ago, YPO's motto is "better leadership through

General George S. Patton
As Patton knew, "glory is fleeting."
Source: Library of Congress, Prints and Photographs Division, LC-USZ62-25122.

education." YPO sponsors a program, called Forum, that brings together senior leaders, in groups of about 10, to discuss common professional and personal issues. Leaders are young CEOs who are members of YPO. In acknowledgment of the adage that it is lonely at the top, young leaders focus on problems that keep them up at night that often are issues they cannot share with colleagues. Just as often, significant others either cannot be told or are fed up hearing about problems. At these times, the Forum group provides advice and counsel from people who have been in the same boat.

The Forum group might help a leader resolve a performance problem with a difficult CFO during a time of a merger. Or, on a more personal note, the group might help a member think about ways to reconcile a strained relationship with a teenage daughter on drugs. In turn, the other leaders benefit personally in helping a peer resolve a problem they do not face now but could face in the future. Temperate leaders surround themselves with people they trust to help them manage their passions and avoid mistakes that result from delusion or blind spots. A Forum group offers leaders a confidential and trusting setting to help them respond to the most difficult problems they confront.

Although such groups offer leaders an outside perspective, leaders also need feedback from colleagues with whom they work regularly. Although every employee is subject to and has participated in informal performance evaluations around the coffee pot, there are few formal ways to learn what we are doing well so we can keep it up or what we are doing poorly so we can cut it out. Often leaders do not learn from what others say about us, since office gossip conversations change quickly when the subject walks into the room. In addition, it is not uncommon that leaders are reluctant to seek or make feedback from others a priority.

As we have seen, tools such as a 360-degree performance evaluation are designed to give us access to those coffee pot conversations about our performance, as it regulates our weaknesses and strengthens areas where we excel. The mechanics of a 360-degree performance evaluation involve securing feedback from peers and people who report to the leader, in addition to getting feedback from those to whom the leader reports. This "up, sideways, and down" feedback provides a way to evaluate how we can make our strengths stronger while addressing the concerns of others.

The point of a formal 360-degree performance evaluation is to learn from our mistakes and build on our strengths by seeking constructive criticism in a disciplined or temperate way. Even if our employer does not use 360-degree performance evaluations, we can informally seek advice and feedback from family, friends, and colleagues about what we do well and how we can improve.

10-5 Corporate Temperance

The idea of excess offers another handle on the challenges of temperance. Excess is always "too much," "too far," or "too long." The root meaning of *excess* is captured in the adverb *too*. *Too* is a word that exaggerates; it means "to go beyond." Excess goes beyond the norm or the standard. Temperance appropriately moderates "too."

Unlike the virtue of justice, temperance is not necessarily tied to the issue of legality. However, it does often deal with excesses that can be linked to prudence and justice. For example, although the word *temperance* is not widely used to describe the debate over how to regulate excessive market timing and late trading, along with its close cousin, prudence, temperance is implicated. Unlike the scandals of corporations such as WorldCom, the financial impact of the mutual fund scandal is limited.

However, reputational risk can lead to financial risk. The mutual fund scandal raises questions of trust in the minds of those who pay the bills for the funds managers. Mutual fund leaders were excessive in serving themselves rather than their clients and in taking risks that were not prudent or temperate. This is in direct opposition to the notion of a mutual fund as risk aversion.

The leaders of funds such as Strong Mutual and Putnam lost their jobs due to late trading and market timing. The former is illegal because stocks are traded after prices for the day have been set. The latter is risky but not illegal. It involves speculating quickly on when to buy and sell. However, it needs to be said that speculative investing differs significantly from the more prudent investment philosophy of buy and hold.

Mutual funds are attractive to the 95 million risk-averse investors who trust the industry with their $7.1 trillion in savings for college tuition and retirement income. The idea of "mutual" is portrayed well in the last line of the Declaration of Independence: "we mutually pledge to each other our lives, our fortunes and our sacred honor."[10]

To regulate something means to bring "excess" within the rules or the range of acceptability. By definition, regulation is a device of temperance. Regulation attempts to return that which has gone "beyond" back within appropriate parameters. Two regulators—New York State Attorney General Eliot Spitzer and William Donaldson, head of the Securities and Exchange Commission—openly debated how to respond with temperance to market timing and late trading. Spitzer brought media attention to expose senior leaders who lost their jobs and face indictments. He hoped others would think twice before being tempted to commit the same acts. Acknowledging that a run on mutual funds would ultimately harm the investors he was trying to protect, Spitzer is trying to respond with temperance. William Donaldson had the same concern as Spitzer. He sought balance—knowing that, if he relied on too light a touch, then another wolf would be free to prey on thousands of lambs.

As is often the case when it comes to regulation, when regulators are too heavy-handed, the industry as a whole can be saddled with burdensome legislation that makes the cure worse than the disease. However, without high-profile consequences to moderate the behavior of other leaders in the industry, another scandal could be around the corner.

Investors also must decide how to temper their response to the mutual fund scandals. Despite losses that have resulted from questions about the fiduciary conduct of their mutual fund managers, they might find it more expensive to switch funds because their share price might be at its lowest value and the sale would create a taxable event. Temperance would suggest that investors contact their fund managers with questions about what actions they can expect to ensure fairness, so their "mutual interests" are honored.

Whereas scandals make the front page of the paper, the more routine corporate temperance challenge has to do with the difficulty of balancing corporate stakeholder interests. The Balanced Scorecard (BSC) developed by Kaplan and Norton is a contemporary version of the "Greek middle way."[11] Classical mythology tells of Icarus, whose intemperance led him to fly so high that the sun melted the wax of his wings, thus causing him to crash into the waves of the sea. His father, Daedelus, flew the middle way and stayed out of trouble. The BSC teaches us to be like Daedelus, to take the middle way and avoid trouble.

If corporate leaders focus only on shareholder wealth at the expense of customers and employees, then the firm will be unable to create "Chainsaw" Dunlap wealth for its owners. However, the reverse is true, too. If a firm considers all of its stakeholders, but fails to earn a profit for its owners, then people lose jobs, as happened to Ben and Jerry's ice cream company. The whole world pulled for two out-of-shape, generous guys who ate lots of ice cream but, when shareholders lost wealth, others were brought in to operate the company.

The BSC is arguably one of the best strategic execution tools. Although its implementation can be complicated, its basic question is straightforward: once a firm has agreed on its strategic direction, how will it measure success?

When this tool is applied well, it involves temperance, since the satisfaction of shareholder, customer, employee, supplier, and regulators is measured and balanced:

1. A sense of team can result from a group of decision makers answering questions that create a shared definition of success. For example, measures are used to provide clarity about the benefits sought by and delivered to customers.
2. Often companies have reasonably sound financial data and anecdotal customer satisfaction data and give limited, if any, thought to process or innovation measures. Since the company is perfectly designed to achieve its current result, the current system offers little hope for new results. BSC can help companies improve customer and shareholder satisfaction by improving processes that support these goals.

How should a firm acquire and allocate resources in a way that adds value to each of its stakeholders? Should earnings be given to the owners, whose funds seeded and grew the firm; to product and operational reinvestment, so that the customers who made earnings possible are satisfied; or to employees, so they continue to be productive and satisfied? The answer to these questions is yes, but the difficulty is balancing among different stakeholders the acquisition and allocation of resources.

Although these decisions are never easy, at least the BSC brings logic and measurement to satisfying stakeholders. In essence, the BSC is a temperance tool since its purpose is to balance stakeholder needs. Chapter 6, on justice, discussed additional applications of the BSC, but temperance also is often an important means of promoting corporate citizenship and the triple bottom line of profitability and social and environmental responsibility.

10-6 Conclusion

Leaders are increasingly being required to operate globally, whereas individuals are looking for balance in their life. Who will travel the planet to create far-flung enterprises, even though these demands will provide little time for family and corporate citizenship in the community in which the leader lives? Corporate governance reform is increasing the transparency under which leaders must operate, while quarterly earnings reward performance rather than character. However, corporate scandals have bankrupted some companies and destroyed market value for others, so character is becoming increasingly important in this transparent world.

The combination of performance, as measured by leaders "making their numbers," and character that inspires and keeps the firm out of trouble is a desirable one. Perhaps some corporate cultures will invest in leaders who have more character than competence, rather than in competent leaders who are short on character. Both character and competence are possible; the goal should be competent leadership by people who also have character.

This desired mix of competence and character requires temperance—discipline and balance. Disciplined people are disciplined in their thought and action. Disciplined leaders are effective in balancing the often competing interests of stakeholders. Through disciplines, individuals develop habits that focus on an inner, an outer and a corporate/community life. Disciplines bring harmony and rhythm to life. Corporations also consider disciplined approaches to their business to ensure performance. The degree to which these modern goals are realized depends on an ancient virtue—temperance.

Chapter Quiz

1. Temperance means all of the following *except*
   a. moderation.
   b. regulate.
   c. legality.
   d. balance.
2. Temperance requires which of the following?
   a. awareness, action
   b. awareness, attention
   c. attention, abstinence
   d. attention, action
3. Which of the following means "to be at work in the world to make it a better place not only for self but for others as well"?
   a. serving leadership
   b. servant leadership
   c. service leadership
   d. self-less leadership
4. Which of the following theologians offered the It-Thou continuum to view human relationships?
   a. Morrie
   b. Buber
   c. Aquinas
   d. Socrates
5. The individual who has temperance has all of the following characteristics *except*
   a. selflessness.
   b. social awareness.
   c. self-awareness.
   d. self-management.
6. To develop character as a business leader, we need to create all of the following disciplined means *except*
   a. inner.
   b. social.
   c. community.
   d. corporate.
7. All of the following are a part of the "inner life" balance *except*
   a. music.
   b. nature.
   c. reading.
   d. religion.

8. Temperance is necessarily tied to all of the following *except*
   a. legality.
   b. morality.
   c. prudence.
   d. justice.
9. Which of the following is the forerunner to the Balanced Scorecard?
   a. Daedelus' middle road
   b. Aquinas' median
   c. Aristotle's mean
   d. Kant's norm
10. The Balanced Scorecard does not provide which of the following?
    a. logic
    b. measurement
    c. social justice
    d. temperance

Note: You can find the correct answers to these questions by taking the quiz and then submitting your answers in the Online Edition. The program will automatically score your submission. If you miss a question, the program will provide the correct answer, a rationale for the answer, and the section number in the chapter where the topic is discussed.

Questions for Thought

1. Why does temperance usually deal with the issue of balance?
2. Why does this chapter discuss temperance as a means rather than an end?
3. The two extremes of intemperance are being a coach potato and being a workaholic. How can the virtue of temperance balance either extreme?
4. It is not unusual to see that temperance balances two or more of the other virtues. For example, begin to think how temperance might balance compassion and justice, as you have already read about this.
5. Explain how it is not possible to be temperate without also being reflective on one's leadership and personal experiences.
6. Mistakes often create imbalance in our professional and personal lives and accordingly become temperance issues. Explain how temperance is necessary to bring work and life into balance.
7. Evaluate your emotional intelligence based on its four dimensions—self-awareness, social awareness, self-management, and social skills.
8. Explore how disciplines and habits form temperance.
9. Which disciplines and habits have helped you develop temperance?
10. Which disciplines and habits might help you grow to develop temperance further?

Web Exercises

This chapter discusses the Young Presidents Organization (YPO). Visit the YPO website at http://www.ypo.org and read up on their mission and goals. In what ways does the YPO promote temperance? What kinds of programs and strategies for being temperate in work and life does the YPO promote?

The American Academy of Family Physicians (AAFP) offers Fifteen Tips for balancing work and personal life at http://www.aafp.org/fpm/20000200/6015ti. html. In what ways is the AAFP promoting temperance? How can you apply these tips to any field? How can you be more temperate in your own life or business dealings?

Case

Temperance: A Life Lived Whole

After climbing into bed, Luke turned off the light in his hotel room and closed his eyes, but he could not turn off his mind. He realized that his body was tired. He had just checked into the hotel after another one of his monthly flights from Chicago to Tokyo. Normally, he used flight time to check the biweekly production results and to think about the myriad of meetings, consultations, and time spent with salespeople he planned for the next week in Tokyo and other places. However, he also thought about the recent issue of a magazine the woman seated next to him on the plane had been reading. The article was entitled, "A Life Lived Whole."[1]

Luke was intrigued with that title. After the usual chitchat with the woman, who turned out to be a college professor, Luke had mentioned that he would enjoy glancing at the magazine. She handed it to him and he began to look at it. Beneath the title of the article—in bold letters—Luke read, "**There is in all things . . . a hidden wholeness.**"[2] Immediately, Luke knew these words articulated a deep longing in his heart and also caused him to wonder whether he would ever find this hidden wholeness.

As the plane flew on to Tokyo, his mind drifted back to his college days. He had been a business major and never regretted that decision. However, he recalled how interesting the two philosophy classes were that he had taken had been. He had lamented having to take them, but even while in the middle of those classes, he admitted they made him think about things that otherwise he would never have pondered. The boldfaced phrase from this article had triggered a recurring question: Just how meaningful was his life? This question usually was accompanied by a slight uneasiness that his life was not as meaningful as it looked to other people . . . nor as meaningful as he might have hoped.

Luke was very successful in his major corporation. Financially, he was very well off, and some people in the large corporation suggested he was being groomed to fill one of the top spots. However, he also had two young children at home; they were growing up, and he felt like he was missing out on some of their key moments. One was in middle school and was active in the school's theatre, as well as the local civic theatre. The other child was ready to enter middle school, and she clearly was a gifted athlete. He experienced some disease at not being present with them at important points in their lives. Quite frankly, he felt cheated that he did not get to experience the pride parents feel when their child succeeds at something.

As Luke lay there in the hotel bed, he opened his eyes to the darkness. His mind went back to the article he had read on the plane. The gist of just one paragraph ran across his mind like one of those streaming commercials on the television screen.

The divided life comes in many and varied forms. To cite just a few examples, it is the life we lead when:

- We refuse to invest ourselves in our work, diminishing its quality and distancing ourselves from those it is meant to serve.
- We make our living at jobs that violate our basic values, even when survival does not absolutely demand it.
- We remain in settings or relationships that steadily kill off our spirit.
- We harbor secrets to achieve personal gain at the expense of other people.
- We hide our beliefs from those who disagree with us to avoid conflict, challenge, and change.
- We conceal our true identities for fear of being criticized, shunned, or attacked.[3]

Not all of these issues were relevant to Luke's own life, but they prompted a thinking process that was still going on in his mind.

In the dark Luke smiled to himself. He was in no crisis; he was not suffering a midlife crisis. Actually, life was going very well . . . except for that faint, but sometimes stronger, sense that his life was not quite balanced. "Yes, that's the word," he thought. "Balance is the key." He suspected that balance would be his way to discover that "hidden wholeness" Parker Palmer, the author of the article, had described. His life was not out of control or "outta whack," as his mother used to say. Those were extreme states. His issue, he concluded, was balance.

He knew he would not come up with answers that night, but he did begin to list in his mind the pieces of his life that were factors in the balance that would help him find that hidden wholeness. Those factors included his family and his work; these were the big ones. But he also realized he wanted to get back into physical shape. He used to be pretty athletic—and it felt good to be in shape—but that was now just a memory. He would love to go back to reading some philosophy and maybe literature dealing with spirituality. He needed assistance to think about meaning in life. And then there was the issue of friendship. He realized he was good at networking, but he allowed himself to wonder if he had any "real friends."

Luke no longer felt depressed that he would never figure it out. He now saw balance as a process and he simply needed to begin working on it. He began to fall asleep with a sense of adventure for life and a question in mind: What will be my steps into living this whole life?

Questions for Discussion

1. If you ask people what they believe, you probably will get an answer pretty quickly. If you ask the same people why they believe the way they do, most may not be as clear. If you ask people how to close the gap between who they are and who they want to be, most will not know where to begin. Discuss.

2. Awareness: As Luke begins the process of balancing his life, what will be his first step? Consider questions such as:
   a. What are the givens in a person's life?
   b. How does Luke spend his time versus how he wants to spend his time?
   c. How can he evaluate the quality of his work, family, friends, and community life?

3. Attention: How does Luke begin to pay attention to working toward balance?
   a. Could you schedule 30 minutes a day to reflect on balance? If not, why not?
   b. Once a week, could you write a 1-page evaluation on the degree your life is in balance?

4. Action: As a result of reflective time, let yourself begin to imagine one or two action steps you would like to take toward a life lived whole.
   a. Every week you are home, plan to spend one hour with each of your children.
   b. Once a month, invite friends over for dinner.
   c. Begin a regular exercise program.
   d. Identify a community organization or activity in which you would like to become involved.
   e. Look at your life and consider one thing that you could drop so your life would be more in balance.

5. What if Luke were female? How would keeping life in balance change if that were the case?

Footnotes

1. Parker Palmer, "A Life Lived Whole," *Yes Magazine,* Winter 2005, http://www.yesmagazine.com/article.asp?/ID=1166.
2. Ibid.
3. Ibid.

Endnotes

1. Anton C. Pegis, ed., *Introduction to St. Thomas Aquinas* (New York: The Modern Library, 1948), 588.

2. Walter Isaacson, *Benjamin Franklin* (New York: Simon & Schuster, 2003), 47.

3. Mitch Albom, *Tuesdays with Morrie: An Old Man, a Young Man and Life's Greatest Lesson* (New York: Doubleday, 1997), 35.

4. "Affluenza," http://www.pbs.org/kcts/.

5. "The Fisherman," http://www.shoptcs.com/CJP/BUS/8.htm.

6. Martin Buber, *I-Thou*, trans. Walter Kaufmann (New York: Touchstone, 1970).

7. Daniel Goleman, Robert Boyatzis, and Anne McKee, *Primal Leadership* (Cambridge, MA: Harvard Business School Press, 2003).

8. Ibid.

9. Sydney Finklestein, *Why Smart Executives Fail* (New York: Portfolio, 2003).

10. Mutual Distrust, *The Plain Dealer*, November 10, 2003, sec. B6.

11. Robert Kaplan and David Norton, *Balanced Scorecard* (Cambridge, MA: Harvard Business School Press, 1996).

Love

11

Outline

Buddha
The Buddha taught people to follow a path that
included compassion and tolerance as part of their lives.
Source: Library of Congress, Prints and Photographs Division, LC-USZ62-95822.

11-1 Love (Care & Compassion)

How does the sixth virtue, love, fit into a world where conventional wisdom tells us to do unto our competitors before they do unto us? As trade barriers decrease and e-commerce increases, companies are on notice to compete or die, making competition even more essential.

To talk about love can be too passionate or comically pitiful. For example, the e-business love calculator uses the combination of a couple's names to determine the probability that the marriage will last. According to Dr. Love, love calculators expect when the man is named Harry and the women is named Linda the marriage has only a 10 percent chance of working out.[1]

The distractions of a word such as *love* are problematic—or, in the case of Dr. Love, meaningless. One way to avoid the problem is to find different language. We suggest three alternative ways to talk about how the virtue of love is lived out in the corporate world: care, compassion, and mercy. Each of these concepts adds value to the business, while doing it with virtue.

11-2 Care

How often do we hear someone say, "Take care," as we open the door to leave? Does this mean anything more than the casual "Hi, how are you?" encounter in the hallway? Even if we were inclined to tell the other person just how we are, they probably are already out of sight or don't care.

Although it has become a throwaway term for us, *care* comes from the Latin word *cura*, meaning "concern," "attention," and "supervision"—all words that have currency in the workplace. The antithesis of care is carelessness, a mode of operation that no leader wants his or her people to embody in their jobs or within their relationships on or off the job. In this sense, we should all be wary of the common phrase "I couldn't care less." One who has no concern for anyone or anything is one who has come to care less—to be careless.

Carelessness is marked by a lack of attention. How many work safety problems on the shop floor are caused because we did not pay attention? Manufacturing facilities post signs reminding employees that safety is everyone's business, urging everyone to pay attention. How do we fail to pay attention? In the first place, we simply may not care, and this carelessness leads to lack of attention. If the results do not matter to us, why pay attention?

Supervision finds a ready home in the business world. In a business setting that has stepped back from a command and control hierarchy, teamwork language is preferred over the term *supervisor*. But, whatever the language, supervision must be undertaken.

Care, concern, attention, and supervision all come into play during a merger and acquisition. Study after study reveals that between 50 percent and 75 percent of mergers and acquisitions fail. KPMG, a large public accounting firm, found that, between 1996 and 1998, 83 percent of the deals studied did not boost shareholder value and 53 percent actually reduced it. At the same time, 82 percent of the executives involved reported that the deals had been successful. Were these executives paying attention?[2]

It is easier to buy a company than to integrate it into an existing enterprise. An ironic illustration of failed integration and failure to build a common culture was provided by the 1997 formation of Franklin Covey, by author Stephen Covey, who wrote *Seven Habits of Highly Effective People*, and Hyrum Smith, the time management expert of Franklin Planners. Although these should have been the right two leaders to blend two businesses, the result was a host of common integration pitfalls: separate headquarters for the two companies; differences in how people were treated; and an "us" versus "them" mentality, which thrived as both sides continued old behaviors despite new organizational structures designed to promote cooperation.³

When a company's efforts are consumed by integration, it can become careless and neglect customers and employees. A wise merger and acquisition team is aware that employees in the trenches as well as those in the corner office are all asking, "What happens to me?" Accordingly, effective merger teams care whether people stay or leave, disrupt or adjust. The manufacturing company Eaton appoints both integration and operating managers to an integration team in order to ensure that attention does get paid to customers during the transition. Customer satisfaction is monitored throughout the integration process, and senior executives visit major customers as early as possible to explain the rationale of the merger and the benefits it will bring them.⁴

Two other aspects of care are captured in the Latin words *sollicitudo* and *diligio. Sollicitudo* means "anxious" or "worry." Solicitous care means someone worries about someone, in the best sense of worry. He or she is anxious for another's well-being. At the heart of this word for care is *sollus*, the Latin word for "wholeness." Solicitude is that care that aims at one's wholeness, one's well-being. It is a desire for one's wholeness when things are disintegrating—when one does not have it all together. It is the anxiety one feels for a co-worker losing his or her job or who may have just learned of a cancer diagnosis. Although this kind of care may not fix everything, solicitude may be the only saving grace possible.

Worry, the most common form of solicitude, generally has a bad reputation in our culture, as we admonish each other not to worry. But as a solicitous word—as a form of care—*worry* can be healthy and helpful when leaders worry about how their followers respond to workplace demands. They should worry about corporate performance, since the only security blanket employees have comes from serving customers well and profitably—no margin, no mission.

The Latin word *diligo* adds a slightly different slant to the idea of care and gives rise to the English word *diligence. Diligo* translates into "cherish," "favor," and "to be partial to." *Cherish* is an affective word. To cherish someone or something is to hold him or her dear, an important attitude of care for any leader. To hold someone or something dear is to value the person, to appreciate his or her worth. There are ways of being, acting, and doing which are endearing. Common courtesies and thoughtfulness go far in establishing and maintaining endearing relationships. To cherish someone does not necessitate a pay raise or a gift.

Research in the field of emotional intelligence (EI) reveals how *sollicitudo* and *diligio* contribute to leadership success, as successful businesses increasingly rely on teamwork. The skill of demonstrating care and compassion for others increases our ability to add economic value. Research demonstrates empirically what we all know intuitively: more than analytical genius is needed for success. A leader is always in relationship to followers. EI is always a factor in this relationship. EI measures our ability to care for others, to read others, to regulate emotions, and to increase self-knowledge. High EI equals higher economic value, as evidenced by a study of a large accounting firm's partners. If a partner possessed significant strength in self-management, then his or her incremental profit was 78 percent higher than partners who lacked this strength. If a partner possessed significant strength in social skills, then his or her incremental profit was 110 percent higher than partners who lacked this strength.[5]

11-3 Compassion

Compassion, meaning to "suffer with," is more powerful than "I care." When we act with compassion, we give ourselves over to another in a deeper, more involved way. Sympathy and compassion bring the dimensions of understanding and sharing to our care. The opposite of compassion, apathy, does not see the other's need or predicament. One who is devoid of compassion often develops contempt for the weak, the hurting, and the needy.

To gain greater clarity in defining the term *compassion* in corporate life, consider that Lubrizol's *Ethical and Legal Conduct Guidelines* translates *compassion* with phrases such as the "Rule of Reciprocity" and "the Golden Rule." Lubrizol offers a dozen global religious traditions and words to express the universal virtue that "we will treat others as we would like to be treated."[6] Lubrizol applies this universal rule to common international business ethical issues, such as employment practices, employee privacy, environmental/health/safety issues, and business expense reports.

Probably the use of passion language in the context of business leaves everyone a bit uneasy, although life lived without love is not life at all. The fifth-century philosopher Augustine put it boldly: "If you do not love anything you will be dolts, dead, despicable creatures. Love by all means, but take care what it is you love."[7]

Augustine's wisdom is twofold. First, he encourages us to love—indeed, to develop the virtue of love. A contemporary writer, Alan Jones, suggests the unnerving concept that "to love is to give yourself away."[8] Our reluctance to give ourselves away through love comes from the fear that we might have nothing left; there may no longer be any "us." But Augustine's advice counters this by saying that if we do not give ourselves away, there will be no "us." If there is not another person or some cause, what is there to us? Following this train of thought, compassion moves love in the direction of sympathy, a love by which we enter into the *pathos* of another, into the depth of the other's suffering and trials of living.

Augustine's second piece of advice is imperative: be careful what you love. What is the object of our love? For what do we ultimately live?

In the 1970s, advertising agency Saatchi & Saatchi was so focused on being number one in the world of advertising that little attention was paid to virtue—compassion for stakeholders—or to the price paid for their acquisitions or the details of integration. The trouble with a goal is that it can be reached, and Saatchi & Saatchi was determined to be the top advertising company on the planet. After a 10-year shopping spree of companies, Saatchi and Saatchi reached its goal in 1987. Annual billings were $7.5 billion, the number of employees reached 18,000, 500 offices were spread across 65 countries, and it was the first company in the world to be listed on the New York, London, and Tokyo stock exchanges. It was the number one ad agency on the planet. Two years later, in 1989, debt increased and revenue declined and the share price lost 98 percent of its value. Five years later, in 1994, a shareholder revolt forced the resignation of Charles and Maurice Saatchi, the brothers who had founded the company 24 years earlier.[9] Creating value for people and doing what is worthy were replaced by growth for the sake of growth, thus destroying value and benefiting no one. Although the Saatchis were brilliant in the world of advertising, Augustine would have cautioned them to examine the object of their love.

11-4 Mercy

The word *mercy* is another way to demonstrate compassion in business. Perhaps in the cutthroat, competitive business world, kindness—or any virtue—seems a bit sappy. Mercy may be seen as a dim hope of the weak or fainthearted, or at best mercy is what one shows an opponent when one is sure of winning.

To be sure, kindness that results from mercy can be superficial or even naïve, but genuine kindness is substantial. Kindness is a graciousness toward others; it is always a gift. The following sentiments of graciousness from a prayer capturing the spirit of thirteenth-century saint Francis of Assisi are universally appreciated:

Where there is hatred, let me sow love;

Where there is injury, pardon;

Where there is doubt, faith;

Where there is despair, hope;

Where there is darkness, light;

And where there is sadness, joy;

Grant that I might not so much seek to be consoled as to console;

To be understood, as to understand;

To be loved as to love;

For it is in giving that we receive;

It is in pardoning that we are pardoned.[10]

The person who shows no mercy is heartless. Heartless is the one who sees the *pathos* of another and remains unmoved. The unmerciful among us can dismiss others, knowing that mercy will open the doors to the vulnerability of caring and possibly drag us through those doors with compassion for the other. Only by not showing mercy can we be safe.

Ruthlessness is an aggressive form of heartlessness. Instead of merely withholding mercy, the ruthless person presses the advantage, demanding when there is nothing left to give. Instead of guilt, the ruthless one typically experiences a sick satisfaction, if not pride, in the face of the "loser."

Mercy transforms any heartless attitude or ruthless action. Our English word *mercy* is rooted in the French *merci,* "thank you." That French word also means "mercy." To offer another mercy is to establish the opportunity for the other to say, "Thank you." Mercy, like any aspect of love, is always a gift, and the only appropriate response to a gift is gratitude.

In the end, care, compassion, and mercy can be best understood through story rather than philosophy. One such story begins with an anonymous professional saying, "I have a client who owed me a good deal of money. Eventually she stopped seeing me, but each month I would send her a bill and receive no response. Finally I wrote to her and said, 'I don't know what difficulty has befallen you that you are unable to pay me, but whatever it is, I'm writing to tell you your debt is forgiven in full. My only request is that at some point in your life, when your circumstances have changed, you will pass this favor on to someone else.'"[11] Is it nothing more than a stupid way to run a business? Or are insight and a mature truth being revealed?

Dragging the virtue of love into the business world is typically not done; in fact, it may be just plain stupid. A corporation does not exist for the purpose of compassion, although compassion might add stakeholder value. Corporations find themselves in the role of balancing economic development and environmental preservation, balancing free trade's positive impact on economic integration and growth with the negative impact of dislocated workers and cultures. As we have seen, balancing is an economic way of discussing temperance and including justice. But just how does compassion fit in the business world? Robert Greenleaf, founder of the Greenleaf Center for Servant Leadership, offers an interesting answer to this question in the following passage:

> I believe that caring for persons, the more able and the less able serving each other, is what makes a good society. Most caring was once person to person. Now much of it is mediated through institutions—often large, powerful, impersonal, not always competent; sometimes corrupt. If a better society is to be built, one more just and more caring and providing opportunity for people to grow, the most effective and economical way, while supportive of the social order, is to raise the performance as servant of as many institutions as possible by new voluntary regenerative forces initiated within them by committed individuals, servants. Such servants may never predominate or even be numerous; but their influence may form a leaven that makes possible a reasonably civilized society.[12]

11-5 Care for Employees

More than good intentions and human relationships are needed to respond to issues such as globalization's benefit of economic growth for the price of unstable employment. Before a company hacks at its payroll, prudent, compassionate leaders might ask whether negative earnings resulted from having too many employees or from serving the wrong markets with the wrong products. Maybe the firm has alternatives to layoffs that will strengthen the company, such as acquiring or selling assets. Maybe employees could be spared and corporate jets, country club memberships, or first-class travel could get the axe.

There are other compassionate alternatives to layoffs that can also add value but that are infrequently considered. No one likes a pay cut but, according to economist Richard Freeman, variable pay could lower unemployment by 1 percent, an amount equal to 1.4 million jobs. While variable pay means that employee compensation goes up and down with earnings, temporary pay cuts are another way to reduce costs and save jobs. Employees could work one day less for one less day of pay or work five days but get paid for four days. Hotel Quest International was in the hotel reservation business but saw revenue plummet when travel declined after the September 11 disaster. To avoid losing an excellent leadership team, the CEO made an offer that was accepted by all members of the team: receive 30 percent less pay through December 31, when compensation was reinstated. Charles Schwab exemplified this model of leadership when he required top executives to take a pay cut. Cuts are more widely accepted if those with the most lead by example.

Accenture, formerly known as Andersen Consulting, may have had trouble with its auditing practice, as with Enron, but the consulting practice offered a creative solution when its business dropped in June 2001. Over 2,000 employees voluntarily accepted the offer of a sabbatical to pursue travel, school, or another job with a noncompeting business or nonprofit. Employees stayed on the payroll for 6 to 12 months at 20 percent of their salary. Additionally, they were allowed to continue benefits, use the firm's laptops, and use the e-mail system. Employees were assured of their old jobs but had no obligation to return. Cisco offered a similar arrangement for employees to work for a local charity for one year at one-third of their salary in addition to health care benefits and stock options. Ogilvy Public Relations Worldwide had experienced one round of layoffs and wanted to avoid another, since there was additional business in its future. The firm asked employees if they would accept a temporary layoff until new projects were available.[13]

These creative responses to worker dislocation represent possible acts of corporate compassion (the golden rule), along with virtues of faith (concern for others); justice (lessening the impact of unemployment); prudence (attracting and retaining talent while balancing the need to control costs); temperance (avoiding the excess of severe cost-cutting, thus minimizing harm to customers, employees, investors, and suppliers); and hope (corporate intention to satisfy stakeholders as the means of enhancing shareholder wealth). Global corporate responsibility that is profitable and that responds to inevitable worker dislocation calls for the best competence and character that can be developed.

11-6 Care for Customers

Corporations compete on a combination of quality, cost, and service. Often quality is a threshold that must be reached simply to stay in business. As global trade barriers continue to fall, consumers have so many choices that no one has to settle for inferior products.

Assuming the product is of sufficient quality, cost becomes a decision point for consumers. It is difficult to compete for customers on cost, since lowering prices in response to a competitor tends to lower profits unless, of course, the economic model is distinctive. Corporations such as Wal-Mart can compete on price due to buying power and logistics expertise. Although price wars are wonderful events for customers, most corporations suffer financially.

Thus, customer service is an increasingly important variable in the competition for consumers. Often companies must compete on the intangible of service—care for customer concerns. When companies demonstrate extraordinary care for customers, they are rewarded financially. Companies can earn six times higher profitability when they achieve a 4.5 in customer satisfaction on a 5-point scale, compared with companies that achieve a 4.0 satisfaction level. When this level of service is achieved, the satisfied customers are likely to recommend the company's products and services to 15 people. In contrast, when customer satisfaction is rated a 1 or 2 on a 5-point scale, customers are likely to tell about 15 other people how horrible the products and services are.[14]

In 1999, the Better Business Bureau in Cleveland selected Mueller Tire for the extraordinary customer service award. Tire sales is a hypercompetitive commodity industry with limited ability to compete on quality and cost. Mueller Tire's research showed that customers viewed buying tires as a hassle, so its business was to reduce the hassle of buying tires. With only 11 stores and a limited advertising budget, its strategy was to rely on customer referrals. Each customer received a brief postpurchase telephone survey concerning satisfaction with the store's service.

In order to ensure that the employees were aligned with the goal of satisfying customers, Mueller Tire compensated them on the basis of customer responses. Each store had the discretion to grant customers a full refund for any dissatisfaction. Customers did not drive their tires over the spikes at an airport car rental and then drive on the rims back to the store, complaining the tires were no good. Most customers were impressed with the strength of the guarantee. The company created a version of a frequent-flyer program in that repeat customers were given discounts and incentives, such as free oil changes. Additionally, customers received discounts for referring new customers. The cultivation of a service culture and the creation of a customer satisfaction system differentiated a company even in a commodity market such as selling tires.[15]

11-7 May 6—the Secret to a Wonderful Life

Two classic Christmas stories, *A Christmas Carol* and *It's a Wonderful Life,* are about businessmen confronted with their deaths. In each case, this confrontation transforms the businessman as he comes to understand that success is measured by love, not money, and that joy rises above circumstances. Even the most jaded viewers of these sentimental tales agree that an untransformed Scrooge could never bring justice to the people he harmed and an unchanged Bailey would never achieve his dream to globe trot as an architect. Who has not at some point acted like Ebenezer Scrooge or George Bailey—stopped caring, lacked compassion, or lost graciousness?

Do you know where you were on May 7, 1997, at 1:30 P.M.? Sandy Stark, then a senior leader at one of the country's largest regional banks, does. Stark started as a secretary in a bank soon after graduating from high school. Over the years she watched people around her getting promoted and noticed that the difference between them and her was a college degree. She corrected this shortcoming by earning a bachelor's degree and, then, in the evening an MBA while still performing effectively at her job. She earned promotions every two to three years, never taking advantage of anyone to get ahead, competing through collaboration rather than ruthlessness. By the age of 38, Stark had become the highest-ranking woman of a far-flung enterprise. As vice chair, her leadership resulted in the number one market share in small business loans in the United States, generating about $2 billion in loans. Over her 20-year career, she was able to see the bank from the viewpoint of a secretary's desk and an executive suite. Her incredible fast-track story provided her with power, influence, and financial success.

At 1:30 on May 7, 1997, Stark was in a meeting, when suddenly the room started to spin and she stared blankly into space while her colleagues waved their hands in front of her eyes. Her secretary called 911, and she was flown by helicopter to a hospital, where she was diagnosed with a brain aneurysm. Because there was too much blood on her brain for doctors to operate immediately, the prognosis was bleak. About two-thirds of those inflicted by an aneurysm die immediately. About two-thirds of those who survive suffer some significant physical deficit. Against the odds, Stark's aneurysm was repaired and, after months of rehabilitation, her recovery was full and complete.

A colleague gave Stark a picture dated May 6, 1997, the day before she was struck by the aneurysm. The picture was of Stark and her team members, standing together during a business trip to Wisconsin. Everyone in the picture except Stark was wearing a "cheese head." She was the only person who would not spend $20 for a cheese head, and her colleagues gave her the picture so she could remember "what happens to you when you do not have your picture taken with a hunk of cheese on your head." The picture is a reminder to Stark that she had no idea on May 6 what was going to happen to her on May 7.

Reflecting on her life up to that date, Stark devised an evaluation system. If that date had been the end of her life, then, on a 5-point scale, how might she grade herself on the following parts of her life?

> *Professional—4—*Her career success far exceeded her expectations, but she was especially pleased that she had received over 500 cards from colleagues. About 300 people reported to her, so she figured that, when the boss has brain surgery, many feel obligated to send the boss a get well card. She also figured some must be authentic. She was pleased that she had been successful; she showed up each day, willing to work hard, solve problems, and not step on others to get ahead.
>
> *Family—2.5 —*Although she said—and believed—her family was important, she spent too little time with them and took too little interest in their lives to measure up to who she wanted to be.
>
> *Community—1—*She simply had been professionally "too busy" to spend time in the community.

Stark believed that she had received a profound gift: the chance to see how well she was answering Augustine's question "for what do I ultimately live?" She was given a chance to review her life as if May 7, 1997, were the date her obituary was published. Unlike Stark, most of us do not know when our May 7 will come. Scrooge was able to view Christmas past, present, and future; Bailey had a visit from an angel, showing him the "what ifs" of an untimely death; Stark had her May 7.[16]

Will Allen Dromgoole offers a thoughtful conclusion to our discussion of care, compassion, and mercy in his poem *The Bridge Builder:*

An old man, going a lone highway,

Came at the evening, cold and gray,

To a chasm, vast and deep and wide,

Through which was flowing a sullen tide.

The old man crossed in the twilight dim;

The sullen stream had no fears for him;

But he turned when safe on the other side

And built a bridge to span the tide.

"Old man," said a fellow pilgrim near,

"You are wasting strength with building here;
Your journey will end with the ending day;
You never again must pass this way;
You have crossed the chasm, deep and wide
Why build you the bridge at the eventide?"
The builder lifted his old gray head:
"Good friend, in the path I have come," he said,
"There followeth after me today
A youth whose feet must pass this way.
This chasm that has been naught to me
To that fair-haired youth may a pitfall be.
He, too, must cross in the twilight dim;
Good friend, I am building the bridge for him.[17]

11-8 Conclusion

While we are not likely to approach a colleague or business employee and tell him or her, "I love you," if we do not exhibit the qualities of love, the business will be poorer. No one wants to follow a leader "who couldn't care less." Equally, no one wants to be a careless leader. To develop the virtue of love necessitates paying attention to people. Love means bringing a compassionate heart to any decision. Compassion does not mean you avoid the tough decision nor does it resolve tough decisions in nice ways.

Love often couples with other virtues. It helps leaders proceed with good faith. It makes courage bolder. It gives heart to justice. Often, it sows the seeds of hope.

Chapter Quiz

Chapter Quiz Quiz

1. The virtue of love is lived out in the corporate world in all of the following ways *except*
   a. care.
   b. compassion.
   c. pity.
   d. mercy.

2. The Latin word *cura* means all of the following *except*
   a. concern.
   b. attention.
   c. supervision.
   d. passion.

3. Carelessness is marked by which of the following?
   a. inattention
   b. denial
   c. ignorance
   d. oblivion

4. The Latin word *diligo* translates into all of the following *except*
   a. cherish.
   b. favor.
   c. anxious.
   d. to be partial to.

5. According to a study of large accounting firms, a partner who possessed significant strength in social skills had incremental profit that was how much higher than partners who lacked his strength?
   a. 40 percent
   b. 50 percent
   c. 85 percent
   d. 110 percent

6. In Lubrizol's *Ethical and Legal Conduct Guidelines,* compassion is translated into which of the following?
   a. rule of concern
   b. rule of reciprocity
   c. rule of trepidation
   d. rule of empathy

7. Which advertising agency lost its position as a global leader due to inattention to compassion for stakeholders?
   a. OMD
   b. AMP
   c. Saatchi & Saatchi
   d. McKinney

8. Which of the following is an aggressive form of heartlessness?
   a. ruthlessness
   b. mercilessness
   c. ignorance
   d. refutation

9. Pay cuts are more widely accepted if which of the following occurs?
   a. All departments suffer equally.
   b. The worst performers are affected first.
   c. Top management accepts the first cuts.
   d. Employees negotiate the percentage cut.

10. Companies that achieve a 4.5 in customer satisfaction on a 5-point scale compared to companies that have a 4.0 earn how many times more?
   a. 2
   b. 4
   c. 6
   d. 8

Note: You can find the correct answers to these questions by taking the quiz and then submitting your answers in the Online Edition. The program will automatically score your submission. If you miss a question, the program will provide the correct answer, a rationale for the answer, and the section number in the chapter where the topic is discussed.

Questions for Thought

1. If you start to toss around the word *love* in a corporate setting, you can get yourself in trouble. What words, ideas, and actions are used in a corporate setting that are consistent with the virtue love?
2. Can you identify and describe nonverbal or subtle indications of love as a virtue in a business setting?
3. Think of an issue or a decision that was made in a company that served justice but that still felt incomplete. Explain how this justice issue might also require compassion.
4. Cite at least one example from this chapter in which compassion was demonstrated and share how it was demonstrated.
5. When a company's revenue is insufficient to cover its wages and benefits, how could compassion creatively enlarge the possibilities for dealing with this problem?
6. How would you distinguish mercy from care in a business setting?
7. Consider the relationship between different levels of power (janitor to CEO) and compassion. How does the power you have impact how you exercise love?
8. Explain how power without love is dangerous.
9. Name one or more reasons leaders either cannot or choose not to be caring or compassionate.
10. What point does Stark's story illustrate in this chapter?

Web Exercises

Visit Google's Jobs site at http://www.google.com/intl/en/jobs/index.html and study the perks, benefits, and culture of the search-engine company. Carefully read The Top Ten Reasons to Work at Google, located at http://www.google.com/intl/en/jobs/reasons.html. In what ways does Google exhibit compassion and even love for its employees? What kids of things does it offer to help keep its employees happy and productive? What kind of emotions do you think its employees feel when they receive these benefits?

Virgin Mobile has consistently won customer service awards. Visit their consumer information site at http://about.virginmobile.com/about/csr/consumers/codeofpractice and read about their policies and goals for service. In what ways does this indicate Virgin Mobile's love and care for its customers? After reading about this company, think of some customer service situations you've been in. What companies cared? How did you know? What characteristics are common among good customer service experiences?

Case

Wal-Mart—Concern for Whom?

Applying the virtue *love* to Wal-Mart is silly, and even the notion of compassion can seem to be a stretch. Perhaps the idea of concern fits better. To what degree does Wal-Mart demonstrate concern for customers, shareholders, employees, suppliers, and the neighborhoods in which it operates its stores?

Merchandising is as old as civilization, and without the use of patents or tariffs to protect market share, Wal-Mart is not only the largest retailer in the world, but it is also the largest corporation in the world. Wal-Mart is bigger than General Motors, ExxonMobil, and General Electric. In 2003, Wal-Mart generated more income than Target, Sears, Kmart, J.C. Penny, Safeway, and Kroger combined. In 1970, Wal-Mart's 30 stores in three states generated sales of $1 billion. In 2004, Wal-Mart's 3,500 stores in 50 states and 1,500 stores in 10 countries generated $250 billion a year. Sam Walton is to retailing what Henry Ford was to cars.[1]

Through a brilliant combination of information technology and globalization, Wal-Mart reversed a 100-year history of retailer dependence on manufacturers. Former Wal-Mart store manager Jon Lehman described the use of technology to track customer buying behavior. "You can find out what size of toothpaste is your best seller, what times of year you sell that toothpaste. You can track sales spikes during the year, during certain seasonable periods, clothes, sizes, colors, flavors—all of those things." The second half of Wal-Mart's success has been formed with China, from which Wal-Mart obtains 80 percent of its goods. Wal-Mart built a procurement center in southern China, where it can pay workers $100 a month to source low-cost products. American consumers benefit from inexpensive goods, and the Chinese are able to grow their economy by learning from Wal-Mart how to enter the largest consumer market in the world.[2]

Wal-Mart does not lack for customers who want access to its stores. Cleveland councilman Roosevelt Coats represents a predominantly African-American ward that is being considered by Wal-Mart as a potential store site. Coats believes his community would be well served by forcing expensive urban city-corner grocery markets or fast-food restaurants to compete with the largest corporation in the world: UBS Warburg concluded that Wal-Mart supercenter prices averaged 14 percent lower than competitors' prices.[3]

Wal-Mart's is America's largest employer, providing jobs for 1.2 million of its associates. Brink Lindsey reminds us that no one drafted Wal-Mart workers and that they must have selected the best option available to them. Some economists even credit Wal-Mart with lowering U.S. inflation and raising U.S. productivity.[4] Emek Basker examined the effect of Wal-Mart on 1,749 counties and concluded that the overall effect on county employment is statistically zero. Perhaps retailing is a zero sum game because the amount of money people spend on retail is constant unless income or populations grows.[5]

For all its success, you need to get in line to join the chorus of Wal-Mart bashers who view the corporation as a tyrant. In a move seen as despicable by some and despite international outrage, Wal-Mart opened a superstore less than a half mile from one of Mexico's archeological sites that dates back to CE 600. In 2004, the day after Thanksgiving, TV newscasts showed a young Wal-Mart team leader screaming with the intensity of guest on *Jerry Springer* that they had to sell $1 million of merchandise that day.[6] These incidents reinforced the view that Wal-Mart's culture consists of profit before people and communities.

In a case brought by Arkansas pharmacists, Wal-Mart admitted to selling drugs below cost, but denied predatory pricing. Ken Stone, a retired professor from Iowa State, claimed that Wal-Mart only reduced prices on high profile items such as lightbulbs and shampoos and that once competitors vanish, so do low prices.

Wal-Mart claimed its national full-time hourly rate averaged $9.46 an hour. Comparable government numbers are $9.94 for wholesale clubs; $9.94 for discount stores; and $10.90 for supermarket and other grocery stores. The University of California at Berkeley Labor Center concluded that union workers in San Francisco averaged $15.31 an hour compared to $9.40 for Wal-Mart workers. A 2002 Harvard business case concluded that Wal-Mart spent an average of $3,500 per employee on health costs; the wholesale/retail sector spent $4,800; and U.S. employers averaged $5,600. Most importantly, because smaller stores cannot compete, Wal-Mart might be destroying a pool of local business leaders, according to a Pennsylvania State University study.[7]

In March 2005, Wal-Mart traded at $50 per share with a price objective of $63 in the following 12 to 18 months. Buchanan recommended that investors buy Wal-Mart stock and stated that the company had acted and will continue to act with integrity by taking action against those that violate company rules. For example, senior leader Tom Coughlin was forced to resign for allegedly accepting unauthorized gifts and for personal reimbursements. Inability to hit a target of $63 a share could result from (1) disruption of product flows from Asia and other low cost supply sources; (2) unionization of Wal-Mart's domestic labor force; (3) the entry of France-based Carrefour into the United States; (4) inability to grow globally; and (5) adverse impact of employee litigation and declines in consumer spending.[8]

Today, Wal-Mart enjoys preeminent market power. Perhaps sometime in the future, shareholders will discount Wal-Mart's earnings if the announcement of a new store results in protests by organized labor and angry neighbors demand that zoning codes be written to protect local businesses against a large white box that increases traffic and the size of parking lots.

Questions for Discussion

1. How would you evaluate Wal-Mart's attitude toward customers, shareholders, employees, manufacturers, and the neighborhoods in which they operate?

2. How might Wal-Mart's attitude toward its employees, suppliers, and neighbors impact its long-term sustainability?

3. Is Wal-Mart good for America?

4. Is Wal-Mart good for China?

Footnotes

1. Phillip Morris, "Cleveland's In Wal-Mart's Cross Hairs," *The Plain Dealer,* December 7, 2004, sec. B9.
2. Hedrick Smith, "Is Wal-Mart Good for America?" http://www.pbs.org/wbgh/pages/frontline/ shows/walmart/view, November 16, 2004.
3. Alison Grant, "When Wal-Mart Moves to Town, Should Consumers, Workers and Competitors Beware of Falling Prices," *The Plain Dealer,* April 10, 2005, sec. G1, G4–G5.
4. Smith.
5. Grant.
6. Morris.
7. Grant.
8. R. F Buchanan, et al., "Hypermarkets and Super Centers Equity Research Recent Development Report," Business and Company Resource Center, http://galenet.galegroup.com/serelet, May 28, 2005.

Endnotes

1. "The Love Calculator," http://www.lovecalculator.com/.
2. Sydney Finklestein, *Why Smart Executives Fail* (New York: Portfolio), 77.
3. Ibid., 100.
4. Ibid., 101.
5. Daniel Goleman, Richard Boyatzis, and Anne McKee, *Primal Leadership* (Cambridge, MA: Harvard Business School Press, 2003).
6. *Ethical and Legal Conduct Guidelines* (Wycliffe, OH: The Lubrizol Corporation, April 2002), 7.
7. Alan Jones, *Passion for Pilgrimage: Notes for the Journey Home* (San Francisco: Harper & Row, 1989), 49.
8. Ibid., 79.
9. Finklestein, 91.
10. "The Peace Prayer of St. Francis," http://www.franciscan-archive.org/index2.html.
11. The Editors of Conari Press, *Random Acts of Kindness* (Berkeley: Conari Press, 1993), 27.
12. Robert Greenleaf, *Servant as Leader* (New York: John Wiley & Sons, 1970), 5.
13. Shari Caudron, "Another God That's Failed," The Conference Board, http://www.conference_board.org/publications.
14. Fariborz Ghadar, "Global Competition Program," (Berea, OH: Baldwin-Wallace College December 9, 2003).
15. Better Business Bureau Customer Service Awards, 1999.
16. Andrew Klaven, "The Secret to a Wonderful Life," *The Plain Dealer,* December 9, 2003, sec. B9.
17. Will Allen Dromgoole, *The Bridge Builder,* http://www.rigsbee.com/bridgebuilder.html.

Chapter

12

Hope

Outline

12-1 Hope (The Future Present)

The seventh, and final, virtue, hope, brings us full circle as it joins hands with the initial virtue, courage. At the outset, we suggested that without courage there would be no energy to live—the gates of Dante's inferno warn, "Leave all hope, ye that enter."[1] To hope requires courage, and the opposite is true as well: without hope, courage is foolishness.

Hope is the lure of the future, the pull of the potential. Hope is always about what has not yet come to pass. Strategic leadership and hope are intertwined, because strategy involves being intentional in setting a future.

Whether hope in a corporation's strategy is well-founded depends on the leader's character. In fact, a questionable character is the most important warning sign in predicting why otherwise smart executives fail. The literature on strategy is exhaustive in its analysis on economic, demographic, and technological trends, in addition to internal strengths and weaknesses. Although analysis is an important element of corporate strategy, it is equally important to ask who the strategists are. Those who formulate the strategy—their virtues, experiences, beliefs, and character—will largely determine corporate success or failure. The firm's history and culture will dictate corporate response to shifting customer preferences and competitive pressures. Ultimately, soft issues, such as culture and openness to change, speak to hope—the unstated assumptions that guide the way all of us navigate the future.

One significant, unstated assumption about hope acknowledges that it is not about guarantees or about being perfect but about learning from mistakes. We have hope in companies that have clear plans to anticipate multiple problems: creating new ventures, managing change and innovation, acquiring and integrating mergers and acquisitions, and responding to competitive pressures. We have less hope in companies that are characterized by a closed-minded and unresponsive culture. We have less hope in companies that reward dissidents with an office next to the boiler room or termination. We have less hope in companies whose decision making is so centralized that people lack empowerment, or so decentralized that no one is responsible.[2]

To hope always takes courage, because formulating strategy often involves apprehension and doubt. The link between hope and courage is "the fundamental knowledge and feeling that there is a way out of difficulty, that things can work out, that we as humans can somehow handle and manage internal and external reality, that there are 'solutions.'"[3] Hope is always just beyond what is presently true.

To anticipate what this means for the business leader, we affirm that hope has to do with the possible, probable, and preferable. Although hope ultimately may be about our preference, that preference is always constrained by what is possible and usually limited by the probable. For example, Jim Collins' three fundamental strategic questions for companies which make the leap from good to great involve hope: (1) what can the company offer customers that will be superior to competitors (in other words, what is possible)?; (2) what will be the economic model of the business (what is probable)?; (3) what initiatives would capture the passion of the firm's employees (what is preferable)?[4]

First of all, hope has to be possible. Second, and equally important, hope must be realistic. Dietrich Bonhoeffer makes a crucial distinction between hope, which is realistic, and a wish dream, which is delusional.[5] Wish dreams might be fun. They might even be fantastic (rooted in fantasy), but fantasy is neither reality nor hope. When leaders fail to learn from their mistakes, they often create strategy that is more fantasy than reality. Otherwise smart executives can fail when they have a false image of reality. Delusional policies can be protected by a culture in which scrutiny is dismissed and leadership habits exacerbate strategic problems.

True hope is realistic and courageous, because courage supplies the energy to hope. But if a situation truly is hopeless, then no amount of energy (courage)—wishing, forcing, or cajoling—will lead to action. There are three dimensions of hope that show how it works—expectation, apprehension and confidence. The impact of hubris and blind spots to create false hopes will be discussed. Finally, the chapter concludes with the importance of reflection and putting our best thoughts into action to live out the virtue of hope.

12-2 Expectation

First, hope is expectation. The language of hope pervades the business world: analysts expect corporations to meet their earnings estimates. This is a position of hope because the earnings estimates are possible, and these estimates are realistic. As we have seen, both possibility and realism are necessary for there to be hope. They give legitimacy to expectation. The root meaning of *expectation* is the Latin *specto,* which means to "look at, aim at, strive for." Striving for is different from guaranteeing, inasmuch as hope only deals expectantly with the future—in the present moment, the "not yet" is not a sure bet.

Because this is true, even the most hopeful companies can fail to hit earning targets. But Wall Street is especially punitive when rosy scenarios trump reality. For example, Jill Barad was promoted to CEO of Mattel after her highly successful career marketing the Barbie doll. However, her marketing talent and continuous optimism wore thin with a skeptical investment community after she missed earning estimates four quarters in a row. She was someone with an ego who demanded loyalty. Her creativity marketing Barbie was necessary, but it was not sufficient to lead an enterprise. Her replacement, Alec Gores, returned the company to profitability in 75 days by using town hall meetings to open up the culture. He learned how upset people were, since they had thoughts about how to make positive change but had lost their hope when they were unable to correct problems. Gores welcomed ideas and empowered people to make decisions, and he held them accountable for performance. In other words, he restored hope.[6]

12-3 Apprehension

When coupled with expectation, the second dimension of hope, apprehension, adds an emotional element—uneasiness, fear, or doubt. Because hope is always located in the "not yet," it is not unusual to be apprehensive that what we hope for might not come. Positively speaking, apprehension is the cautionary aspect of hope. For example, in an economic market where earnings are uncertain and where margins are squeezed, the capital markets are rightfully apprehensive. This apprehension may be very prudent. But sometimes the apprehensive element of hope predominates. Then apprehension is no longer appropriately cautionary. Leaders and followers may become wary, depressed, or worse, despairing.

All of us have had at one time "flimsy hopes." Flimsy hope is possible and at times maybe realistic. But it is also fragile and easily damaged. A flimsy hope leaves us uneasy, and the emotional tone of our uneasiness is that we are wary of trusting. If we are apprehensive, it is hope held lightly. Our expectation may not be very strong: "High probability of failure; certain death; what are we waiting for?" asked Gimli the Dwarf in *The Lord of the Rings*.[7]

An even deeper level of apprehension is fear, which makes our hoping feel almost pointless. Fear erodes hope. Fear corrodes our expectations. We know there is hope, but we fear what we are hoping will not come. There is hope, but we are afraid to invest in it.

Otherwise capable organizations comprising of smart people can feel hopeless in taking the right actions. In 1999, the French were successful in stopping terrorists from crashing a hijacked plane into the Eiffel Tower. Then they warned the FBI that a similar plan was being hatched against U.S. targets. A few months later, the FBI was informed that several foreigners with terrorist connections had enrolled in U.S. flight schools. They were interested in learning how to fly commercial jets, but not how to land them. Among those enrolled were students associated with those who had plotted to crash planes into the Eiffel Tower. Middle East sources even reported that the World Trade Center was a likely target. FBI field agents started to connect the dots and requested searches and wiretaps. However, this request was diluted to appear less urgent than the agents intended. The request was denied and the agents were reassigned.

Some might suggest that the Twin Towers lay in rubble due to government bureaucracy and the incompetence of the FBI, yet is the public sector really unique? It is not surprising that vital information can be identified in one part of an organization and yet another part of the organization does not hear of it, or not know it soon enough. Or sometimes those with authority to act either are never informed or fail to act.

If the apprehensive aspect of hope is dominant, leaders can become depressed. There may be legitimate hope, but depression robs them of those feelings of hope—they do not "feel hopeful." Hope should be buoyant. But when hope becomes fearful, hope becomes submerged or falls. Things may not be hopeless, but we may be afraid to care.

Hopelessness starts to grip employees who can see what is wrong but who know that their ideas will be ignored, at best, or, worse, that they as the messenger will be "shot." For example, for years Rubbermaid was well respected and admired, but under the leadership of Wolfgang Schmitt the company paid too little attention to production and distribution efficiencies and too much attention to the supervision of middle and senior leaders. The company identified its core competency as innovation but suppressed innovative thinking. Stanley Gault, the former CEO, said that Wolfgang Schmitt would not listen or take advice. The paradox of poor oversight is that insufficient time is spent on serving customers and excessive energy is spent on micromanagement. This results in a culture in which employees spend more energy pleasing the boss than pleasing customers.[8]

The final level of apprehension is doubt. We find it hard to believe that we are so apprehensive that hope is tenuous. Because hope always deals with that which has not come to be, it is always possible to doubt. Some of us have a view of reality that makes hope difficult. Indeed, "seeing reality" itself is a form of hope, or hopelessness. Generally, people do not just see reality as it is. In fact, seeing reality also means we are interpreting reality.

Specifically, there are at least three ways of seeing reality: through hostile, indifferent, or supportive lenses.[9] If we view reality as hostile, then it easily follows that we are apprehensive about any hopes we might have. At best, hope seems dubious. Reality seen as hostile does not invite trust. We are more likely to be wary. Leaders who see reality this way inevitably communicate that to their followers. In this view of reality, the world is "out to get us."

Even if we consider reality to be indifferent, we may doubt that hope has a role in our life. Certainly, an indifferent world is not going to give anything. An indifferent world is not a providential world—a world that provides. At best, this world seems simply not to care. Even if it is not hostile, it is a world that is care-less. Over time this can lead to despair, and despair extinguishes the dimmest of hopes.

The third way of seeing reality does seem to make hope easier. When we see reality as basically supportive, it typically feels more hopeful. With this view of reality we can trust our expectation that things will come true. If we sense the world is essentially providential, we are eager to engage what is to come. And we feel more confident in our creativity and ability to shape reality. Leaders who work with this view of reality are usually more inspirational.

Whichever view of reality we hold, we must remember that the future is always present as hope but not guarantee. One purpose of leadership is to shape the hopes of those who follow. It is fascinating, and often a challenge, to understand why we place hope in leaders. If there is hope, we are trusting that things will work out; we expect success.

We may not really know why leaders succeed or fail; however, this does not prevent people from making claims for success or failure. The following is a list of common reasons for failure offered by about 200 senior executives who lead large corporations, along with more realistic, truthful views of those reasons.

- *Executives were stupid.* In fact, those who operated large corporations had usually earned degrees from selective schools and were often recognized as experts in the business they led.
- *Executives had no way of knowing what was coming.* In most circumstances, the forces that required the business to change were seen, discussed, and then dismissed, even while managers tried to keep senior leaders informed.

- *Executives failed to execute.* Although the business had experienced huge losses on one side of its operations, other operations were well run. Failures had more to do with a flawed view of the firm's real position in the marketplace and a closed-minded culture. Operational problems were just a symptom.
- *Executives were goofing off.* Middle managers often conclude that, if senior leaders were motivated to perform better, then trouble could be avoided. However, anyone who has tried to get on the calendar of a senior leader knows the schedule is oppressive and that most of his or her activities outside the job are work-related, such as community involvement to demonstrate civic responsibility. Furthermore, senior leaders usually benefit personally if the company adds value. The challenge for senior leaders is to balance work and life responsibilities, as they risk their health, their family life, and their reputation in order for the company to succeed.
- *Executives lacked leadership ability.* In fact, most executives knew how to get people to do what they wanted and had a clear vision of the company, although they may not have accepted obstacles that had to be overcome to realize a vision.
- *Executives lacked resources.* Large companies failed on a large scale precisely because they had enormous resources.
- *Executives were crooks.* Of course, there were some dramatic exceptions, but the clear majority of leaders were honest. Even in cases of corruption, why did those who were honest not expose the corrupt? Recent scandals have brought to light revolting sums of theft, but the uncomfortable fact is that the size of the theft was insufficient to bring down the company.[10]

In other words, employees perceive that leadership failure occurs for reasons that do not square with reality. Recall that hope must be realistic. Employees and leaders are well served by understanding that the common reasons smart executives fail have less to do with being dumb, lazy, and dishonest and more to do with the intangible nature of character.

12-4 Confidence

As the third dimension of hope, confidence counterbalances apprehension. This means that, where one's hope is mostly apprehensive, there will be little confidence. And the reverse is true. When one's hope is expressed very confidently, there apparently is little or no apprehension. Thus, hope is always a mixture of expectation, apprehension, and confidence. Like apprehension, confidence has three levels—namely, trust, sureness, and arrogance. As we saw for apprehension, the final level—in this case, arrogance—moves at least to the boundary of hope—if not beyond hope itself.

As the first level of confidence, trust characterizes a hope that feels ready to move ahead, to proceed. This is the kind of hope that is revealed in such statements as "He trusts his abilities," "She trusts what she knows to be true," and "He knows he can do that." All three are statements of hope inasmuch as they are expectations. Perhaps the key word to describe this kind of "trusting confidence" is *readiness* to trust oneself—one's abilities, knowledge, gifts, and so on. One is ready to engage the future, to take on the task, to be the person one is called to be. In most ways this kind of readiness, which comes with confidence, counters the uneasiness that is characteristic of the apprehensive dimension of hope. And this kind of trust seems easiest if we view reality as supportive. To trust, to be ready, and to be confident always involve an implicit "yes."

The second, bolder level of confidence is sureness. To be sure goes beyond simple trusting; it adds a bit of swagger to confidence. Dick Thornburgh exemplifies some of this swagger in fulfilling his passion to make business leaders more ethical. Thornburgh was governor of Pennsylvania during the Three Mile Island nuclear plant accident in the 1970s, was U.S. attorney general during the savings and loan scandal of the 1980s, and more recently investigated WorldCom. He has been well positioned and always willing to take on trouble. In the case of WorldCom, he concluded that "the checks didn't balance and the balances didn't check."[11] He was concerned that Bernie Ebbers, the former CEO, had operated without oversight and dominated the board. Thornburgh is not confident that the Sarbanes-Oxley law will ensure good governance, but he finds it helpful that CEOs and CFOs must now sign financial statements submitted to the Securities and Exchange Commission (SEC). He also believes legislation tends to overreact to problems such as those created by WorldCom. However, he is confident that sooner or later the good guys usually win.

Of course, Thornburgh's confidence that the good person will always catch the bad person is not a guarantee that will happen, but the probabilities are pretty high. This kind of "sure confidence" is stronger than trust, because there is more optimism: "Not only do I trust I can do it, but I'm sure I can." And this statement edges us toward the third level of confidence, arrogance.

Is arrogance is a legitimate form of confidence? It goes beyond being sure; arrogance, as a form of hope, is as close as hope can get to a guarantee. But if it is hope, it can never be a guarantee, even though the arrogant one may think in those terms. It does reveal the Achilles heel of arrogance—guarantees do not fail, but arrogance can.

Arrogance sometimes is strength of character, but arrogance certainly and easily can be a weakness of character. And weakness of character is often a doorway to failure. Again, we do well to look at failures in leadership. As suggested, the sharp observer knows that smart executives fail for reasons that have less to do with being dumb, lazy, and dishonest and more to do with the intangible nature of their character. Even when they are well meaning and competent, the warning signs for trouble are seven unhealthy habits common to smart executives who fail:

- *We are number one.* They believe they can control events and have the illusion of personal preeminence. It may not be intentional, but they treat employees as objects to serve their ends and customers as if they are lucky to do business with the superior corporation that they lead.
- *We blend personal and corporate interests.* When a leader's identity is one with the company, it can result in decisions that are great for the leader but not for the company. At best, ego does not allow the leader to cut losses of initiatives associated with their name. At worse, they start down the slippery slope of using corporate funds for personal reasons.
- *We have all the answers; just ask us.* In a world where the business environment is uncertain, they push for rapid closure. They are not open to learning, dissent goes underground, and followers stop following. They are control freaks, who freeze all decisions until stamped with their personal approval.
- *We require our way or the highway.* If you are not with them, then you are against them. The "Saddam Hussein School of Management" ruthlessly eliminates all dissent.
- *Peacocks.* Media presence and the lecture circuit can favorably impact quarterly earnings, given executives' charm and acumen. Image is everything, as evidenced by buying naming rights of pro sports facilities and using financial statements as public relations tools.
- *We ask, "What problem?"* They treat major obstacles with a wave of the hand as a minor speed bump. More commitment can solve any problem. When in doubt, charge.
- *We know it worked before.* In a world where tomorrow is uncertain, they select yesterday's answer. The one great idea that got them a top job becomes the answer to all future problems, even when inappropriate.

This list of reasons for failures introduces two additional pitfalls to hope: hubris and blind spots. Blind spots, by definition are weaknesses unknown to us. Hubris is more intentional. We need to look at each one.[12]

12-5 Hubris: Pride before the Fall

Glory is fleeting in that success often precedes failure. For example, the employees of a company that is first in its industry can often be polite to outsiders but enjoy showing off their brilliance. "We know more than you, so pay attention and see how it is done" may well be true, but the "we are with the government and we are here to help you" attitude is alienating.

The Schwinn Company watched as previously loyal dealers began selling competitor's mountain bikes in response to consumer dissatisfaction with Schwinn's bikes. Mountain bike entrepreneur Gary Fisher was told by a Schwinn representative, "We know bikes. You guys are all amateurs. We know better than anybody."[13] When Schwinn started to manufacture offshore to reduce its costs, it only succeeded in creating formidable Chinese competitors. Schwinn's culture resisted change and did not adapt to shifting customer preferences, but it continued to make small changes to perfect its bikes; however, these changes made no difference to its customers.

In another example, Johnson and Johnson's (J&J) 90 percent market share dominated business in stents used extensively by cardiologists to open clogged arteries. Cardiologists requested some improvements to the J&J product, changes that would result in stents that were easier to handle, were flexible, and came in varying lengths, so they could better adapt to different patient organ sizes and shapes. Since there was no competition to challenge its preeminence, J&J refused to make changes for about two years. When Guidant entered the market and offered the stents cardiologists wanted, within 45 days it had captured 70 percent of the market. When doctors and hospital administrators were asked how J&J lost its market, simple answers pointed to J&J's lack of respect for customers' ideas and inability to listen.[14]

Motorola had the capability to make digital cell phones and had extensive data to indicate that the market demanded digital over its analog phones. The firm probably could have dominated the digital cell market, but highly decentralized business units, combined with a "trust us, we know what is best for you" attitude, led the company to stick with analog. Between 1994 and 1998, Motorola's U.S. market share peaked at 60 percent and dipped to 34 percent, while the share of competitor Nokia, which did make digital phones, increased from 11 percent to 34 percent. In June

1998, Motorola announced plans to lay off 20,000 employees, most of whom were innocent bystanders of the company's disaster.[15]

Shifting customer preferences and competitive responses require that companies constantly keep a finger on the pulse of the marketplace. Lou Gerstner, the former CEO of IBM, or Big Blue, believed that the company's decline was caused by too much time focused on internal measures and too little time focused on customers and competitors.

Corporate leaders would be wise to avoid what venture capitalists call "sucking your exhaust."[16] Clear warning signals include an aggressive sense of control, significant emphasis on personal achievement, self-righteous resentment about failures, defensiveness, overconfidence, and denial. Interestingly, the signs of hubris are often coupled with genius. Venture capitalists wish these same geniuses would wear their "humility sweater" to safeguard against the pitfalls of pride.

Realistic hope in corporate strategy involves taking into account issues of character and issues of competence. Pride is one thing that should always be missing in a person of character. And character informs competence, so that senior leaders listen and learn from customers and competitors. Humbly, they recognize that mistakes are inevitable and they build systems to respond appropriately. In essence, character leads executives to act responsibly.

12-6 Blind Spots

Any experienced driver knows about the blind spot in driving. Even if the car has a good rearview mirror, there is a spot where the mirror does not reflect an approaching car. The driver does not create the blind spot, but it is there. A car might be next to us, but we cannot see it. In this sense, blinds spots are passive; nonetheless, they can cause grief. Coca-Cola is a generally well-run company, but it had a blind spot to complaints about Belgian schoolchildren getting sick from its products. It was slow to recognize that its brand was at risk and then reacted with statements written by lawyers. When even the best companies can on occasion act like zombies, we should all be concerned. Interestingly, a zombie company that is adrift is often full of executives who are brilliant, adaptable, and clearly in touch with external events. What makes otherwise brilliant executives look silly are policies or a culture that inhibits action and discourages people from taking responsibility.[17]

12-7 Responsibility: The Confidence of Hope

Victor Frankl
Frankl is the originator of the phrase "He who has a why to live for can bear with almost any how."
Source: AP/Wide World Photos

Victor Frankl survived three years in a Nazi death camp. People were treated as animals and responded in kind. While most of us have no idea what it means to experience such unthinkable hatred and persecution, we do understand that people would choose self-preservation over concern for others. What we would not expect to find is a small number who would give away food when they were hungry and give away a blanket when they were cold. Even in the midst of humiliation, torture, and death, a small number of prisoners responded to their adversity with integrity and character.

Frankl asked what was different among those who gave rather than took, despite extreme suffering. He concluded the difference was not wealth or poverty, education or lack thereof, culture or lack of sophistication or religiosity. The commonality among the givers was that they all had a reason or purpose in life. They all believed that, even though they could not control the trouble that had found them, they could always control their response. This distinction is huge.

Frankl left no room for excuse. He did not allow for a lack of character due to victim status. He believed we have complete control in our choice to be responsible, even in a Nazi death camp. Interestingly, he also found that those who responded well to their situation were realistic in their hoping. Realizing that their fate might be sealed and there was no room for wishful thinking, they accepted their reality with integrity and were more likely to survive the ordeal.[18]

As we have already seen, if reality is experienced as basically supportive, then it is easier to hope with confidence. Marcus Borg puts it succinctly when he says, "If we see reality as supportive and nourishing, then another response to life becomes possible: trust."[19] Borg's reference to trust should remind us of our early discussion of the virtue of faith, which was described as trust. Hence, the virtue of hope implicates two other virtues, courage and faith.

Recall the root of *faith—fid*, as in *fiducia*. It is a simple move to see that to have confidence means to "have faith with" or, as Borg says, to "trust." This brings us close to the real meaning of the confidence of hope. We have faith or trust that that which we hope for will come to be. It is important to remember that confidence does not make the mistake of seeing hope as a guarantee. But it does trust what one hopes.

Hope is also power. It is not the abusive power of manipulation but power of the possible. It is the power to stand in the today and welcome the tomorrow. Even as we welcome the tomorrow, we can shape it. Hope does not create the tomorrow, but hope is the power to receive, shape, and live the tomorrow when it comes. Hope may not create the future, but it is creative. Often the "not yet" is creatively shaped by what we are being or doing now. Hope positions how the future comes to be present.

A compelling story of the power of hope is illustrated by Jim Collins' "Stockdale paradox." This story expresses again how hope sustains us through adversity. Stockdale was a prisoner of war in Vietnam. He was beaten, starved, and isolated from fellow prisoners. He coped by concluding that his life would never be worse than it was then and that, once he was released, his life would never be better.[20]

Collins' Level 5 leaders all possess Stockdale's kind of hope. They are realistic and responsible about the hope they have for the corporation's strategy by looking out the window and in the mirror. These leaders formulate strategy by looking out the window to understand factors external to the company while looking in the mirror to take full responsibility to ensure the firm delivers on its promises. These leaders credit others for success and take responsibility for failure driven by external factors that are often beyond their control. In contrast, like Narcissus, ego-centered leaders look in the mirror to admire all their personal achievements. They look out the window to blame poor performance on external factors.

Character is often the unexamined element in corporate strategy and leadership. The corrupt behavior of the corporate leaders at Enron, WorldCom, Tyco, and too many others to name contributed to a human cry for corporate governance reform. We put faith in reforms, such as increasing the number of outside directors who own stock and separating the role of CEO and board chair. However, there seems to be no difference in shareholder wealth between firms that do or do not enact these reforms. Responsible conduct cannot be legislated. Board effectiveness is driven by how well directors function as a group and with the CEO. Effectiveness depends on where they place their priorities. Responsible and constructive conflict that promotes diversity of perspectives, while maintaining respectful and healthy relationships, will in the end define board effectiveness.

12-8 Corporate Conduct and Hope

Finkelstein's study that examined why smart executives fail, concluded that character was the reason: "perhaps the single most important indicator of potential executive failure is the one that is hardest to precisely define—the question of character. A person who has high ethical standards and deep competence, who desires to succeed by helping others to be better than they would otherwise be on their own, who can face reality even when it's unpleasant and acknowledge when something is wrong, and who engenders trust and promotes honesty in the organizations they create and lead."[21]

Our expectations to be hopeful about corporate strategy should be based more on leader ability to build a healthy culture that adapts to changing circumstances by learning from mistakes—theirs and others'. When this ability is missing, then we rightfully are apprehensive or doubtful good things will happen. Although this is easier said than done, it is a realistic hope that we bet on organizations that adapt to changing market conditions with creativity and open-mindedness. Entrepreneurial people of character are disciplined, are honest, and do not need bureaucracy that adds to corporate overhead and detracts from profitability in tangible and intangible ways. The all-knowing and powerful CEO does not really need people except when he or she wants something done.

Finkelstein developed a set of questions to grade a company on openness to learning. Even though a company earns a good grade in answering all of these questions today, the wise company remembers that the exam is given again tomorrow. All companies are subject to the possibility of failure, even if their executives are smart:

1. Do you believe that the CEO and senior leaders are open to different ideas?
2. Do people believe they can take mistakes to senior management?
3. Does your company have an informal or a formal process for learning from mistakes?
4. Is it standard practice to challenge those who say, "This is how we have always done it?"
5. Is there a set of corporate values that people really believe in and use to handle gray areas of business?[22]

Companies can build in safeguards against blind spots and hubris that provide greater assurance for stakeholders to have realistic hope. GE designed an initiative, entitled "workout," that places managers in an auditorium with all those who report to them and their bosses. Ideas are generated by staff that require the boss to respond in one of three ways: (1) "Great idea, let's implement," (2) "Not a good idea for the following reasons," or (3) "Give me time to study and I will get back to you by . . ." GE also created a "reverse mentoring" program for young managers capable of teaching senior executives about the Internet. Both of these initiatives support GE's intention to break down bureaucracy and hierarchy.

In the same vein, Colgate has "continuous improvement reviews," whereby project teams list past mistakes, select those likely to recur, and offer possible resolutions to each pitfall. This information is archived and constantly improved to benefit future teams.

Initiatives such as GE's workout and reverse mentoring and Colgate's continuous improvement reviews are effective responses to potential blind spots and hubris. Of course, other methods can be effective; the key is responding to the human failings that reside in all of us.

12-9 Leadership Conduct and Hope

Hope firmly grounded in reality has a far better chance for success. Understanding the cost of leadership as well as its benefits can serve executives and their corporations well. Leadership offers the satisfaction of being part of something larger than oneself. It clearly offers the status of personal achievement and associated awards. However, there are significant costs that are not always understood by aspiring or even current leaders. Leadership involves living in a fish bowl, where people are constantly observing what one says and does. This means one cannot always express oneself freely. One is no longer part of the group. Although one is rarely alone, one is often lonely. The problems that come one's way are often those on which people already have an opinion but do not want the responsibility for. Or there may be situations that are too complex for others to resolve. To complicate matters further, honest feedback rarely travels up, so it is difficult to assess how one is doing. Leadership requires significant energy and fortitude to handle long hours and difficult problems that can negatively impact family life. The pay may or may not result in prosperity, but job insecurity often goes along with the potential financial benefits.[23]

Leadership responsibility places individuals under extreme pressure. Problems will arise that cannot be shared at work, and significant others cannot always be helpful. For these reasons, wise leaders participate in formal or informal groups of peers who can discuss openly and in total confidence personal and corporate problems that are keeping them up at night. Some use executive coaches and some form kitchen cabinets comprised of informal trusted advisors. As seen earlier, developmental tools such as a 360-degree performance evaluation can help individuals uncover hidden strengths and provide warning signals about blind spots and hubris. The point is that we all can benefit from responsible, thoughtful, and honest sounding boards that focus us to build stronger companies and communities. Ultimately, leaders serve their own interests if the company adds value in a way that demonstrates character.

12-10 Conclusion

No matter what we learn about the costs and benefits of leadership or common reasons smart executives fail, awareness and insight do not assure wise action. We can be aware and attempt to pay attention to how blind spots and hubris get us off track, but we will also need discipline to learn from our inevitable mistakes. We need to wear our "humility sweater" and avoid "sucking our exhaust." We attempt to avoid human failings. And if we do fail, we can learn ways to deal with that. And interestingly, all this should give us more reason to hope. Humans do have the capacity to look forward to the future with hope.

Chapter Quiz

1. Hope has to do with all of the following *except*
   a. the possible.
   b. the probable.
   c. the profitable.
   d. the preferable.
2. Which of the following is *not* a dimension of hope?
   a. expectation
   b. confidence
   c. apprehension
   d. desire
3. Which of the following is the final level of apprehension?
   a. fear
   b. doubt
   c. suspicion
   d. anxiety

4. All of the following are ways to see reality *except*
   a. supportive.
   b. hostile.
   c. clarity.
   d. indifferent.

5. Which of the following is the counterbalance to apprehension?
   a. confidence
   b. faith
   c. buoyancy
   d. trust

6. What is true about arrogance?
   a. It is a strength of character.
   b. It is a weakness of character.
   c. It is not applicable to character.
   d. It is an asset and liability of character.

7. Guidant was able to overtake what percentage of Johnson & Johnson's market share in surgical stents by respecting and acting on customers' ideas?
   a. 10 percent
   b. 30 percent
   c. 50 percent
   d. 70 percent

8. According to Marcus Borg, the virtue of hope implicates which of the following virtues?
   a. courage and faith
   b. courage and love
   c. love and prudence
   d. love and faith

9. Which of the following is the primary reason why smart executives fail?
   a. lack of hope
   b. lack of character
   c. lack of prudence
   d. lack of faith

10. What was the purpose of General Electric's "workout" program?
   a. to review employees' performance
   b. to evaluate executives' accomplishments
   c. to review the company's blind spots and hubris
   d. to evaluate the company's employment hierarchy

Note: You can find the correct answers to these questions by taking the quiz and then submitting your answers in the Online Edition. The program will automatically score your submission. If you miss a question, the program will provide the correct answer, a rationale for the answer, and the section number in the chapter where the topic is discussed.

Questions for Thought

1. How do leaders decide what is possible?
2. What tools are available to a leader to determine what is probable?
3. How can a preferred strategy shape the hopes of employees?
4. Describe how business leaders express their hope with the language of expectations. For example, think about earnings expectations.
5. Since hope never comes with a guarantee, what are typical fears and doubts that could be associated with hope?
6. How could confidence be associated with hope?
7. Consider and describe how blind spots imperil hope in a business setting.
8. Consider and describe how hubris imperils hope in a business setting.
9. Describe a situation in which you did not have control. Was hope possible? What options did you consider? If there was more than one option, which one was preferable?

Web Exercises

The Bank of Hawaii asks Hawaiian businesses to participate in a business confidence study each year to help predict the state's economy. Visit the 2005 results of this survey at http://www.boh.com/econ/survey/index.asp and think about what the figures expressed mean to both business leaders and to employees/ prospective employees who live in Hawaii. How do surveys such as this one foster hope or a lack of hope?

Visit http://www.trump.com/main.htm and view information about Donald Trump and his companies. Is Trump a "Peacock?" How does his celebrity status affect his business dealings and personal decisions in business? How would his businesses fare if he was less visible as a celebrity?

Duck and Weave under Pressure

Analysts have learned that a publicly traded company invested $200 million to create a customer relationship management (CRM) system to increase revenue. Because revenue generation will determine whether the company will remain independent, analysts are watching this project closely.

Sam is the project leader, but he is about to retire and has no reason to worry about his job. He leads by fear.

Linda is one of three sponsors for the project and has allocated 50 percent of her 120-member staff to working full-time on this initiative. Through the rumor mill, she learned that the technology portion of the project was likely to miss its deadline by three to six months. The CRM is a self-funded project. The budget assumed revenue increases would more than cover increased technology costs, so a delay in implementation means the project no longer can sustain itself financially.

Bob was leading the technology portion of the project. He wanted to fudge the timetable and spread blame across the company so he wouldn't be held responsible. He feared he would lose his job if he told the truth in a public setting. Linda suggested that Bob outline a plan that was as close to meeting the original goal as possible and that included several options that could be considered for an open discussion. Linda told Bob she would help him deliver the message, so Bob agreed.

Linda met with Sam privately. She told him the company had not learned to move beyond obstacles. The culture caused an inability to overcome obstacles to reach a goal, and the effect was lackluster earnings. Linda requested that Sam set a new tone for an upcoming emergency meeting. She pleaded with Sam to listen to Bob's description of the task and stressed the need to work together constructively. She asked that Sam review Bob's options to meet the CRM deadline and then commit to working together to bring everything to a productive outcome. She told him it would be vital that he resist blaming or taking potshots at a person or department. He didn't explain why, but Sam asked Linda not to tell Kevin, Linda's boss, about the situation and Bob's plans. Kevin was much like Sam, prone to outbursts and blaming others before knowing the facts. However, Linda didn't think it would be in her interest for Kevin to learn the bad news from somebody else. She also thought it was right to intentionally keep Kevin uninformed. She told Sam she would think about his request.

After thinking about Sam's appeal, Linda's instinct led her to the conclusion that Sam might want to be the person to tell Kevin. She also concluded that she needed to be better prepared before her meeting with Kevin. At this point, it wasn't clear to Linda that she understood the problem and possible options, so she spent a day and a sleepless night gathering facts. The next day, she worked up the courage to deliver the bad news to Kevin that the CRM project was behind schedule. Linda requested that Kevin not add to the problem and to wait for the resolution plan, which was starting to take shape. As it turned out, the "heads up" to Kevin gave him time to reflect upon the situation, ask the right questions, and avoid being stunned.

Linda told Sam that she had thought about his request, but had decided to tell Kevin. Initially he was upset, but it was difficult to challenge Linda for keeping her boss informed. Linda reminded Sam that overcoming obstacles required keeping people informed and exploring sound solutions without assigning blame. Sam seemed to relax when Linda shared that Kevin agreed to give the solution a chance.

Linda reminded Sam of their agreement to set a collaborative tone at the meeting that would identify problems and solutions to address the missed deadline. Sam asked Linda to sit next to him in the meeting. Sam started the meeting by saying that he had given Linda permission to kick him if he lost control. He set the right tone to generate creative ways to solve the problem. After hours of tedious discussion, he started to adopt his more typical counterproductive behavior. She kicked him more than once and, although the meeting was less than ideal, it did lead to an agreement with widespread commitment. Ultimately the CRM was implemented almost within budget, but successful enough to have a material impact on earnings.

It was not without good reason that Sam demanded followers execute CRM plans: this project needed to succeed for the company to maintain control over its destiny. Yet, the CRM required follower ownership, so could commitment be achieved only by fear?

Linda was caught in a delicate balance between maintaining her integrity and hanging onto her job. Yet, the more challenging or threatening the situation, the greater the stature of the person who responds well to trouble.

Questions for Discussion

1. How does the way people respond to the fear of losing their job influence hope?
2. How did other virtues encourage or discourage hope in this case?
3. If trust is essential to leading change, how can trust be created when it has been absent?

Endnotes

1. Dante Alighieri, *The Divine Comedy,* The Carlyle-Okey-Wicksteed Translation (New York: The Modern Library, 1950), 22.
2. Sydney Finkelstein, *Why Smart Executives Fail* (New York: Penguin Group, 2003).
3. William F. Lynch, *Images of Hope: Imagination as Healer of the Hopeless* (Notre Dame: Notre Dame University Press, 1965), 32.
4. Jim Collins, *Good to Great: Why Some Companies Make the Leap . . . and Others Don't* (San Francisco: HarperCollins, 2001).
5. Dietrich Bonhoeffer, *Life Together: A Discussion of Christian Fellowship,* trans. John W. Doberstein (New York: Harper & Row, 1954), 26.
6. Finklestein.
7. J.R.R. Tolkein, *The Lord of the Rings: The Two Towers,* DVD directed by Peter Jackson (New Line Home Entertainment, 2003).
8. Finklestein.
9. Marcus J. Borg, *Jesus A New Vision: Spirit, Culture, and the Life of Discipleship* (San Francisco: HarperSan Francisco, 1991), 103.
10. Finkelstein, 3–7.
11. Michael Liedtke, "Thornburgh Aims to Improve the Ethics of Business Leaders," *The Plain Dealer,* January 2, 2004, C2.
12. Finkelstein, 74.
13. Finkelstein.
14. Ibid.
15. Ibid.
16. Ibid., 48.
17. Ibid., 182.
18. Victor E. Frankl, *Man's Search for Meaning* (New York: Perseus, 2000).
19. Borg, 103.
20. Collins.
21. Finkelstein, 263.
22. Ibid., 269.
23. Robert Lee and Sara King, *Discovering the Leader in You* (San Francisco: Jossey-Bass and the Center for Creative Leadership, 2001).

weorth

Worth and Worthiness

13

Outline

Bill Gates and Abraham Lincoln
(*left*) Bill Gates represents worth. (*right*) Lincoln represents worthiness.
Sources: (*left*) © Reuters/CORBIS. (*right*) Library of Congress, Prints and Photographs Division, LC-D416-31.

This chapter purposely uses the language of "worth" as a concluding way to think about both value and virtue. The word *worth* goes back to the Old English word *weorth,* which has a range of meanings: "value, desirable, useful, estimable."

One way of asking what our life is worth can be answered economically. We subtract what we owe (liabilities) from what we own (assets) to calculate our net worth. Clearly, some people are economically worth more than others. Bill Gates and a monk are polar examples of net worth. Bill Gates and all competent business leaders hopefully are able to increase the value of their assets and add value to others with whom they are in contact: shareholders, stakeholders, and recipients of their charity. Our business model appropriately applauds competency, which increases economic worth and encourages value addition all the way around.

We all know that this is not the only goal in life, however. Or if value creation is the only goal, then probably we have aimed too low. If this is our sole goal, then our life is worth less than it otherwise could be. Obviously, this is where the shift in the meaning of worth takes place. In addition to economic value, rich human life must also aspire to virtue. In this sense, the rich life is the good life, in which character counts. One of the

Latin words for *worth* is *dignus,* the root of the word *dignity.* Indeed, dignity is a good way to talk about the noneconomic worth of life. A person of character is a person of dignity—a person of worth. In this sense, there may be no discrepancy between Bill Gates and a monk. Both can be persons of dignity—persons of great worth.

Probably it is better to talk about people of character as "worthy" people. In this sense, people acquire worth—become worthy—as they develop character. We all know that people can be poor in character, just as they can be poor economically. In fact, one might be born into wealth and, in that way, already be worth quite a bit. In this context, worth is inherited. One can also be born into a family that has character, but character is not inherited in the same way as money or property. Our parents' character may be influential, but it is not inherited. To become worthy, one has to learn and develop for oneself.

In addition, we can see that the pursuit of virtue also has practical benefits to adding value. Using this language, we can say that worthiness is the end and worth is the means. Again, the goal of human life is character and the means of a good living is competence. To pull this off, wisdom is needed to integrate the two. In fact, many might see wisdom itself as a virtue. In our list of seven virtues, prudence has many of the same functions as wisdom. Combining character and competence allows us to see how pursuing virtue often enhances value. For example, business is difficult to conduct if people question our worthiness. We stay out of trouble by offering a value proposition to others that integrates virtue.

Another way to express worth and worthiness is "generalized reciprocity," which means some form of the golden rule that is found in all civilized societies. A nineteenth-century French visitor to America, Alexis de Tocqueville, was impressed with the way Americans resisted the attitude "Do unto others before they do unto you." Americans resisted not by following an idealistic code of selflessness but by following "self-interest rightly understood."[1] David Hume, an eighteenth-century Scottish philosopher, provides another clear example of generalized reciprocity:

> Your corn is ripe today; mine will be so tomorrow. Tis profitable for us both that I should labor with you today, and that you should aid me tomorrow. I have no kindness for you, and you know you have as little for me. I will not, therefore, take any pains upon your account; and should I labor with you upon my own account, in expectation of a return, I know I should be disappointed, and that I should not in vain depend on your gratitude. Here then I leave you to labor alone; you treat me the same manner. The seasons change; and both of us lose our harvest for want of mutual confidence and security.[2]

Reciprocity builds "social capital" in ways that serve the giver, not just the receiver. Amazingly, social capital (the level of reciprocity earned among those we know) predicts occupational success, social status, and economic rewards even more than do education and experience, according to studies conducted around the planet. As a predictor, social capital is very useful, but sometimes the predictions do not issue in good news. Unfortunately, where social capital is most needed is where it is most absent. Impoverished communities typically comprise people who lack friends and supporters. Social capital is not a mushy, idealistic concept but is necessary for communities to work.

How do we use wisdom to develop social capital in a way that builds net worth and is worthy? In this concluding chapter, we will use wisdom as an overarching, integrating approach that involves being aware, paying attention, and acting to apply the seven classical virtues to our life.

13-1 Awareness

Probably we all have made things happen, have watched things happen, and have asked what has happened. There is a before and after, as we move from a clueless state to an aware state. To make this move requires that we are open to new insights. To remain unaware means to continually miss things and opportunities. This is true of businesses, too.

A company can be unaware of a shift in customer preferences or competitor responses. Strategic analysis is intended to help leaders become aware of the external and internal factors that influence corporate ability to create wealth. Recall from Chapter 3 the example of retailers' losing business to the Internet and catalogues. They lost business because they were unaware that their competitive advantage was to let people try on clothes. Despite being experienced merchandisers, they were blind to their facilities' being too small and to their staff's discouragement to customers who wanted to see how clothes fit. Every business has its own version of being unaware of their fitting room.

Recall from Chapter 7 that Gilkey revealed how the lawyer within us rationalizes actions as moral, when those around us clearly see us as self-serving. We need reflection to avoid fooling ourselves. Reflection presupposes awareness. In other words, developing character depends on our ability to detect when we select pleasure over service to others. Given our apparent infinite capacity to deceive ourselves, we need to understand the barriers to a moral life. Developing our character requires that we understand our interests, who we are, and human nature. Becoming aware of our moral blind spots is an important step in building character.

We all have blind spots in that we are quick to express what we believe, but we are less likely to be clear about why we believe what we do or how we live a life of virtue. For example, are we aware of how we learned about character? In reflecting on this question, we probably draw on stories and people that involved courage, temperance, justice, prudence, faith, love, and hope. We are likely to remember people and experiences, teachers and parents, who taught us about character. Stories and personal experiences involving character might reveal to us why we believe what we do and how we might live a life guided by virtue; they might also disclose our blind spots to us.

13-2 Attention

There is no assurance that awareness will lead us to pay attention. We can be aware of someone in a room, but not care about them or pay any attention to their presence. However, the moment a thought results in engagement, we move beyond awareness. For example, the entrepreneur suddenly pays attention to ways to solve customer problems, or a monk pays attention to the way virtue is part of his everyday life. When we pay attention, we wonder, listen, and try to understand what is happening. Attention has a focus which awareness does not have.

Recall that Scott Technology asked fire chiefs about equipment that helped them put out fires. They learned about an infrared light attached to a firefighter's helmet that would help him or her locate someone lying on the ground in a smoke-filled room. They learned that, although the light helped save lives, it did not help when someone was under a bed or in a closet. By paying attention to the needs of those putting out fires, Scott designed an infrared light that attached to a firefighter's shoulder using Velcro and an extension wire. This way, the light pointed in the direction he or she was looking but could be removed from his or her jacket without removing a helmet and mask.

Similarly, to add value, we must pay attention to customers. To develop virtue, we must pay attention to how the virtues play a role in our everyday life and, ultimately, define our destiny. A reflective person knows that a busy life requires time for contemplation in order to pay attention to his or her life. Those who are reflective do not all follow the same method to aid their reflection. Some use journals, meditate, read, pray, take nature walks, listen to music, exercise, and the like.

Building social capital by joining groups can help us pay attention to our life. Groups can even lead to health and happiness. Statistically speaking, you are more likely to live a longer life by joining a group than if you quit smoking. Having friends over monthly for meals, joining a book club, and belonging to professional organizations all contribute to our well-being and the well-being of others.[3] Just as those who pay attention to adding value use tools, such as a Balanced Score Card, that promote disciplined execution, developing virtue requires a disciplined, habitual way to do so. For example, a person who wants to live a just life will need to learn how to attend to any situation to determine what is just. Over time, this intentional attention becomes habitual and then the person simply acts justly as a matter of course.

13-3 Action

Action can be momentary or sustained through habit and discipline. If virtue is the desired end, habit and discipline are the means. In the same way, if value is the desired end, habit and discipline are the means.

Consider the role that discipline and ability play according to Bill Walsh's theory of the "middle six" (six of the 11 players fielding a football team), which he used to explain the San Francisco 49ers' football success in winning Super Bowls during the 1980s. Walsh strategically melded the NFL players' differing abilities and disciplines by building a system around his stars. He focused on his middle six players. He also accepted that some players could not or would not change the way they played. He concluded that every team has superstars. In his era, the 49er superstars were Joe Montana, Jerry Rice, and Roger Craig. They had the most ability, arrived early to practice, and left late. In other words, they had the most talent and discipline. Walsh built a system that played to the strength of his most motivated and talented players.

On the other end, every football team has two or three players who have marginal NFL level ability or who have ability but lack discipline. Walsh concluded that he had limited impact on the unwilling or unable. The remaining players constituted the "middle six," people of average NFL ability and discipline. Walsh asserted that, if his system built on the strength of his most able and disciplined and if he could coach his middle six to outperform the other team's middle six, and if he limited his time on those who could not or would not improve, then he would win more games than he lost.[4]

In 2004, Gallup studied a corporate version of the middle six. Gallup measured level of engagement among employees and its impact on productivity. The average company has 28 percent of its employees actively engaged (motivated, disciplined, productive); 55 percent of its employees disengaged (motivated to keep the job but not willing to go beyond the call of duty); and 17 percent actively destructive, working against the goals of the company. When companies are able to change the ratio of the percent engaged, disengaged, and destructive, productivity increases significantly.[5]

Jim Collins asserted that disciplined people, not surprisingly, think and act in a disciplined way that eliminates bureaucracy, lowers costs, and increases the commitment of the best. Tools such as the Balanced Score Card provide companies with a disciplined way to focus the attention of the middle six and to support the stars, so that strategy can be executed.

Just as disciplined sports teams win more than they lose and profitable companies hit or exceed earnings targets, so does a life that integrates virtue and value happen only by intention and discipline. MBA students can integrate value and virtue by selecting a professional experience that kept them up at night. One student recalled his position as a loan officer. He worked for a credit card company that made high-risk, high-interest loans to people with substandard credit. Managers were pressured to increase lending and maintain an acceptable delinquency rate. The business was like a dog chasing its tail—lend more risky loans to substandard customers, which increased delinquency rates and the pressure to collect. Manager turnover was high, but compensation was generous. The MBA worked for a manager who was attracted by the financial opportunity to support his family. The manager enjoyed his family, coached Little League, and was active with his church and community. This otherwise good manager missed loan targets, increased delinquency rates, and found himself on the wrong side of his boss. He responded to the pressure to perform by claiming fraudulent expenses to cover delinquency rates. When this failed, he refinanced loans and forged customer names. The shell game was uncovered when he applied customer payments to delinquent loans. He was fired, repaid fraudulent claims, and returned bonuses to avoid persecution.

The MBA and co-workers were aware of what the manager was doing, although not to the full extent. All remained silent because they liked him and felt sorry for him. The manager never put pressure on others; in fact, he often treated people to lunch and dinner. In reflecting on the incident, the MBA student saw the issues of virtues everywhere. He realized he had lacked courage to act, since he was worried about losing his job. He had failed to fulfill his fiduciary responsibilities. He concluded that temperance and prudence might have saved this manager from getting in so deep that he lost his job and reputation.

The student concluded that he had had a choice to act morally but had failed. Years later this student still regretted that value (high compensation and shareholder wealth) had trumped virtue. Of course, the manager's lack of virtue (fraud) had also been bad for business, since customers do not take kindly to forged signatures and shareholders get hurt when earnings targets are missed.

This example shows that the goal of reflection and discipline is not perfection but progress. The idea is to avoid sleep-walking through life. With this thought in mind, consider the following four questions, which can be used by an MBA class, by a liberal arts class, in an executive forum, or by any thoughtful person.

1. Did I reflect on my life?
- Create a habit of reflection to pay attention to character issues.

2. In what acts of compassion was I involved?
- An act of compassion is a private way to support another person.

3. In what acts of social justice was I involved?
- Social justice is a public act to right a social wrong.

4. Did I learn from my mistakes?
- Progress, not perfection, is the goal.

These four questions describe a way of life for a person striving to develop character. Although competence is related to our natural talents and abilities, disciplined reflection that focuses us on compassion, justice, and learning from our inevitable gaffes will lead to developing and deepening character.

Although we can be rich and lack character, a truly rich person strives to live and act with character. Bill Gates epitomizes a person who competently has acquired incredible wealth but who also is trying to live with character by sharing his wealth. Is he perfect? The U.S. Justice Department and his competitors may think otherwise. Has he shown that character development is always a work in progress? Absolutely.

In 2004, Gates' competence in building a net worth of $46 billion made him the richest man in the world. As Microsoft's largest shareholder, Gates earned an additional $3.3 billion, all of which was donated to his foundation, when the firm announced a shareholder dividend disbursement of $75 billion. Skeptics suggest his motive was to placate shareholders and to resolve lawsuits. CEO Steve Ballmer believes the company is now positioned to grow.[6] Regardless of whether motives included lawsuit resolution, shareholder satisfaction, corporate growth, or social justice, the Gates foundation was gifted an additional $3.3 billion to donate. This is a remarkable philanthropic initiative—an act of character.

A letter written by Bill and Melinda Gates captured their focus on character: "The last few decades of the 20th century brought an incredible burst of innovation, particularly in medical science and information technology. But many of those innovations have yet to reach people living in poverty. . . . This new century brings with it exciting advances in health and learning. We all share the responsibility of ensuring that these opportunities are not out of reach for the people who need them most."[7] The three *As* are clearly present in these words of Gates: awareness of injustice, attention to education and health inequities, and action in the form of a foundation are spelled out. And because it involves action, character goes beyond words.

Issues of poverty and disparity are not solely economics issues, since they call for virtue. These issues appeal to justice, compassion, and prudence. They ask people to trust that human predicaments can be solved, or at least shared. They challenge those materially better off to temper and moderate lifestyles, so that sharing can happen. These issues beg for people of courage and hope.

13-4 Conclusion

Gates' letter captures the motivation of their action: "Our grant making is grounded in the belief that the death of a child in Africa is no less tragic than the death of a child in America and the understanding that those of us who were born in rich countries have a fundamental responsibility to help those who weren't."[8]

Every human life is a story. Bill Gates' story is dramatic. But then, every one of us is living our own drama. How will it end? What will be told? It can be a story guided by character and produced by competence. It can be a good story.

Chapter Quiz

1. The Old English word *weorth* means all of the following *except*
   a. estimable.
   b. useful.
   c. substitutable.
   d. value.

2. Dignity is a noneconomic measure of which of the following?
   a. worth of life
   b. worth of accomplishments
   c. worth of experience
   d. worth of sacrifices

3. How is worthiness acquired?
   a. inherited
   b. adopted
   c. learned
   d. experienced

4. Which of the following best predicts occupational success, social status, and economic rewards?
   a. education
   b. experience
   c. social capital
   d. monetary capital

5. If virtue is the desired end, then which of the following are means?
   a. discipline and action
   b. discipline and habit
   c. action and habit
   d. action and morality

6. Bill Walsh employed which of the following theories to strategically meld players' differing abilities and motivations?
   a. middle four
   b. middle six
   c. top four
   d. top six

7. According to a Gallup poll, what percentage of employees is "actively engaged"?
   a. 28 percent
   b. 38 percent
   c. 48 percent
   d. 58 percent

8. According to a Gallup poll, what percentage of employees is "disengaged"?
  a. 25 percent
  b. 35 percent
  c. 45 percent
  d. 55 percent
9. Which of the following best allows us to develop and deepen character?
  a. abilities
  b. experience
  c. reflection
  d. education
10. In the letter written by Melinda and Bill Gates, all of the following were present as attestations of their character *except*
  a. action.
  b. attention.
  c. awareness.
  d. anxiousness.

Note: You can find the correct answers to these questions by taking the quiz and then submitting your answers in the Online Edition. The program will automatically score your submission. If you miss a question, the program will provide the correct answer, a rationale for the answer, and the section number in the chapter where the topic is discussed.

Questions for Thought

1. Consider how you understand yourself in the world as a business leader. Write an essay that includes your thinking on the following four views:
  a. View of reality
   • Indifferent—reality is not out to get us and is not looking out for us.
   • Hostile—reality is out to get us.
   • Supportive—reality has our best interests at heart.
   • View of the nature of business
   • View of human nature (are people basically good or bad?)
   • View of a company
2. Articulate your own leadership style reflecting on the following:
  a. Describe how each of the seven virtues is already present as a part of this style.
  b. Give an example of your own leadership and personal life to illustrate virtues that you have developed.
  c. If virtues are missing from your leadership style, how might you incorporate them?

3. Articulate your competencies.
   a.   Describe how your competencies enable you to add value.
   b.   Are there ways to enhance the competencies you already have?
   c.   Do you see ways of adding new competencies?

4. In what situations (or can you imagine) have you seen two or more virtues involved at the same time? What were these virtues, and how did you see them interacting?

5. As you reflect on the seven classic virtues, do you think there are two or more virtues that are often in conflict with each other? What are these virtues, and how do they seem to conflict?

6. As you reflect on the seven classic virtues, do you think there are two or more virtues tat often compliment one another? Identify which virtues compliment each other, and explain how they do so.

Web Exercises

Reciprocity in business can be rare, but when it exists, it is very valuable. Progressive Auto Insurance (http://www.progressive.com) will give you a quote on your auto insurance from their company as well as quotes from three or four competing companies. How does this help Progressive? How does it help other companies? Can competing companies realistically expect to have even a small amount of reciprocal business?

Athletes are often known to have charities through which to disperse some of their wealth. Visit these three charities and compare them. Do any seem more worthy than others? How do you determine for yourself what each is worth in terms of contributions of the community at large?

The Tiger Woods Foundation: http://www.twfound.org

The Lance Armstrong Foundation: http://www.laf.org

Billie Jean King's Women's Sports Foundation: http://www.womenssportsfoundation.org

Case

An Earth-Friendly Brewery

Occasionally, stray dogs attracted by french fry–scented exhaust chase "the fatty wagon" that transports customers from the Great Lakes Brewing Company to Jacobs Field. Vermicompost and used vegetable oil are filtered to fuel the diesel-powered van. The firm recently received a $150,000 Ohio Department of Development's Office of Energy Efficiency grant to use cooking oil, diesel, or natural gas to supplement current boiler operations for heat and electricity in the restaurant and brewery.

Socrates called worms the "intestines of the earth" because they eat everything except plaster and glass. These waste-munching legless wonders devour recycled barley, hops, and yeast that remain after brewing. Vermicompost also produces a fertilizer that produces vegetables for the restaurant. Local community gardens grow faster and greener. A local baker who produces 50 to 70 soft pretzels daily, approximately 200 pizzas a week, and 75 to 100 loaves of barley bread also uses worm bins. The cost savings amount to only about 15 percent of the cost of the ingredients, but the baker likes the idea of using a viable product that can be recycled.

"If you can help your community and society as a whole, and make money in the process, what's wrong with that?" asks Dan Conway. Partially filled bottles of beer past their expiration date and those rejected from the assembly line can still be consumed. This beer is used to make salad dressing, cheddar cheese soup, and beer brats for a nearby market.

Trash removal fees have been reduced by 40 percent by recycling all cardboard (5,000 pounds per month), glass (800 pounds per month), plastic (shrink-wrap) and paper from the brewery, restaurants, and offices. All paper products (menus, memos, napkins, product packaging) are printed on 100 percent recycled paper. All carton containers are being changed to nonbleached, recycled material.

"There is no away anymore. Away went away. You're just pushing it on to somebody else," stated co-owner Pat Conway. An idealistic target of 100 percent recycling may not happen, but capital investments have been recouped in operational savings. In the future, new "green products" will generate new sources of revenue. "You don't have to be a tree-hugging, pipe-smoking, bearded leftist to think this can work. Common sense, and frugal, honest, and forward-thinking business practices can help the bottom line, and the environment and society," concludes Pat Conway.

Source: Brian Albrecht, "An Earth-Friendly Brew," *The Plain Dealer Sunday Magazine,* January 16, 2005, pp. 7–9, 20.

Questions for Discussion

1. How is Great Lakes Brewing Company focused on people, planet, and profits?
2. How does this case illustrate ways to create worth and to do what is worthy?

Endnotes

1. Robert D. Putnam, *Bowling Alone: The Collapse and Revival of American Community* (New York: Touchstone Books, 2000), 136.
2. Ibid., 134.
3. Ibid.
4. Bill Walsh and Richard Rapaport, "To Build a Winning Team: An Interview with Head Coach Bill Walsh," *Harvard Business Review,* January, 1 1993.
5. Curt Coffman, "On Engagement and Productive," (Cleveland, OH: Union Club, April 5, 2004).
6. Byron Acohido and Adam Shell, "Microsoft Plans Big Dividend," *USA Today,* July 21, 2004, 1.
7. Bill & Melinda Gates Foundation, http://www.gatesfoundation.org/AboutUs/ LetterFromBillMelindaGates/.
8. Ibid.

Postscript

Postscript from a CEO

Westfield has included the character/competence framework in our leadership development programs because of its practical orientation and its support of our strategic intent to share knowledge and build trust. Peter Rea and Alan Kolp offer a thoughtful guide to help leaders build their character and competence that has supported Westfield's goals and will also support the goals of other companies.

As the complexity of business continues to increase, the profit, nonprofit, and government sectors need leaders who can add economic value produced by their competence and guided by their virtue. The capital markets, insurance, banking, financial services, and auditing can only work when those involved can be trusted due to their competence and character. Just as we must uncover a culture that lacks character, we should celebrate and invest in businesses where character is present.

Trust cannot be taken for granted. Board and senior leaders must work hard to cultivate a culture of character. We need the ideas expressed in this book to clarify ways to make business decisions based on character and competence.

While much has been written about corporate scandals since the beginning of this century, what's missing is a practical guidepost that can help leaders and executives create and strengthen a culture of integrity. Peter Rea and Alan Kolp reveal ways that self-delusion and rationalization need to be checked by trusted advisors, candid feedback, and humility to learn.

Leading with Integrity demonstrates that over the long haul, character is nondiscretionary. The best asset a leader can offer business is character. Those who are in business for the long haul know that over time, character always matters. No company that tries to "look good" for the sake of appearance will ever have a culture of integrity without watchdogs and fear. Character cannot be legislated, but it can be learned with the help of *Leading with Integrity*. Rather than rely on the latest management fad, this text relies on ideas that have stood the test of time. An investment in this book is an investment in the character and competence of leaders and their culture.

Robert Joyce

Professional Responsibilities[1]

Increasingly, professional organizations and corporations are creating codes of ethics or statements about responsibility. An example of this trend includes the professional responsibilities of project management. Project management is a vital skill given that all professional leaders at multiple levels must be competent at scoping and executing projects.

Professional responsibilities for a project manager are both broad-based and encompassing. There are five tasks included under professional responsibilities:

- **Ensure Individual Integrity and Professionalism:** The project manager is expected to act in a professional manner at all times. This includes adhering to all legal requirements, maintaining moral and ethical standards, and protecting the community and all stakeholders even though there may be some conflicting interests among the shareholders. The project manager must be knowledgeable in legal requirements (including professional standards legal requirements), multinational, ethnic, ethical and cultural standards at both the project's location and within the team. Understanding the values set forth by the stakeholders is also necessary.
- **Contribute to the Project Management Knowledge Base:** Project managers are expected to contribute to the project management knowledge base by sharing project management knowledge on such topics as current research, best practices, lessons learned, and continuous improvement efforts. The intent of this contribution is to advance the profession, improve the quality of project management, and improve the capabilities of one's colleagues. Contributions can take the form of articles, presentations, books, and various other media.
- **Enhance Individual Competence:** Project managers are expected to enhance their own individual competencies in the same manner as they contribute to the profession. Usually, the project managers that contribute to the profession enhance their own competencies at the same time.

- **Balance Stakeholder Interests:** All stakeholders may have different values and interests. These competing interests mandate that project managers not only understand stakeholder needs and objectives, but also possess strong conflict resolution skills, negotiation skills, and communication skills.
- **Interact with the Team and Stakeholders in a Professional and Cooperative Manner:** Project managers are expected to understand the ethnic and cultural norms of both the team members and the stakeholders. This leads into the category of cultural diversity and socioeconomic influences such as political differences, national holidays, communication preferences, religious practices, ethical and moral beliefs, and other demographic considerations. Project managers must be willing to embrace diversity, be open-minded, exercise self-control, exhibit empathy, and exercise tolerance with a willingness to compromise.

Code of Professional Conduct

In addition to the five tasks described under professional responsibility, PMI® has developed a Code of Professional Conduct that reinforces these five tasks. The code applies to everyone working in a project environment, not merely the project manager. As such, the code emphasizes that PMP®s must function as "role models" and exhibit characteristics such as honesty, morality, and ethical behavior.

The code has two major sections:

- Responsibilities to the Profession
- Responsibilities to the Customers and the Public
- Responsibilities to the Profession include the following subsections:
  - **Compliance with All Organizational Rules and Policies:** This area emphasizes the need for honesty in providing PMI,® with PMP® application information, testing honesty, and reporting of information to both stakeholders and PMI.® This also includes reporting violations of the Code of Professional Conduct to PMI.®
  - **Candidate/Certificant Professional Practice:** This area emphasizes truthfulness, following legal requirements and maintaining ethical standards.
  - **Advancement of the Profession:** This area focuses on sharing non-proprietary intellectual property but safeguarding classified information.
- Responsibilities to the Customers and the Public have two subsections:
  - **Qualifications, Experience and Performance of Professional Services:** This subsection is basically similar to the previous subsections but focuses on honesty and integrity in dealing with customers and the public.
  - **Conflict of Interest:** This subsection emphasizes the professional relationship and trust that must exist in dealing with the customer, the customer's intellectual property, and that the project manager should avoid situations leading to a conflict of interest.

Special Topics for Professional Responsibility

There are numerous situations that can create problems for project managers in dealing with professional responsibilities expectations. These situations include:

- Maintaining professional integrity
- Adhering to ethical standards
- Recognizing diversity
- Avoiding/reporting conflicts of interest
- Not making project decisions for personal gains
- Receiving gifts from customers and vendors
- Providing gifts to customers and vendors
- Truthfully reporting information
- Willing to identify violations
- Balancing stakeholder needs
- Succumbing to stakeholder pressure
- Managing your firm's intellectual property
- Managing your customer's intellectual property
- Adhering to security and confidentiality requirements
- Abiding by the Code of Professional Conduct

Several of these topics are explained below.

Conflict of Interest: A conflict of interest is a situation where the individual is placed in a compromising position where the individual can gain personally based upon the decisions made. This is also referred to as personal enrichment. There are numerous situations where a project manager is placed in such a position. Examples might be:

- Insider knowledge that the stock will be going up or down
- Being asked to improperly allow employees to use charges numbers on your project even though they are not working on your project
- Receiving or giving inappropriate (by dollar value) gifts
- Receiving unjustified compensation or kickbacks
- Providing the customer with false information just to keep the project alive

Project managers are expected to abide by the PMI® Code of Professional Conduct that makes it clear that project managers should conduct themselves in an ethical manner. Unjust compensation or gains are not only frowned upon but also unacceptable. Unless these conflict of interest situations are understood, the legitimate interests of both the customer and the company may not be forthcoming.

Inappropriate Connections: Not all stakeholders are equal in their ability to influence the decisions made by the project manager. Some stakeholders can provide inappropriate influence/compensation such as:

- A loan with a very low interest rate
- Ability to purchase a product/service at a price that may appear equivalent to a gift
- Ability to receive free gifts such as airline tickets, tickets to athletic events, free meals and entertainment, or even cash

Another form of inappropriate connections would be with family or friends. These individuals may provide you with information or influence by which you could gain personally in a business situation. Examples of affiliation connections might be:

- Receiving insider information
- Receiving privileged information
- Opening doors that you could not open by yourself, at least without some difficulty

Acceptance of Gifts: Today, all companies have rules concerning the acceptance of gifts and their disclosure. While it may be customary in some countries to give or accept gifts, the standard rule is usually to avoid all gifts. Some companies may stipulate limits on when gifts are permitted and the appropriateness of the gift. The gifts might be cash, free meals, or other such items.

Responsibility to Your Company (and Stakeholders): Companies today, more than ever before, are under pressure to maintain ethical practices with customers and suppliers. This could be interpreted as a company Code of Ethics that stipulates the professional behavior expected from the project manager and the team members. This applies specifically to the actions of both the project manager as well as the team members. Some companies even go so far as to develop "Standard Practice Manuals" on how to act in a professional manner. Typical sections of such manuals might be:

- Truthful representation of all information
- Full disclosure of all information
- Protection of company-proprietary information
- Responsibility to report violations
- Full compliance with groups auditing violations
- Full disclosure, and in a timely manner, of all conflicts of interest
- Ensure that all of the team members abide by the above items

Multiple-Choice Questions on Professional Responsibility

1. You have been sent on a business trip to visit one of the companies bidding on a contract to be awarded by your company. You are there to determine the validity of the information in their proposal. They take you to dinner one evening at a very expensive restaurant. When the bill comes, you should:
    a. Thank them for their generosity and let them pay the bill
    b. Thank them for their generosity and tell them that you prefer to pay for your own meal
    c. Offer to pay for the meal for everyone and put it on your company's credit card
    d. Offer to pay the bill, put it on your company's credit card, and make the appropriate adjustment in their bid price to cover the cost of the meals
2. You are preparing a proposal in response to a Request for Proposal (RFP) from a potentially important client. The salesperson in your company working on the proposal tells you to "lie" in the proposal to improve the company's chance of winning the contract. You should:

    a. Do as you are told

    b. Refuse to work on the proposal

    c. Report the matter to either your superior, the project sponsor, or the corporate legal group

    d. Resign from the company

3. You are preparing for a customer interface meeting and your project sponsor asks you to lie to the customer about certain test results. You should:

    a. Do as you are told

    b. Refuse to work on the project from this point forth

    c. Report the matter to either your superior or the corporate legal group for advice

    d. Resign from the company

4. One of the project managers in your company approaches you with a request to use some of the charge numbers from your project (which is currently running under budget) for work on their project (which is currently running over budget). Your contract is a cost-reimbursable contract for a client external to your company. You should:

    a. Do as you are requested

    b. Refuse to do this unless he allows you to use his charges number later on

    c. Report the matter to either your superior, the project sponsor, or the corporate legal group

    d. Ask the project manager to resign from the company

5. You have submitted a proposal to a client as part of a competitive bidding effort. One of the people evaluating your bid informs you that it is customary for you to send them some gifts in order to have a better chance of winning the contract. You should:

    a. Send them some gifts

    b. Do not send any gifts and see what happens

    c. Report the matter to either your superior, the project sponsor, or the corporate legal group for advice

    d. Withdraw the proposal from consideration

6. You just discovered that the company in which your brother-in-law is employed has submitted a proposal to your company. Your brother-in-law has asked you to do everything possible to make sure that his company will win the contract because his job may be in jeopardy. You should:

    a. Do what your brother-in-law requests

    b. Refuse to look into the matter and pretend it never happened

    c. Report the conflict of interest to either your superior, the project sponsor, or the corporate legal group

    d. Hire an attorney for advice

7. As part of a proposal evaluation team, you have discovered that the contract will be awarded to Alpha Company and that a formal announcement will be made in two days. The price of Alpha Company's stock may just skyrocket because of this contract award. You should:

    a. Purchase as much Alpha Company stock as you can within the next two days

    b. Tell family members to purchase the stock

    c. Tell employees in the company to purchase the stock

    d. Do nothing about stock purchases until after the formal announcement has been made

8. Your company has decided to cancel a contract with Beta Company. Only a handful of employees know about this upcoming cancellation. The announcement of the cancellation will not be made for about two days from now. You own several shares of Beta Company stock and know full well that the stock will plunge on the bad news. You should:
   a. Sell your stock as quickly as possible
   b. Sell your stock and tell others whom you know own the stock to do the same thing
   c. Tell the executives to sell their shares if they are stock owners
   d. Do nothing until after the formal announcement is made

9. You are performing a two-day quality audit of one of your suppliers. The supplier asks you to remain a few more days so that they can take you out deep sea fishing and gambling at the local casino. You should:
   a. Accept as long as you complete the audit within two days
   b. Accept but take vacation time for fishing and gambling
   c. Accept their invitation but at a later time so that it does not interfere with the audit
   d. Gracefully decline their invitation

10. You have been assigned as the project manager for a large project in the Pacific Rim. This is a very important project for both your company and the client. In your first meeting with the client, you are presented with a very expensive gift for yourself and another expensive gift for your wife. You were told by your company that this is considered an acceptable custom when doing work in this country. You should:
    a. Gracefully accept both gifts
    b. Gracefully accept both gifts but report only your gift to your company
    c. Gracefully accept both gifts and report both gifts to your company
    d. Gracefully refuse the acceptance of either gift

11. Your company is looking at the purchase of some property for a new plant. You are part of the committee making the final decision. You discover that the owner of a local auto dealership from whom you purchase family cars owns one of the properties. The owner of the dealership tells you in confidence that he will give you a new model car to use for free for up to three years if your company purchases his property for the new plant. You should:
    a. Say thank you and accept the offer
    b. Remove yourself from the committee for conflict of interest
    c. Report the matter to either your superior, the project sponsor, or the corporate legal group for advice
    d. Accept the offer as long as the car is in your spouse's name

12. You company has embarked upon a large project (with you as project manager) and as an output from the project there will be some toxic waste as residue from the manufacturing operations. A subsidiary plan has been developed for the containment and removal of the toxic waste and no environmental danger exists. This information on toxic waste has not been made available to the general public as yet, and the general public does not appear to know about this waste problem. During an interview with local newspaper personnel you are discussing the new project and the question of environmental concerns comes up. You should:

   a. Say there are no problems with environmental concerns

   b. Say that you have not looked at the environmental issues problems as yet

   c. Say nothing and ask for the next question

   d. Be truthful and reply as delicately as possible

13. As a project manager, you establish a project policy that you, in advance of the meeting, review all handouts presented to your external customer during project status review meetings. While reviewing the handouts, you notice that one slide contains company confidential information. Presenting this information to the customer would certainly enhance good will. You should:

   a. Present the information to the customer

   b. Remove the confidential information immediately

   c. Discuss the possible violation with senior management and the legal department before taking any action

   d. Discuss the situation first with the team member that created the slide, and then discuss the possible violation with senior management and the legal department before taking any action

14. You are managing a project for an external client. Your company developed a new testing procedure to validate certain properties of a product and the new testing procedure was developed entirely with internal funds. Your company owns all of the intellectual property rights associated with the new test. The workers that developed the new test used one of the components developed for your current customer as part of the experimental process. The results using the new test showed that the component would actually exceed the customer's expectations. You should:

   a. Show the results to the customer but do not discuss the fact that it came from the new test procedure

   b. Do not show the results of the new test procedure since the customer's specifications call for use of the old test procedures

   c. Change the customer's specifications first and then show the customer the results

   d. Discuss the release of this information with your legal department and senior management before taking any action

15. Using the same scenario as in the previous question, assume that the new test procedure that is expected to be more accurate than the old test procedure indicates that performance will not meet customer specifications whereas the old test indicates that customer specifications will be barely met. You should:

   a. Present the old test results to the customer showing that specification requirements will be met

   b. Show both sets of test results and explain that the new procedure is unproven technology

   c. Change the customer's specifications first and then show the customer the results

   d. Discuss the release of this information with your legal department and senior management before taking any action

16. Your customer has demanded to see the "raw data" test results from last week's testing. Usually the test results are not released to customers until after the company reaches a conclusion on the meaning of the test results. Your customer has heard from the grapevine that the testing showed poor results. Management has left the entire decision up to you. You should:

    a. Show the results and explain that it is simply raw data and that your company's interpretation of the results will be forthcoming

    b. Withhold the information until after the results are verified

    c. Stall for time even if it means lying to the customer

    d. Explain to the customer your company's policy of not releasing raw data

17. One of your team members plays golf with your external customer's project manager. You discover that the employee has been feeding the customer company-sensitive information. You should:

    a. Inform the customer that project information from anyone other than the project manager is not official until released by the project manager

    b. Change the contractual terms and conditions and release the information

    c. Remove the employee from your project team

    d. Explain to the employee the ramifications of his actions and that he still represents the company when not at work; then report this as a violation

18. Your company has a policy that all company-sensitive material must be stored in locked filing cabinets at the end of each day. One of your employees has received several notices from the security office for violating this policy. You should:

    a. Reprimand the employee

    b. Remove the employee from your project

    c. Ask the Human Resources Group to have the employee terminated

    d. Counsel the employee as well as other team members on the importance of confidentiality and the possible consequences for violations

19. You have just received last month's earned value information that must be shown to the customer in the monthly status review meeting. Last month's data showed unfavorable variances that exceeded the permissible threshold limits on time and cost variances. This was the result of a prolonged power outage in the manufacturing area. Your manufacturing engineer tells you that this is not a problem and next month you will be right on target on time and cost as you have been in the last five months. You should:

    a. Provide the data to the customer and be truthful in the explanation of the variances

    b. Adjust the variances so that they fall within the threshold limits since this problem will correct itself next month

    c. Do not report any variances this month

    d. Expand the threshold limits on the acceptable variances but do not tell the customer

20. You are working in a foreign country where it is customary for a customer to present gifts to the contractor's project manager throughout the project as a way of showing appreciation. Declining the gifts would be perceived by the customer as an insult. Your company has a policy on how to report gifts received. The best way to handle this situation would be to:

    a. Refuse all gifts

    b. Send the customer a copy of our company's policy on accepting gifts

    c. Accept the gifts and report the gifts according to policy

    d. Report all gifts even though the policy says that some gifts need not be reported

21. You are interviewing a candidate to fill a project management position in your company. On his resume, he states that he is a PMP.® One of your workers who knows the candidate informs you that he is not a PMP® yet but is planning to take the test next month and certainly expects to pass. You should:

    a. Wait until he passes the exam before interviewing him

    b. Interview him and ask him why he lied

    c. Inform PMI® of the violation

    d. Forget about it and hire him if he looks like the right person for the job

22. You are managing a multinational project from your office in Chicago. Half of your project team are from a foreign country but are living in Chicago while working on your project. These people inform you that two days during next week are national religious holidays in their country and they will be observing the holiday by not coming into work. You should:

    a. Respect their beliefs and say nothing

    b. Force them to work because they are in the United States where their holiday is not celebrated

    c. Tell them that they must work non-compensated overtime when they return to work in order to make up the lost time

    d. Remove them from the project team if possible

23. PMI, informs you that one of your team members, who took the PMP® exam last week and passed, may have had the answers to the questions in advance provided to him by some of your other team members who are also PMP®s and were tutoring him. PMI® is asking for your support in the investigation. You should:

    a. Assist PMI® in the investigation of the violation

    b. Call in the employee for interrogation and counseling

    c. Call in the other team members for interrogation and counseling

    d. Tell PMI® that it is their problem, not your problem

24. One of your team members has been with you for the past year since his graduation from college. The team member informs you that he is now a PMP® and shows you his certificate from PMI® acknowledging this. You wonder how he was qualified to take the exam since he had no prior work experience prior to joining your company one year ago. You should:

    a. Report this to PMI® as a possible violation

    b. Call in the employee for counseling

    c. Ask the employee to surrender his PMP® credentials

    d. Do nothing

25. Four companies have responded to your RFP. Each proposal has a different technical solution to your problem and each proposal states that the information in the proposal is company-proprietary knowledge and not to be shared with anyone. After evaluation of the proposals, you discover that the best technical approach is from the highest bidder. You are unhappy about this. You decide to show the proposal from the highest bidder to the lowest bidder to see if the lowest bidder can provide the same technical solution but at a lower cost. This situation is:

    a. Acceptable since once the proposals are submitted to your company, you have unlimited access to the intellectual property in the proposals

    b. Acceptable since all companies do this

    c. Acceptable as long as you inform the high bidder that you are showing their proposal to the lowest bidder

    d. Unacceptable and is a violation of the Code of Professional Conduct

Answers to the Multiple-Choice Questions

1.	B	14.	D
2.	C	15.	D
3.	C	16.	A
4.	C	17.	D
5.	C	18.	D
6.	C	19.	A
7.	D	20.	D
8.	D	21.	C
9.	D	22.	A
10.	C	23.	A
11.	C	24.	A
12.	D	25.	D
13.	D		

Endnote

1. © 2004 by Dr. Harold Kerzner. All rights reserved.

The Tylenol Tragedies:

A Case Study on Managing Crisis Projects

Abstract

Both the academic community that teaches management policy and strategy coursework and the practitioners appear to be in agreement on the importance of planning, whether it is strategic planning or operational planning. But what if a major crisis happens, especially one that could have an extremely serious consequence upon the financial health, image or reputation of the company? Based upon the seriousness of the crisis, there may not be sufficient time to prepare a plan. Yet, action must be taken as quickly as possible.

During the last week of September and the first week of October in 1982, seven people died ingesting Extra-Strength Tylenol capsules laced with cyanide. Four years later in 1986, the same situation of product tampering of Tylenol occurred again, this time with the death of only one person. During both crises, Johnson & Johnson set the standard on how crises should be managed. Academia has been teaching the Tylenol case study for over two decades as an example of morality and ethics in business and what constitutes effective corporate responsibility.

Understanding Crisis Management

For some time, corporations in specific industries have found it necessary to simulate and analyze worse case scenarios for their products and services. These worst-case scenarios have been referred to as contingency plans, emergency plans or disaster plans. These scenarios are designed around "known unknowns" where at least partial information exists on what events could happen.

Crisis management focuses on the "unknown unknowns" which are tragedies without precedent. Crisis management requires a heads-up approach with a very quick reaction time combined with a concerted effort on the part of possibly all employees. In crisis management, decisions have to be made quickly, often without even partial information and perhaps before the full extent of the damage are known.

In a crisis, events happen so quickly and so unpredictably that it may be impossible to perform any kind of planning. Roles and responsibilities of key individuals may change on a daily basis. There may be very active involvement by a majority of the stakeholders. Company survival could rest entirely on how well a company manages the crisis.

The History of Tylenol

In 1982, Johnson & Johnson was a health care giant with annual sales of over $5.4 billion. Johnson & Johnson owned 150 companies, one of which was McNeil Consumer Products, the maker of Tylenol.

Beginning in 1960, McNeil carefully promoted Tylenol to physicians, hospitals and pharmacies as an alternative pain reliever for people who suffered from the side effects of aspirin. By 1976, McNeil began aggressively advertising Tylenol to the general public, building on its reputation as a "professional product."

With a massive advertising budget, Tylenol's market share dominated other non-prescription painkillers such as Anacin, Bayer aspirin, Bufferin, and Excedrin. By 1982, Tylenol commanded an astounding 37 percent share of the $1 billion plus analgesic market. So much advertising and marketing money was poured into Tylenol that none of the other makers of acetaminophen pain relievers could threaten its dominance. Surprisingly enough, acetaminophen is the only active ingredient in Tylenol, and any drug company could produce the product.

Tylenol accounted for 7 percent of Johnson & Johnson's worldwide sales and 15 percent to 20 percent of its 1981 profits. Even though the U.S. economy was in the midst of a recession in 1981, Johnson & Johnson's earnings were up 16.7 percent, and 1982 looked even better. McNeil executives were predicting that Tylenol could achieve a 50 percent market share within the next few years. Within the previous years (during the recession), the stock had climbed from the low 20's to 46 the night before the poisonings. McNeil and Johnson & Johnson were certainly in an enviable position.

The Tylenol Poisonings

In September 1982, seven people died after taking Extra-Strength Tylenol laced with cyanide. All of the victims were relatively young. These deaths were the first ever to result from what came to be known as product tampering. All seven individuals died within a one-week time period. The symptoms of cyanide poisoning are rapid collapse and coma and are difficult to treat.

On the morning of September 30, 1982, reporters began calling the headquarters of Johnson & Johnson asking about information on Tylenol and Johnson & Johnson's reaction to the deaths. This was the first that Johnson & Johnson had heard about the deaths and the possible link to Tylenol.

The news quickly spread to the fifth floor of Johnson & Johnson's headquarters building in New Brunswick, New Jersey. The Chairman of Johnson & Johnson was James Burke, 57, a 30-year veteran of Johnson & Johnson. The news came as a shock to Chairman Burke. Despite the company's size, the news could have a huge, damaging impact on earnings.

Chairman Burke assigned David Collins, 48, to take charge of coordinating the company's response to the Tylenol crisis. Collins was a former general counsel and company group chairman. A month earlier he had been named to Johnson & Johnson's 12-man executive committee and given the additional job of Chairman of McNeil Consumer Products.

In addition to the personal qualifications of David Collins, there were several reasons why Burked asked him to take charge. First, Burke was a strong proponent of decentralized decision making. Second, Tylenol was a McNeil product and Burke was hoping to insulate the parent company, Johnson & Johnson, from bad publicity. Third, Collins was the Chairman of McNeil and, therefore, had the authority to commit McNeil resources to the crisis.

Collins was asked by Burke to take a lawyer, a public relations aide and a security person and fly immediately to McNeil, 60 miles away in Fort Washington, Pennsylvania, to handle things from there. It was important to Burke to isolate the parent company as much as possible from the potentially bad news that could possibly affect other Johnson & Johnson products. Burke was hoping that the news media would view Tylenol as a McNeil product rather than a Johnson & Johnson product. Having the crisis managed from McNeil rather than Johnson & Johnson corporate certainly seemed the right thing to do at the time.

With very little information available at that time, and very little time to act, the crisis project was managed using three phases. The first phase was discovery, which included the gathering of any and all information from every possible source. The full complexity of the problem had to be known, as well as the associated risks. The second phase was the assessment and quantification of the risks and the containment of potential damage. The third phase was the establishment of a recovery plan and risk mitigation. Unlike traditional "life cycle" phases, which could be months or years in duration, these phases would be in hours or days.

By the time Collins arrived at McNeil, the switchboards were lighting up at both McNeil and Johnson & Johnson. At first the calls came from the newspapers, TV, and radio stations, some as far away as Honolulu and Ireland. But as the story started to break, even more calls began to pour in from pharmacies, doctors, hospitals, poison control centers, and hundreds of panicked consumers, many asking for clarifications (which Johnson & Johnson couldn't give), and many others making what turned out to be false reports of possible poisonings.

"It looked like the plague," remarked Collins. "We had no idea where it would end. And the only information we had was that we didn't know what was going on." Collins's first move was to call an old roommate of his from Notre Dame, a lawyer who handled some of Johnson & Johnson's business in Chicago, and ask him to get down to the Cook County Medical Examiner's Office, find out as much as he could, and call him back at McNeil. "I needed my own eyes and ears on the scene," he said.

However serene the impeccably landscaped McNeil plant grounds appeared to Collins as his helicopter touched down on the pad, inside, the natural order of things was in turmoil. Harried managers were running back and forth between telephone banks and McNeil President Joseph Chiesa's office, bringing in new reports of fatalities and other supposed poisonings. Each bit of information was scribbled with a laundry marker on drawing paper held by a big easel. As the reports accumulated, the sheets were ripped from the easel and pinned up on the walls. Soon the room was papered with a confusing mass of information with arrows drawn between them: victims, causes of deaths, lot numbers on the poisoned Tylenol bottles, the outlets where they had been purchased, dates when they had been manufactured, and the route they had taken through the distribution system—all the way back to the 14 stainless steel machines in Fort Washington that encapsulate and spew out pills at the rate of over 1,000 a minute.

From the start, the company found itself entering a closer relationship with the press than it was accustomed to. Johnson & Johnson bitterly recalled an incident nine years earlier in which the media circulated a misleading report suggesting that some baby powder had been contaminated by asbestos. But in the Tylenol case, Johnson & Johnson opened its doors. For one thing, the company was getting some of its most accurate and up-to-date information about what was going on around the country from the reporters calling in for comment. For another, Johnson & Johnson needed the media to get out as much information to the public as quickly as possible and prevent a panic.

The dangers of trying to manage the news were firmly in mind when the company had to reverse itself on whether any cyanide was used on the premises. It was Collins's first question to McNeil executives when he got off the helicopter. He was told no, but later in the day he learned to his dismay that cyanide was in fact used in the quality assurance facility next to the manufacturing plant to test the purity of raw materials. The public relations department released this startling bit of information to the press the next morning. While the reversal embarrassed the company briefly, Johnson & Johnson's openness made up for any damage to its credibility—the last thing the company could afford to lose under the circumstances.

By the end of the first day, a Thursday spent largely sorting out facts from false alarms, Collins and the other McNeil executives felt strongly that the poisonings did not occur at their plant, either accidentally or intentionally. If someone had dumped a dose of cyanide small enough to escape detection into one of the drug mixing machines, the mixture would have been so diluted as to be nearly harmless, and the contaminated pills would have ended up all around the country, not simply on Chicago's West Side. Moreover, all the samples tested from the lot reported to have poisoned the first five Chicago victims turned out to be normal.

Regardless, the company couldn't take the chance that the whole lot had not been poisoned and recalled all 93,000 bottles scattered across the country, an expensive process for which the telegrams to doctors, hospitals, and distributors alone cost a half million dollars. McNeil also suspended all advertising for Tylenol.

An Important Discovery

The first phase of the crisis ended early Friday morning when the company learned that the sixth victim had been poisoned with Tylenol capsules from a lot manufactured at McNeil's other plant in Round Rock, Texas. That proved the tampering had to have taken place in Chicago and not in the manufacturing process, because poisoning at both plants would have been almost impossible. The discovery was important for the company because it signaled the end of its initial helter-skelter involvement with fact gathering and the beginning of its effort to assess the impact the poisonings would have on its product. Also, Johnson & Johnson had to figure out what to do about it. But for Collins, who had gone to bed exhausted at a nearby motel at 2 A.M. only to be re-awakened an hour later by a phone call reporting the Round Rock development, its significance—like so much else that first day—was not immediately apparent. "The fact the second batch came from Round Rock didn't say a damn thing to me," he admitted, "except that, oh Jesus, now I've got two lots to recall instead of one."[1] This was both bad and good news for Collins. The bad news, obviously, was that two lots had to be recalled. The good news, however, was that it now seemed unlikely that the tampering occurred at McNeil.

Had the incident not been so extraordinary, Johnson & Johnson, ardent in its commitment to decentralization, would have expected McNeil Consumer Products to cope with the problem on its own. Reassuring as it was to have the resources of Johnson & Johnson at its disposal, McNeil executives didn't seem altogether thrilled by the new scrutiny they were getting from above. "Managing a crisis is one thing," said McNeil President Chiesa, "but managing all the helpful advice is another."

In Johnson & Johnson's eyes, the Tylenol crisis was a major public health problem—and a major threat to the company. Johnson & Johnson carefully restricts the company name to relatively few items, such as baby products and Band-Aids. "One of the things that were bothering me," said Burke, "is the extent to which Johnson & Johnson was becoming deeply involved in the affair. The public was learning that Tylenol was a Johnson & Johnson product, and the dilemma was how to protect the name and not incite whoever did this to attack other Johnson & Johnson products." According to company surveys, less than 1 percent of consumers knew before the poisonings that Johnson & Johnson was the parent company behind Tylenol; now more than 47 percent were aware of that fact.[2]

On the weekend of October 9th, Lawrence G. Foster, Johnson & Johnson's vice president for corporate public relations, told the chairman that the crisis had unquestionably become a Johnson & Johnson problem. The company was at risk. Financially it wouldn't topple—Tylenol accounted for only a small fraction of the profits—but there was an international reputation at stake.

On October 10th, Mr. Burke made up his mind. All 150 sister companies would pitch in; there would be no new name or second "fighting" brand. Tylenol would fight under its own flag. It was hell or high water.

The next morning, Monday, Mr. Burke and Mr. Clare, Johnson & Johnson's president, huddled for three hours and concurred on the strategy. Other top executives were notified that afternoon. "It would almost be an admission of some kind of guilt in my opinion to walk away from that name," Mr. Nelson agreed. "We'd be very foolish. And even if a third of this business never came back, we'd still have the top-selling pain reliever in the world. . . . It's better than a sharp stick in the eye."

On Tuesday morning, October 12th, at a meeting of 50 company presidents and corporate staffers, Mr. Burke declared, "This is an unequivocal decision."

Suddenly the corporation had some direction. Bleary eyes got a little brighter; snippy impatience was leavened with occasional humor. The executives even knitted themselves together with shared bromides, such as, "We're the guy who got hit by the truck," or, "Is there more upside than downside if we make this move?"[3]

Burke quickly decided to elevate the management of the crisis to the corporate level, personally taking charge of the company's response and delegating responsibility for running the rest of the company to other members of the executive committee.

The members of the executive committee responsible for developing strategies for the crisis project, as well as crisis decision making, were:

- James Burke, Johnson & Johnson Chairman
- David Clare, Johnson & Johnson President
- George Frazza, General Counsel
- Lawrence Foster, Vice President of Public Relations

- David Collins, McNeil Consumer Products Chairman
- Wayne Nelson, Group Chairman
- Arthur Quilty, Executive Committee member

There were several reasons why Burke decided to take control of the situation himself. First, Burke believed that the crisis could become a national crisis with the future of self-medication at stake. Second, Burke recognized that the reputation of Johnson & Johnson was now at stake, even though all of the spokespeople up to this point were carefully labeled as McNeil employees. Third, and perhaps the toughest decision of all, was Burke's belief that McNeil may not be able to battle the crisis alone.

The fourth reason was the need for a Johnson & Johnson corporate spokesperson. James Burke was about to become the corporate spokesperson. This was one of the few times that a CEO appeared on television. Burke's first decision was to completely cooperate with the news media. The general public, medical community and Food and Drug Administration were immediately notified.

There was some concern that pulling the capsules off of the shelves would provide instant gratification to the killer, resulting in the tampering of other Johnson & Johnson products. Also, there could be a whole series of "copycat" tampering that could affect the entire industry.

There was also a discussion over offering a reward for information leading to prosecution of the killer. At first, they settled for a $1 million reward leading to the culprit's conviction. However, the FBI feared that this would result in more blind leads than the agency could handle. The reward was then reduced to $100,000 and announced at a news conference.

Instead of providing incomplete information or only the most critical pieces and stonewalling the media, Burke provided all information available. He quickly and honestly answered all questions from anyone. This was the first time that a corporate CEO had become so visible to the media and the public. James Burke spoke with an aura of trust.

Tylenol quickly captured the nation's attention. Queries from the press on the Tylenol story exceeded 2,500. Two news clipping services generated in excess of 125,000 clippings. One of them said the Tylenol story had resulted in the widest domestic coverage of any story since the assassination of President John F. Kennedy. Associated Press and United Press International gave it second place as the impact story of 1982—only coverage of the nation's economy ranked higher. The television and radio coverage was staggering.[4]

Before the first week came to an end, more than 100 state and Federal agents were spread across the Chicago area in a painstaking effort to reconstruct the route of the poisoned capsules. The route of the contaminated Tylenol capsules was as follows:

- The capsules were manufactured in Fort Washington, Pennsylvania, and Round Rock, Texas.
- From the plants, McNeil then shipped the capsules to 35 states, including Illinois.
- In Chicago, McNeil delivered the capsules to almost 100 wholesalers, some of whom would keep them in the warehouse for a few days.
- Sometime in August, the wholesalers sold the Tylenol capsules to retail outlets.

The investigators believed that the tampering occurred after the capsules reached Illinois. This was based upon the theory that potassium cyanide is corrosive and would eventually destroy the gelatin shell. Investigators began experimenting with potassium cyanide and its decomposition to see if they could pinpoint the precise point in time when the tampering occurred.

Other investigative teams were focusing on possible disgruntled workers or former employees in one of a number of companies that physically handled the product along its route. The initial conclusion was that the poisoning was a willful act and not a manufacturing accident.

While the first phase had been one of problem identification and containment, the second phase was one of communication. Burke allotted the next week to establishing a good working relationship between the company and the police and health authorities investigating the crime. On Monday, he went to Washington to meet with the FBI and the Food and Drug Administration. Burke had begun to advocate a recall of all Extra-Strength Tylenol capsules but—in a surprising role reversal—both the FBI and the FDA counseled him against recalling the drug precipitously. "The FBI didn't want us to do it," explained Burke, "because it would say to whoever did this: 'Hey, I'm winning. I can bring a major corporation to its knees.' And the FDA argued a recall might cause more public anxiety than it would relieve."

On Tuesday, however, following what appeared to be a copycat strychnine poisoning with Tylenol capsules in California, the FDA agreed with Burke that he had to recall all Tylenol capsules—31 million bottles with a retail value of over $100 million. "Often our society rails against bigness," Burke said, "but this has been an example where size helps. If Tylenol had been a separate company, the decisions would have been much tougher. As it was, it was hard to convince the McNeil people that we didn't care what it cost to fix the problem."[5]

There were several options available to Burke and the strategy committee. Some of the options included:

- Do nothing and hope the problem goes away. This was unlikely since the media and the consumers were expecting action. More and more people were now aware of the problem. (Although this was an option, Johnson & Johnson would never sit by idly and do nothing.)
- Tell the Johnson & Johnson story in hopes that the public will be sympathetic and Tylenol can recover quickly.
- Take aggressive action in a search for the killer, placing all blame elsewhere.
- Replace the capsules with another type of product (i.e., caplets).
- Recall only those batches that were contaminated.
- Recall all Extra-Strength Tylenol capsules.
- After recall, relaunch the product under the same name but different packaging.
- After recall, relaunch the product under a different name and different packaging.

Deciding which option to select would certainly be a difficult decision. Looking over Burke's shoulder were the stakeholders who would be affected by Johnson & Johnson's decision. Among the stakeholders were stockholders, lending institutions, employees, managers, suppliers, government agencies, and the consumers.

Consumers: The consumers had the greatest stake in the crisis because their lives were on the line. The consumers must have confidence in the products they purchase and believe that they were safe to use as directed.

Stockholders: The stockholders had a financial interest in the selling price of the stock and the dividends. If the cost of removal and replacement, or in the worst-case scenario of product redesign, were substantial, it could lead to a financial hardship for some investors that were relying on the income.

Lending Institutions: Lending institutions provide loans and lines of credit. If the present and/or future revenue stream is impaired, then the funds available might be reduced and the interest rate charge could increase. The future revenue stream of its products could affect the quality rating of its debt.

Government: The primary concern of the government was in protecting public health. In this regard, government law enforcement agencies were committed to apprehending the murderer. Other government agencies would provide assistance in promoting and designing tamper-resistant packages in an effort to restore consumer confidence.

Management: Company management had the responsibility to protect the image of the company, as well as its profitability. To do this, management must convince the public that management will take whatever steps are necessary to protect the consumer.

Employees: Employees have the same concerns as management but are also somewhat worried about possible loss of income or even employment.

Whatever decision Johnson & Johnson selected was certain to displease at least some of the stakeholders. Therefore, how does a company decide which stakeholders' needs are more important? How does a company prioritize stakeholders?

For Jim Burke and the entire strategy committee, the decision was not very difficult—just follow the corporate credo.

For more than 45 years, Johnson & Johnson had a corporate credo, shown later in this appendix, which clearly stated that the company's first priority is to the users of Johnson & Johnson's products and services. Everyone knew the credo, what it stood for, and the fact that it must be followed. The corporate credo guided the decision-making process, and everyone knew it without having to be told.

When the crisis had ended, Burke recalled that no meeting had been convened for the first critical decision: to be open with the press and put the consumer's interest first. "Every one of us knew what we had to do," Mr. Burke commented. "There was no need to meet. We had the credo philosophy to guide us."

By mid-week, an extortion note threatening a second wave of poisonings turned up at McNeil. "Imagine our reaction," explained Collins. "We get this note that says send $1 million to a bank account number at Continental Bank in Illinois. We had to laugh. This guy's gotta be an idiot. We're still not convinced he did it."

Through advertisements promising to exchange capsules for tablets, through thousands of letters to the trade, and through statements to the media, the company was hoping to demystify the incident. "There was a lot of noise out there, most of it associating Tylenol with death," said Chiesa. "We wanted to clear up any misunderstanding, to make sure everyone had all the facts we did, that the problem was limited to one area of the country, and only a few bottles of Tylenol capsules were contaminated.[6]

Advice was pouring in by the sackful. A Pittsburgh man offered some new names for Tylenol—perhaps Lespane or Apamin or Painex. There was a suggestion from Atlantic City that Tylenol be canned like chili. An Ontario couple sent $10—which was returned—as a contribution to the reward.

A psychic in Schenectady, N.Y., breezily notified the company that the killer was a Chicago pharmacist "dressed in a white smock, buttoned up to the neck, and white trousers." A boy sent a $5 billion extortion note, carefully composed of letters clipped from the newspaper, and included his home address. The Colorado School of Mines offered to extract cyanide from any contaminated capsules so thoroughly that they could still be marketed. Thanks anyway, the company politely replied.

"There are some very real problems with all the suggestions put forth," Mr. Burke argued. "Tylenol II: Change the color from red to green because red is stop, green is go; change the name.

"The public collectively just isn't easy to fool. When the public is watching carefully, they make incredibly smart decisions. They're just so much smarter collectively than we are individually."[7]

Worst-Case Scenario

From the start, Burke squelched one obvious option: abandoning Tylenol and reintroducing the pain reliever under a new name. Despite the long odds many outside marketing experts gave against a complete comeback, and the fact that sales of Tylenol products initially dropped 80 percent, company executives said they never had any question about whether to bring back Tylenol. Said Wayne Nelson, Collins's predecessor at McNeil, who was now a company group chairman, "Even in our worst-case scenarios where we get back only half the base we had before, it would still be the market leader."

By the second weekend, Burke had moved on to the third phase: rebuilding the brand. "We were still in a state of shock," explained Burke. "It's like going through a death in the family. But the urgency of bringing about Tylenol's recovery makes it important we move out of the mourning stage faster than usual."

Good News, Bad News

It seemed clear that the company would have to come up with a new tamper-resistant package, as would the rest of the drug industry. But how consumers ultimately felt about the product—and what conflicts the poisonings posed in their minds—would be the determining factor in the comeback. Burke called in Young & Rubicam, Johnson & Johnson's oldest advertising agency, to begin polling consumer attitudes. Initially he wanted to know how the public was reacting to the crisis, but he also knew the surveys would be indispensable in building a data base for what was obviously going to be, as he put it, "a very complicated communications problem."

One of the more astonishing things learned from the first surveys was than an overwhelming number of people—94 percent of the consumers surveyed—were aware that Tylenol had been involved with the poisonings. The implications of that figure, when coupled with other data, were both good and bad.

The good news, said Burke, was that 87 percent of the Tylenol users surveyed said they realized the maker of Tylenol was not responsible for the deaths. The bad news was that although a high percentage didn't blame Tylenol, 61 percent still said they were not likely to buy Extra-Strength capsules in the future. Worse, 50 percent felt that way about Tylenol tablets as well as capsules. In short, many consumers knew it wasn't Tylenol's fault but said they were not going to buy it anyway, revealing a fear associated with the name that was not likely to dissipate soon.

The most heartening piece of information in the surveys—and the one on which the company based its comeback strategy—was that the frequent Tylenol user seemed much more inclined to go back to the product than the infrequent user. The message: the company can forget about making new converts in the next year or two. Instead, it would concentrate on bringing back to the fold the loyal customers of the past.

"People forget how we built up such a big and important franchise," said Burke. "It was based on trust. People started taking Tylenol in hospitals or because their doctors recommended it. In other words, they were not well and in a highly emotional state." The contrary view, it can be argued, is that those same people who originally bought Tylenol because they didn't want to take a chance on aspirin's side effects are the last people who would want to take a chance now with the emotionally charged brand name.

The competition was not standing idly by. American Home Products had increased production of its acetaminophen, Anacin-3, at both its plants from two to three shifts on a round-the-clock basis. Bristol-Myers did not discuss any marketing plans it had for its acetaminophen, Datril, except to say that demand was up considerably and the company was looking into new packaging for all its analgesic products.[8]

Tamper-Resistant Packaging

After the tamperings in the Chicago area in the fall of 1982, the over-the-counter medications and the packaging industries examined a broad range of technologies designed to protect the consumer against product tamperings. Johnson & Johnson conducted an exhaustive review of virtually every viable technology. Ultimately, they selected for Tylenol capsules a triple safety sealed system that consisted of glued flaps on the outer box, a tight printed plastic seal over the cap and neck of the bottle and a strong foil seal over the mouth of the bottle.

The decision to reintroduce capsules was based on marketing research done during that time. This research indicated that the capsules remained the dosage form of choice for many consumers. Many felt it was easier to swallow, and some felt that it provided more potent pain relief. While there was no basis in fact for the latter perception—tablets, caplets and capsules are all equally effective—it was not an irrelevant consideration. "To the extent that some people think a pain reliever may be more powerful, a better result can often be achieved," said Burke. "This is due to a placebo effect but is nonetheless beneficial to the consumer."

Given these findings and Johnson & Johnson's confidence in the new triple-seal packaging system, the decision was made to reintroduce Extra-Strength Tylenol pain relievers in capsule form.

The Race Begins

It would not be easy designing a new tamper-resistant package. There were a thousand tasks, and each time one was completed, two others seemed to spring up in its stead. Nothing was more crucial than the new packaging, and the chairman headed the task force on tamper resistance himself. Everyone in the industry realized that the first product on the market to be sheathed in some kind of anti-tampering protection would reap enormous psychological benefits. And that meant dollars—each share of the analgesic market was worth $15 million to retail sales.

A small team was formed at McNeil, quickly christened Machiavelli & Co., which tried to outwit the dozen or so tamper-resistant methods available. "Tylenol had been on TV right along side a skull and crossbones." Mr. Clare said, "So we knew whatever the rest of industry was going to do, we had to do more."

After a mad scramble among the drug companies for machines and material, McNeil settled on a triple seal: A glued carton; a shrink sleeve on the bottleneck; and foil covering beneath the cap. It was decided that the first "put ups," or shipments, would be Extra-Strength Tylenol capsules in bottles of 50, the most popular size.

By this time, the engineers and executives were beginning to think of the whole ordeal as a kind of over-the-counter space race. Production went to three shifts, seven days a week. There were agonizing logistical roadblocks—the shrink sleeve, for instance, had to be mounted by hand, despite a search through Asia and Europe for enough machinery.

Carton machinery had to be reconfigured to glue rather than fold boxes. New graphics had to be designed. They wanted to call the anti-tampering device the Tylenol "safety seal," but first they had to hunt down the man who owned the trademark to that phrase and license it from him for $2,000 a year.[9]

"There probably are as many emergency plans worked out and ready to go within the Johnson & Johnson organization as there are in any other company that tries to prepare for unforeseen emergencies," David R. Clare, president of Johnson & Johnson and chairman of its Executive Committee, commented. "But the events surrounding the Tylenol crisis were so atypical that we found ourselves improvising every step of the way.

I doubt that even now we could devise a plan of action to deal with all aspects of the Tylenol situation. Events happened so quickly and so unpredictably that it would be impossible to anticipate the critical decisions that had to be made."[10]

Estimates on the extra cost ranged from a penny to 4 cents a bottle. But somehow no one had thought of whether to pass it along to the customer until Joe Chiesa, the McNeil president, suddenly announced on a television talk show late one night that the company would eat the price increase. The Johnson & Johnson executives were stunned. Of course! Brilliant!

"If he hadn't made that judgment, I think we would have horsewhipped him," Mr. Burke quipped.

The packaging frenzy came to a climax on Thursday afternoon, November 4th. Mr. Burke, Mr. Frazza and Mr. Collins swooped down to Washington in the company chopper for an emergency meeting with Richard Schweiker, secretary of health and human services, and Dr. Hayes of the FDA. In mid-meeting, the chairman pulled out samples of the newly packaged capsules.

Both Mr. Schweiker and Dr. Hayes had trouble getting the bottles open. The secretary turned to Mr. Burke and said, "Everybody else is going to have a package. You've got an armored tank."

Amid this small triumph there were dozens of other critical decisions to make. No mine field was more hazardous than advertising. If the product wasn't aggressively peddled, the market would wither away permanently. But, if the company was perceived as pushy or manipulative, consumers would balk at returning to the fold.

Mr. Burke and his executives watched nearly six hours of taped consumer reactions to Tylenol. They commissioned survey after survey of public sentiment. The polls showed that one American in five still didn't know the tampering had occurred outside the plant, but they also showed that millions would be willing to take Tylenol capsules again if the bottles were made tamper-proof.

The campaign began to take shape. Three commercials were filmed, all geared at luring back former users since the surveys indicated that consumers who had never taken Tylenol before were a hopeless cause for now. A print ad was drafted for release November 21st that said, "The Makers of Tylenol want to say 'THANK YOU, AMERICA' for your continuing confidence and support."[11]

The Marketing War

The makers of Tylenol embarked on an extremely delicate mission of psychological warfare. Timing was crucial. If Johnson & Johnson brought Tylenol back before the hysteria had subsided, the product could die on the shelves. If the company waited too long, the competition could gain an enormous lead.

Sophisticated though the consumer surveys were, they didn't give a clear answer on timing. "The problem with consumer research," said an impatient Joe Chiesa, "is that it reflects attitudes and not behavior. The best way to know what consumers are really going to do is put the product back on the shelves and let them vote with their hands."

With carefully measured public service–like ads vowing to regain consumer trust, the company had set a discreet tone for its new campaign. Said Collins, "We're coming back against a tragedy, so there's no way we can come riding in on elephants, blowing horns and saying here we are."

Perhaps even more important was the effort that most of the public didn't see. At the end of October, a month to the day after the crisis began, Burke mobilized 2,259 salespeople from all of Johnson & Johnson's domestic subsidiaries to persuade doctors and pharmacists to begin recommending Tylenol tablets to patients and customers. It was the same road the makers of Tylenol took when they began marketing the product 22 years ago. Tylenol was not out of the game, but it was back at square one.[12]

Everything was in place. Return to the marketplace would be announced in a New York news conference on Thursday, November 11th, and transmitted by satellite to 30 cities. Then Mr. Burke would fly to San Diego for a "high road" speech to a convention of editors, stressing that "we don't want to let the bastard (the killer) win."

The rest would be up to the consumer. And the courts would decide whether Johnson & Johnson should have foreseen the lunatic in Chicago. The question persists: Should the packages have been tamper-resistant?[13]

From the day the deaths were linked to the poisoned Tylenol until the recall on Thursday, November 11th, Johnson & Johnson succeeded in portraying itself to the public as a company willing to do what was right, regardless of cost.

Serving the public interest has simultaneously saved the company's reputation. That lesson in public responsibility—the public relations—will survive at Johnson & Johnson, regardless of what happened to Tylenol.

The Tylenol Recovery

From crisis to comeback, the following is just a partial list of activities undertaken by the company:

- McNeil established toll-free consumer hot lines in the first week of the crisis to respond to inquiries related to the safety of Tylenol. Through November, more than 30,000 phone calls had been handled through this medium.
- A full-page ad was placed in major newspapers across the country on October 12th, offering consumers the opportunity to exchange capsules for tablets.
- In October, Johnson & Johnson communicated by letter on two separate occasions with its domestic employees and retirees, keeping them updated on important information and expressing thanks for continued support and assistance. In part, the communication urged employees and friends of Johnson & Johnson to request that Tylenol tablets be returned to those local drug stores and retail outlets where they had been removed.
- A 60-second spot was broadcast in October and November featuring Dr. Thomas Gates, medical director for McNeil, alerting consumers to the impending return of the Tylenol capsules in tamper-resistant packaging. An estimated 85 percent of all TV households in the U.S. saw the commercial an average of 2.5 times during the first week of airing.
- Members of the corporate relations department of Johnson & Johnson visited more than 160 congressional offices in Washington to accomplish a number of goals related to the Tylenol comeback. These included voicing support for federal criminal legislation making product tampering a felony and endorsing public service announcements by the Food & Drug Administration on tamper-resistant packaging. Resolutions are now under consideration in Congress to commend the FDA, the industry and Johnson & Johnson for the prompt and effective response to the Tylenol crisis.
- Johnson & Johnson executives made personal appearances or were interviewed for such print and video feature presentations as *Fortune, The Wall Street Journal, 60 Minutes, The Donahue Show, ABC Nightline* and *Live at Five* (New York). A number of additional executives were briefed for interviews on Tylenol that were being requested by TV and radio talk shows.
- Four videotaped special reports on the Tylenol crisis and comeback were prepared and distributed or shown to employees and retirees. The tapes, which lasted more than three hours, covered all important aspects of the evolving Tylenol story and treated at length the November 11 teleconference and the appearance of James E. Burke, Chairman of the Board, on the *Donahue Show.*
- The Johnson & Johnson quarterly report in October informed stockholders of the impact of the Tylenol capsule withdrawal.
- A four-minute videotape was prepared for use by television programs covering tamper-resistant packaging. The footage depicted the production of Tylenol in the new tamper-resistant packaging and established the important triple-seal features as the standard for the industry.
- As a matter of policy, all letters directed to Johnson & Johnson and McNeil on Tylenol from consumers were answered. By late November, the company had responded to more than 3,000 inquiries and letters of support.[14]

By Christmas week, 1982, Tylenol had recovered 67 percent of its original market. The product was coming back faster and stronger than the company had anticipated.

Among the key components of the McNeil/Johnson & Johnson Tylenol comeback campaign were the following:

- Tylenol capsules were reintroduced in November in triple-seal, tamper-resistant packaging, with the new packages beginning to appear on retail shelves in December. Despite the unsettled conditions at McNeil caused by the withdrawal of the Tylenol capsules in October, the company, with its new triple-sealed package, was the first in the industry to respond to the national mandate for tamper-resistant packaging and the new regulations from the Food & Drug Administration.
- In an effort to encourage the American consumer to become reaccustomed to using Tylenol, McNeil Consumer Products Company provided the opportunity of obtaining free $2.50-off coupons good toward the purchase of any Tylenol product. Consumers simply phoned a special toll-free number to be placed on the list of those receiving the coupons. The same offer was made on two separate occasions in November and December through high-circulation newspapers containing the $2.50 coupon. McNeil estimates that these two programs would stimulate millions of trials of Tylenol before the end of the year.
- McNeil sales people were working to recover former stock levels for Tylenol by implementing an off-invoice pricing program that provided the buyer with discounts linked to wholesale purchasing patterns established prior to October. Discounts went as high as 25 percent.[15]

Three years later, by 1985, the company had recovered virtually its entire market share, outselling the next four analgesics combined. The company had spent more than $175 million to survive and conquer what was potentially one of the biggest disasters in the drug industry. This included more than $60 million in one year's advertising to re-introduce its new Tylenol. The Tylenol disaster had far-reaching effects in that virtually all nonprescription drugs, as well as other products, were now packaged in tamper-resistant packages.

Some people believed that James Burke almost single-handedly saved Tylenol, especially when Wall Street believed that the Tylenol name was dead. Burke had courageously made some decisions against the advice of government agents and some of his own colleagues. He appeared on a variety of talk shows, such as the *Phil Donahue Show* and *60 Minutes*. His open and honest approach to the crisis convinced people that Johnson & Johnson was also a victim. According to Johnson & Johnson spokesman, Bob Andrews, "The American public saw this company was also the victim of an unfortunate incident and gave us our market back."

Both Johnson & Johnson and James Burke received nothing but accolades and support from the media and general public in the way the crisis was handled. A sampling of opinion from newspapers across the United States includes:

- *Wall Street Journal:* "Johnson & Johnson, the parent company that makes Tylenol, set the pattern of industry response. Without being asked, it quickly withdrew Extra-Strength Tylenol from the market at a very considerable expense . . . the company chose to take a large loss rather than expose anyone to further risk. The anti-corporation movement may have trouble squaring that with the devil theories it purveys."
- *Washington Post:* "Though the hysteria and frustration generated by random murder have often obscured the company's actions, Johnson & Johnson has effectively demonstrated how a major business ought to handle a disaster. From the day the deaths were linked to the poisoned Tylenol . . . Johnson & Johnson has succeeded in portraying itself to the public as a company willing to do what's right regardless of cost."

- *Express and News* (San Antonio, Tex): "In spite of the $100 million loss it was facing, the company . . . never put its interests ahead of solving the murders and protecting the public. Such corporate responsibility deserves support."
- *Evening Independent* (St. Petersburg, Fla): "The company has been straight-forward and honest since the first news of the possible Tylenol link in the Chicago-area deaths. Some firms would have tried to cover up, lie or say 'no comment.' Johnson & Johnson knows better. Its first concern was to safeguard the public from further contamination, and the best way to do that was to let people know what had occurred by speaking frankly with the news media."
- *Morning News* (Savannah, Ga.): "Tylenol's makers deserve applause for their valiant attempt to recover from the terrible flow they have suffered . . ."[16]

Federal and local law enforcement agencies had logged into the computer some 20,000 names of potential Tylenol killers, and 400 of them were scrutinized extensively. Two of them were eventually convicted. James Lewis, 40 years old, admitted writing a letter to Johnson & Johnson threatening more deaths unless he was paid $1 million. He was found guilty of extortion and received a 10-year sentence in Federal prison.

Six weeks after the murders, after receiving a tip, police questioned Roger Arnold, 48 years old, a laborer in the Jewel Food Stores warehouse. He was released due to lack of evidence. The next June, according to the police, he shot and killed a man he believed to be a tipster. He was convicted of second-degree murder. Neither Lewis, nor Arnold nor anyone else was convicted for the original Tylenol deaths.

The Corporate Culture

The speed with which a company can react to a crisis is often dependent upon the corporate culture. If the culture of the firm promotes individualism and internal competition, employees will feel threatened by the crisis, become non-supportive and refuse to help even if it were to be in their own best interest. Such was not the case at Johnson & Johnson. The culture at Johnson & Johnson was one of cooperation. Employees were volunteering to assist in any way possible to help Johnson & Johnson and McNeil out of the crisis.

On November 11, 1982, Mr. Burke announced that Johnson & Johnson would give consumers a free $2.50 coupon good towards the purchase of any Tylenol product. The free coupon could be obtained by calling an 800 number which Mr. Burke gave out at a teleconference for the media, portions of which were rebroadcast on local TV and radio news shows.

Within minutes after the conference closed, a telephone center that had been set up at McNeil headquarters in Fort Washington, Pa., was swamped with calls—and would continue to be inundated for the next two weeks.

In fact, the number of calls proved to be much more than McNeil management had anticipated. The day after the teleconference, Peter Scarperi, vice president of finance and a member of the management board, appealed to McNeil employees to pitch in and handle the phones on a volunteer basis—on the weekend. How fast was the response? "Within an hour we had all the people we needed for nearly the entire weekend," said Mr. Scarperi.[17] During the 11-day period following the announcement, McNeil received 136,000 calls. By the first week of December, there were over 210,000 calls by consumers.

Emblematic of the responsiveness, determination, and spirit characterizing the manner in which the crisis and the recovery program had been handled—both inside and outside the company—is the story of McNeil's employee buttons. The following is reprinted from TYLINE, a McNeil employee publication:

> "Like everyone, (McNeil employee) Tony McGeorge wanted to be of help any way he could. 'It was so frustrating not to be able to do more,' he said. 'So I headed up an ad hoc employee morale committee (with Logan P. Hottle, director, professional sales staff), and we came up with a suggestion for the button.'

> "The button, of course, is the thumbs-up 'We're coming back' badge worn all over McNeil. The committee received approval for the idea late one Friday afternoon. They called an outside manufacturer and described how the button should look . . . The manufacturer called his production facility in California at 5:30 P.M. Eastern time.

> "The finished buttons were delivered by McNeil by that Sunday noon—free of charge, a gift from the manufacturer."[18]

Four Years Later: The Second Tylenol Tragedy[19]

On Monday afternoon, February 10th, 1986, Johnson & Johnson was informed that Diane Elsroth, a young woman in Westchester County, New York, died of cyanide poisoning after ingesting Extra-Strength Tylenol capsules. Johnson & Johnson immediately sent representatives to Yonkers to attempt to learn more and to assist in the investigation. Johnson & Johnson also began conferring by telephone with the FDA and the FBI both in Washington and at the respective field offices.

Johnson & Johnson endorsed the recommendation of the FDA and local authorities that people in the Bronxville/Yonkers, N.Y., area not take any of these capsules until the investigation was completed. Although from the outset Johnson & Johnson had no reason to believe that this was more than an isolated event, Johnson & Johnson concurred with the FDA recommendation that nationally no one take any capsules from the affected lot number ADF 916 until further notice. The consumers were asked to return products from this lot for credit or exchange. The tainted bottle was part of a batch of 200,000 packages shipped to retailers during the previous August, 95 percent of which had already been sold to consumers. Johnson & Johnson believed other people would have reported problems months ago if the batch had been tainted either at the manufacturing plant or at distribution sites.

Once again Johnson & Johnson made its CEO, James Burke, its lead spokesperson. And once again the media treated Johnson & Johnson fairly because of the openness and availability of James Burke and other Johnson & Johnson personnel. Johnson & Johnson responded rapidly and honestly to all information requests by the media, a lesson remembered from the 1982 Tylenol tragedy.

Johnson & Johnson responded to hundreds of news media inquiries, providing up-to-the minute information, and also held three major press conferences in a week's time at its headquarters. It established a free, "800" telephone hotline through which consumers and retailers could contact McNeil Consumer Products Company to receive the latest information and advisories. And it suspended all television advertisements as of the evening of February 10th.

On February 11th, Johnson & Johnson initiated a pick-up of the entire Tylenol capsule inventory from all retail outlets in a three-mile radius of the store where it is believed the bottle of poisoned capsules was purchased. Laboratories of the FDA and McNeil Consumer Products Company began chemical analyses of capsules retrieved from the Westchester County area. Additionally, as they did in 1982, Johnson & Johnson began polling consumers through independent research organizations to track their awareness and understanding of the extent of the problem and attitudes toward our products.

On the afternoon of February 11th, Johnson & Johnson called a major news conference to aid in the accuracy of the information communicated to the public and to make certain that they were aware of the nature of the problem. The FDA also picked up and analyzed thousands of Tylenol capsules from this area that led to the finding of a second bottle that contained five capsules of cyanide on February 13th.

The second bottle confirmed to be tainted came from the shelves of a Woolworth's store in the New York City suburb of Bronxville, about two blocks from an A&P Food Store that was the source of the capsules taken by Diane Elsroth. The second bottle apparently was manufactured at a different plant than the first.

Within minutes of notification that the FDA had found a second bottle of contaminated capsules, Johnson & Johnson issued a nationwide release to the news media urging consumers not to use Tylenol capsules until further notice. On the evening of the 13th, Johnson & Johnson initiated a withdrawal of all capsule put-ups from wholesalers, retailers and consumers in the Westchester County area. Johnson & Johnson also began urging the trade nationwide to remove all capsule put-ups from their shelves.

At the second news conference on February 14th, Johnson & Johnson again requested retailers to remove Tylenol capsule products from their shelves. All consumers were advised to return those products to Johnson & Johnson. A reward of $100,000 was offered for information leading to the identification of the person or persons responsible for the poisoned Tylenol capsules in Westchester County.

During exhaustive deliberations over the weekend of February 15th and 16th, Johnson & Johnson concluded that the company could no longer guarantee the safety of capsules to a degree consistent with Johnson & Johnson's standards of responsibility to its consumers. The packaged capsules were tamper-resistant, not tamper-proof. Thus, on Monday, February 17th, Johnson & Johnson announced at the third press conference that Johnson & Johnson would no longer manufacture or sell any capsule products made directly available to the consumer, and that they had no plans to reenter this business in the foreseeable future. "We were aided in this judgment by the knowledge that we had the caplet available, a solid dosage form that all our research showed was an acceptable alternative to the majority of our capsule users," remarked Burke. "We also announced on February 17th that we would replace all capsules in the hands of consumers and the trade with caplets or tablets. We issued a toll-free 800 number consumers could call for a product exchange or a full refund, and we announced a Tylenol capsule exchange address."

Withdrawal from the Direct to Consumer Capsule Business

Clearly, circumstances were different in 1986. In light of the Westchester events, Johnson & Johnson no longer believed that they could provide an adequate level of assurance of the safety of hollow capsule products sold direct to consumers. For this reason, they made the decision to go out of that business. "We take this action with great reluctance and a heavy heart," Burke said in announcing the action. "But we cannot control random tampering with capsules after they leave our plant. Therefore, we feel our obligation to consumers is to remove capsules from the market to protect the public." The company, Burke said, had "fought our way back" after the deaths of seven people who ingested cyanide-laced Tylenol capsules in 1982, and "we will do it again. We will encourage consumers to use either the solid tablets or caplets," said Burke. "The caplet is especially well-suited to serve the needs of capsule users. It is oval-shaped like a capsule, 35 percent smaller and coated to facilitate swallowing. It is also hard like a tablet and thus extremely difficult to violate without leaving clearly visible signs. We developed this dosage form as an alternative to the capsule. Since its introduction in 1984, it has become the analgesic dosage form of choice for many consumers."

"While this decision is a financial burden to us, it does not begin to compare to the loss suffered by the family and friends of Diane Elsroth," Burke said, his voice quavering as he referred to the woman who died. He said he had expressed, on behalf of the company, "our heartfelt sympathy to Diane's family and loved ones."

In abandoning the capsule business, Johnson & Johnson had taken the boldest option open to it in dealing with an attack on its prized Tylenol line. At the same time, the company used the publicity generated by the latest Tylenol scare as an opportunity to promote other forms of the drug, particularly its caplets. Johnson & Johnson initially balked at leaving the Tylenol capsule business which represented about one-third of the $525 million in Tylenol sales in 1985. Mr. Burke said he was loath to take such a step, noting that if "we get out of the capsule business, others will get into it." Also, he said, pulling the capsules would be a "victory for terrorism."

In Washington, Food and Drug Administration Commissioner, Frank Young, said the agency respected Johnson & Johnson's decision. "This is a matter of Johnson & Johnson's own business judgment and represents responsible actions under tough circumstances," the agency said in a statement, adding that it "didn't suggest, direct or pressure Johnson & Johnson into this action." Meanwhile, other over-the-counter drug makers said Johnson & Johnson's decision was premature, and some indicated that they wouldn't abandon capsules.

People thought that the 1982 tampering incident meant an end to Tylenol. Now the same people believed that Tylenol would survive because it had demonstrated once that it could do so. If survival would be in caplets, then industry would eventually follow. The FDA was planning to meet with industry officials to discuss what technological changes might be necessary to respond effectively to this problem. At stake was a re-examination of over-the-counter capsules that included dozens of products ranging from Contac decongestant to Dexatrim diet formula.

Conclusion[20]

During congressional testimony, Burke said, "I have been deeply impressed by the commitment and performance of government agencies, especially the FDA and the FBI. I cannot imagine how any organizations could have been more professional, more energetic or more rational in exercising their responsibilities to the American public.

"In addition, the media performed a critical role in telling the public what it needed to know in order to provide for its own protection. In the vast majority of instances, this was accomplished in a timely and accurate fashion. Within the first week following the Westchester incidents, polling revealed nearly 100 percent of consumers in the New York area were aware of the problem. I believe this is an example of how a responsible press can serve the public well being.

"The wide availability of self-medications through the open market in the United States is part of our unparalleled health care delivery system. We must work together to maintain the advantages of this system. For industry and government, this means doing what is appropriate to provide for the safety of consumer products. At the same time, we must maximize the freedom and accessibility needed for maintaining full advantage of an open marketplace—not the least of which is enlightened product selection. For the consumer, this means continued education and awareness. As has often been noted, no system yet designed can absolutely guarantee freedom from product tampering; the careful consumer must always be the most important single element in providing for his or her own safety."

Accolades and Support

Once again, Johnson & Johnson received high marks, this time for the way it handled the second Tylenol tragedy. This was evident from the remarks of Mr. Simonds, McNeil's vice president of marketing. "There's a real unity of purpose and positive attitude here at McNeil. Any reservations people had about the effect of removing capsules from the company's product line are long since resolved. We realized there was no good alternative" to the action announced by Johnson & Johnson Chairman James E. Burke, he says, "as we simply could not guarantee the safety of the capsule form."

As in the aftermath of the 1982 tragedies, Mr. Simonds adds, "everybody at McNeil pulled together." More than 300 McNeil employees manned the consumer phone lines, with four of them fielding calls in Spanish.

The employees were buoyed by unsolicited testimonials from consumers. One man in Savannah, Ga., wrote Mr. Burke that "You and your people deserve the right to walk with pride!" Members of a fifth-grade class in Manchester, Mo., wrote that they "will continue to support and buy your products."

Many of the correspondents did not know what they could do to help but clearly wanted to do something. A man in Yonkers, N.Y. (near where the tampering occurred), for example, wrote, "In my small way I am donating a check in the amount of $10 to offset some of the cost of this kind of terrorism. I would like to donate it in the names of my two children, Candice and Jennifer. Now it (the capsule recall and discontinuation) will only cost Johnson & Johnson $149,999,990." (The check was returned with thanks.)

Nor were the testimonials and words of thanks just from consumers. The *New York Times* said that in dealing with a public crisis "in a forthright way and with his decision to stop selling Tylenol in capsule form, Mr. Burke is receiving praise from analysts, marketing experts and from consumers themselves."

The Cleveland *Plain Dealer* said "the decision to withdraw all over-the-counter capsule medications, in the fact of growing public concern about the vulnerability of such products, was sadly but wisely arrived at."

The magazine *U.S. News and World Report* wrote, "No company likes bad news, and too few prepare for it. For dealing with the unexpected, they could take lessons from Johnson & Johnson."

And columnist Tom Blackburn in the *Miami News* put it this way: "Johnson & Johnson is in business to make money. It has done that very well. But when the going gets tough, the corporation gets human, and that makes it something special in the bloodless business world."

Perhaps most significantly, President Reagan, opening a meeting of the Business Council (comprised of corporate chief executives) in Washington, D.C., said, "Let me congratulate one of your members, someone who in recent days has lived up to the highest ideals of corporate responsibility and grace under pressure. Jim Burke of Johnson & Johnson, you have our deepest admiration."

That kind of support from many sources spurred McNeil, and the results are evident. "There is absolutely no doubt about it. We're coming back—again!"[21]

Johnson & Johnson Credo

We believe our first responsibility is to the doctors, nurses and patients, to mothers and all others who use our products and services. In meeting their needs everything we do must be of high quality. We must constantly strive to reduce our costs in order to maintain reasonable prices. Customers' orders must be serviced promptly and accurately. Our suppliers and distributors must have an opportunity to make a fair profit.

We are responsible to our employees, the men and women who work with us throughout the world. Everyone must be considered as an individual. We must respect their dignity and recognize their merit. They must have a sense of security in their jobs. Compensation must be fair and adequate, and working conditions clean, orderly and safe. Employees must feel free to make suggestions and complaints. There must be equal opportunity for employment, development and advancement for those qualified. We must provide competent management, and their actions must be just and ethical.

We are responsible to the communities in which we live and work and to the world community as well. We must be good citizens—support good works and charities and bear our fair share of taxes. We must encourage civic improvements and better health and education. We must maintain in good order the property we are privileged to use, protecting the environment and natural resources.

Our final responsibility is to our stockholders. Business must make a sound profit. We must experiment with new ideas. Research must be carried on, innovative programs developed and mistakes paid for. New equipment must be purchased, new facilities provided and new products launched. Reserves must be created to provide for adverse times. When we operate according to these principles, the stockholders should realize a fair return.

Source: Reproduced by permission of Johnson & Johnson. This is the 1979–1989 version of the Credo. Small changes were made to the Credo in 1989.

Tylenol Tragedy Questions

1. Aquinas stated that good falls under one of the four philosophical virtues—prudence, justice, temperance and fortitude (courage). He concluded when we choose good or refrain from evil, we have been prudent. When we demonstrate integrity in our behavior with others, we have been just. When we struggle to pursue our desires at the expense of others, we have been temperant and courageous. Aquinas viewed prudence as the "virtue, which commands," justice as the "virtue about due actions between equals," temperance as the virtue "which suppress desires for the pleasure of touch," and fortitude as the virtue "which strengthens against dangers of death." Apply the virtues of prudence, justice, temperance and fortitude to the Tylenol case.[22]

2. Why did Jim Burke originally want McNeil to handle the crisis by themselves without any help from Johnson & Johnson?

3. Why did he later change his mind and make it a Johnson & Johnson problem?

4. What percent of Johnson & Johnson's 1981 profits were attributed to Tylenol?

5. How did Johnson & Johnson handle its relationship with the press right at the beginning when the deaths were first discovered and attributed to poisoned Tylenol capsules?

6. What were the three crisis life cycle phases adopted by Johnson & Johnson?

7. What was the primary concern during the first phase?

8. Why was it "good news" that the contaminated capsules came from two different lots manufactured in two different states?

9. At what level of management were the members of the crisis management committee?

10. Why did Jim Burke personally take charge of the crisis project?

11. What options were available to Burke and Johnson & Johnson during phase 3 of the 1982 poisonings?

12. Who were the stakeholders and how was each affected?

13. What is corporate credo? Is a credo a means of accelerating decision making?

14. Why did the government *not* want Johnson & Johnson to remove all of the Tylenol capsules from the shelves?

15. What strategy did Johnson & Johnson adopt to recover its market share?

16. Was Johnson & Johnson perceived as the culprit or the victim?

17. What options were available to Johnson & Johnson after the 1986 Tylenol tragedy?

18. Why was it easier for Johnson & Johnson to recapture their market share after the 1986 crisis than after the 1982 crisis?

19. Is it possible to develop a perfectly tamper-proof package?

20. How do you protect a firm's reputation during a crisis?

21. Why was Johnson & Johnson's handling of the crisis viewed as successful and Nestlé's (see Appendix C) viewed as a disaster?

Endnotes

1. Adapted from Thomas Moore, "The Fight to Save Tylenol," *Fortune*, November 29, 1982, pp. 44–49, ©1982 Time Inc. All rights reserved.
2. Ibid.
3. Adapted from Rick Atkinson, "The Tylenol Nightmare: How a Corporate Giant Fought Back," *The Kansas City Times*, November 12, 1982, p. 3.
4. Lawrence G. Foster, "The Johnson & Johnson Credo and The Tylenol Crisis," *New Jersey Bell Journal*, 6, No. 1, (Spring 1983), p. 3.
5. "The Fight to Save Tylenol," p. 48.
6. Ibid.
7. "The Tylenol Nightmare," p. 3.
8. "The Fight to Save Tylenol," p. 49.
9. "The Tylenol Nightmare," p. 4.
10. "The Johnson & Johnson Credo and The Tylenol Crisis," p. 2.
11. "The Tylenol Nightmare," p. 4.
12. "The Fight to Save Tylenol," p. 49.
13. "The Tylenol Nightmare," p. 4.
14. "The Tylenol Comeback," A Special Report from the Editors of *Worldwide*, A Publication of Johnson & Johnson Corporate Public Relations, undated, reprinted from Johnson & Johnson Worldwide, 17, No. 5 (December, 1982).
15. Ibid.
16. Ibid.
17. Ibid.
18. Ibid.
19. This entire section has been adapted from James E. Burke's speech presented to the U.S. Senate Committee on Labor and Human Resources, February 28, 1986.
20. Ibid.
21. "Tylenol Begins Making a Solid Recovery," *Worldwide*, A Publication of Johnson & Johnson Corporate Public Relations, 1986.
22. Peter Gomes, *The Good Life: Truths That Last in Times of Need*, Harper: San Francisco, 2002, pp. 215–16.

Nestlé's Marketing of Infant Formula:

A Case Study of Criticism and Corporate Response

Introduction

Corporations have an obligation to provide social responsibility, hopefully, without any impact on the profitability of the firm. During the past 40 years, laws, guidelines, and social responsibility codes have been enacted. But what happens if the guidelines, codes, and laws are non-existent? What happens if the corporation truly believes that they are serving humanity, but at the same time part of society believes that an injustice has occurred? Such was the case of Nestlé's where corporate management emphatically believed that they were serving humanity with the distribution of infant formula to Third World nations. However, infant mortality occurred, estimated to be in the thousands, as a result of Nestlé's aggressive marketing campaign.

Background to Social Responsibility

The role of business today is more than just producing goods or services for a profit. Businesses must respond to the needs of its stakeholders, especially those groups that can bring significant pressure to bear. If the special interest groups cannot convince the firm to demonstrate social responsibility, then government agencies will step in and enact laws that can affect the operation of the business as illusrated in Exhibit 1.[1] These laws exist for the purpose of enforcing a firm's social responsibility.

Exhibit 2 identifies ways corporations can be socially responsible and profitable.[2]

Recognizing the need for social responsibility is easier than actually doing it. Social responsibility can be identified either by the actions of the company or by the individual actions of its officers. In 1997, Ted Turner, who owned 10% of Time Warner Inc., donated $1 billion, one-third of his net worth, to United Nations Charities. Turner stated, "I'm putting every rich person in the World on notice that they're going to be hearing from me about giving money. If you want to lead, you got to blow the horn and get out in front of the parade."[3] Most corporations do not have CEO's like Ted Turner or Bill Gates whose personal wealth and donations can be viewed as the corporation's social responsibility.

When a corporation, rather than its officers must act in a socially responsible manner, responsibility usually falls upon the shoulders of marketing to determine how best to satisfy the firm's socially responsible obligations. Such was the case of Nestlé. Senior management at Nestlé, which had the ultimate responsibility for integrating social responsibility into the strategic plan, thought that they were "doing a good service for humanity" by introducing the infant formula to Third World nations. Senior management truly believed that they were saving lives. Nestlé's marketing personnel believed that the best way to execute the desires of management was with an all-out aggressive marketing campaign, not fully realizing the adverse consequences.

According to Milton Friedman, "There is one and only one social responsibility of business—to use its resources and engage in activities designed to increase profits as long as it stays within the rules of the game, which is to say, engages in open and free competition without deception or fraud."[4] Applying this definition to the Nestlé's case, we could argue that their aggressive marketing campaign may have been deceptive. But who determines whether or not it was deceptive if legislation does not exist as a guide or standard?

Archie Carroll contends that business managers have four responsibilities: economic, legal, ethical and discretionary, with the last two making up social responsibility (see Exhibit 3):[5]

> **Economic:** Management within an organization is responsible for producing goods and services that are valuable to society so that the firm may repay its creditors and shareholders.
> **Legal:** Management is expected to abide by laws that governments are responsible for setting or have set.
> **Ethical:** An organization's management is responsible for following the generally held beliefs about behavior in a society.
> **Discretionary:** Organizations maintain responsibilities that they choose to voluntarily take on.

Without any legal precedence on how to market to Third World nations, Nestlé believed they were in accordance with ethical standards. The trial in Switzerland, where Nestlé was defending their marketing tactics, showed just the opposite. The court ruled that Nestlé was legally correct in their marketing approach but ethically incorrect.

As a result of the Nestlé trial, the World Health Organization eventually drew up ethical guidelines on how to market infant formula in Third World nations. The Nestlé case is in support of Carroll's belief that, if a firm does not accept its social responsibility through proper ethical and discretionary actions, then society will enact legal responsibilities through government intervention.

Firms can be ethically and socially responsible and remain profitable even to the point of maintaining a competitive advantage. Consider the following:[6, 7]

- Ben and Jerry's Ice Cream: Their environmental concerns enabled them to charge premium prices and gain market share.
- Maytag: They avoided spending time and money on contracting because of their trusting relationships with suppliers and distributors.

- Procter and Gamble: They can recruit exceptional employees at less than the market rate.
- Levi Strauss: They are highly welcomed in foreign countries and markets.
- Rubbermaid: They received great capital supplements from investors who strongly believed that highly reputable companies are promising long-term investments.

Nestlé's believed up until the very end that they were acting in a socially responsible manner and doing a good deed for humanity despite the fact that newborn infants were dying. Acting socially responsible can be detrimental at the same time as providing benefits. Consider the Kathy Lee Gifford story. When Kathy Lee Gifford learned that the plant in Honduras, which was manufacturing products under her name, was a sweatshop employing children, she immediately severed ties with the plant. Yet very little attention was given to a *Wall Street Journal* article by Lucy Martinez-Mont, a professor of economics in Guatemala:

> "The likely impact of Ms. Gifford's crusade on Central America frightens me. If it drives businesses to leave the region altogether, it will kill jobs and worsen living conditions for the poor . . . People choose to work in the maquila shops of their own free will, because these are the best jobs available to them. Given that unemployment compensation is unheard of in Central America, a lousy job is better than no job at all."[8]

The Marketing Campaign

Nestlé's Infant Formula

Nestlé's entrance into the infant formula industry was derived from a desire to increase profitability and gain a market share. Nestlé began developing and marketing its infant formula in the 1920's, when the product was proven to be nutritionally superior to condensed milk for the baby and a successful alternative to breastfeeding. Nestlé entered the Third World markets in Brazil and expanded over the last fifty years into approximately twenty additional Third World markets. Nestlé manufactured three broad categories of infant formulas: Starter formulas, Follow-Up formulas, and Weaning foods. Nestlé positioned the formulas as supplements to breast milk or, in cases where the mother was incapable of breast-feeding, as a substitute for breast milk.[9] It is important to note that Nestlé never intended that the infant formula serve as a replacement for breast milk, but rather as a supplement.

The product, itself, is of high quality and nutritionally superior to other alternatives in processed products. The product can meet a nutritional need as a supplement to breast-feeding and as a second-best alternative when women are unable or unwilling to breast-feed.[10] Therefore, the product can be socially useful and the product, itself, is not the problem, but rather the misuse of the product.

Product Misuse

The product is only successful for the infant if it is mixed with water fed through clean and sterile bottles, and stored in refrigerators. Many poor consumers do not have access to clean and drinkable water. They sometimes use the main water supplies, rivers or lakes, which are also used for laundry and bathing. They may also not have the funds to afford fuel required for boiling water. Sanitary facilities and disposal systems are often undeveloped and contaminated. An unsanitary bottle or liquid can produce harmful infections to the infant. Parents in Third World countries may also be illiterate and not fully able to follow product directions. Mothers do not properly mix formulas or follow correct sanitary procedures. Their lack of financial resources also restricts them from purchasing additional needed formula, causing mothers to dilute the formula mix to make the formula stretch further.[11]

All of these forms of product misuse cause serious and fatal health effects to infants. The environmental restrictions, along with the improper resources and guidance make it a very risky market for Nestlé to target, unless consumers are provided with a basic understanding of sanitation and nutrition. Nestlé failed to assure this type of awareness.

Nestlé's Marketing Practices

Product misuse and infant fatalities occurred as a result of Nestlé's inadequate distribution and marketing of its formulas.

There are five main marketing techniques used by Nestlé that have been noted as being the major cause of product misuse and infant mortality: mass media advertising, informational brochures, free samples, product promotions via medical professionals, and "milk nurses."[12] The use of these marketing techniques has created massive controversy among Nestlé's opponents.

Mass Media Advertising

Nestlé conducted mass media advertising via posters, billboards, loudspeaker vans, radio, television, and magazines. Nestlé's efforts were highly criticized for advertisements that overemphasized the product in comparison to breast-feeding and didn't differentiate when infant formula should be used in place of breast-feeding. Ads showed healthy babies being fed the formula, leaving readers with the impression that their babies would be healthy only if fed infant formula.

Nestlé did not target specific groups for advertisement. They simply targeted everyone, even those who might not have been appropriate for the product. Because many readers in Third World countries were illiterate, without proper guidance, consumers continued to misuse the product.

Information Brochures

Nestlé distributed information packets and brochures through hospitals and clinics. Again, pictures were used to overcome the literacy barrier. Readers were misled into believing, according to the advertisements, that infant formula was just as beneficial as breast-feeding. Much like Nestlé's mass media advertising efforts, information brochures were successful in bringing in more infant formula consumers.

Free Samples

Nestlé provided free samples to hospitals and clinics where consumers could try the product for free. The problem was that mothers became hooked on the product early on in the infant's life and the option of breast-feeding was eliminated. Once the infant formula was fed to the baby, the mother loses her ability to breast-feed, which created a further need for the infant formula.

Promotion via Medical Professions

Medical professionals were targeted because of their potential influence over consumers. Parents view them as objective authorities that provide the proper advice and product for their child. Consumers believed that because the infant formula was recommended by the hospital, it must be the best. Medical facilities recommended the product to patients, but didn't provide any further directions or guidance for proper care or possible alternatives.

"Milk Nurses"

Along with the use of medical professionals, Nestlé used "milk nurses" to promote and advertise the infant formula. These were company-paid representatives who promoted the product to the medical professionals, health care facilities, mothers, and consumers. Although these nurses dressed in white uniforms and were often medically trained, they were employed by Nestlé and receiving a salary and sales bonus. Consumers associated the nurse image and the infant formula with the "right thing to do." These nurses, however, did not provide adequate education or guidance; they attempted to make the product well known and to sell as much as possible.[13]

Multinational Advertising in Third World Countries

In Nestlé's case, the issue arises as to whether their mass media advertising campaigns and messages are considered false or deceptive in the eyes of the Third World consumers. Many government agencies and federal laws are set up to regulate this type of advertising. Specifically, international advertising regulations are most closely structured and monitored by the Federal Trade Commission (FTC). The FTC can challenge "unfair or deceptive acts or practices in order to promote truth in advertising and fair merchandising."[14]

Additional laws, such as the Lanham Act, are also a method of regulation. Section 43(a) of the Act has the same goal as the FTC: focusing on the falsity or deceptiveness of the advertisement. The laws allow citizens to raise suits in federal courts for deceptive advertising, and its focus is not on the intent of the advertiser but instead on the effect of the advertisement on the viewer.[15]

Nestlé's advertising practices go much deeper into not only the legal issues surrounding its marketing and advertising practices, but the ethical and moral debate of administering social responsibility in Third World countries via its advertisements.

Nestlé's Standpoint

To Nestlé, the infant formula market in Third World countries was considered a potentially huge profit-bearing market. Each baby was considered a target for the infant formula. Nestlé also claimed to bear some social responsibility and ethical reasoning to their tactics as well. Nestlé argued that it was important to introduce infant formula marketing in the Third World countries because infants needed supplements that can't be provided often by mothers because they are undernourished or may not be able to produce enough nourishment. Nestlé's belief was that infant formula would provide a safer alternative than some other methods, which do not provide adequate nutrition. Nestlé also argued that women in these countries need the convenience of infant formula to feed their children because they have heavy work schedules. When questioned on their marketing practices,

Nestlé stated that proper instructions on how to prepare and use the formula are explicitly written out on all products.[16]

The Rising Opposition

As word spread about the tragic events of infant formula occurring in Third World countries, many critics started to raise their voices and demand changes in Nestlé's marketing practices. The first major opposing voice was that of Dr. Derrick Jelliffe, was the head of the Caribbean Food and Nutrition Institute in Jamaica. He announced his concerns to Nestlé's marketing practices in Third World countries, and phrased the term, "commerciogenic malnutrition," to detail the practice of infant formula misuse that leads to diseases and death.[17] He voiced his concerns so strongly that others began to voice their opinions and form organizations structured to address the infant formula problems. In 1972, the Protein Advisory Group (PAG) developed Statement 23, which detailed the problems of past promotions and highlighted the importance of industry, government, and health professionals maintaining an increased responsibility in infant formula marketing. The statement indicated steps that could be taken to resolve the problems of infant formula and the marketing tactics.[18]

PAG Statement 23 created additional awareness of the situation and in 1974, the War on Want, a British charity organization, published a powerful article that attacked Nestlé, called "The Baby Killers." Less than a year later, the Third World Action Group published a similar article, called "Nestlé Kills Babies," which accused Nestlé of unethical and immoral behaviors associated with its infant formula marketing practices in Third World countries. Nestlé sued the group for defamation and won. However, the court case drew further attention to the issue, and Nestlé was asked to stop marketing its infant formula in Third World countries or to revise its advertising and marketing practices. Nestlé made no modifications. The company strongly believed that what they were doing was legally right.

Pressure from health, citizen, and social groups grew. The Nestlé case was becoming highly known and publicity continued to escalate. In 1975, The International Pediatric Association recommended a resolution to stop the distribution of free samples and to enforce controls on Nestlé's marketing practices. Also in 1975, the International Council of Infant Food Industries (ICIFI) was organized to cultivate free exchange of information and cooperation. This coalition was initiated to construct industry-wide self-regulation. Nestlé felt the only way it could remain competitive and safely change marketing practices was to get everyone to go along with it. Critics believed the code did not enforce strict enough marketing practices in Third World countries. Some companies implemented their own codes as a way of ensuring social responsibility.

The Nestlé Boycott

In late 1976, INFACT (Infant Formula Coalition Action) was formed. On July 4, 1977, INFACT launched an international boycott against all Nestlé products, with the intention of increasing public awareness and creating economic pressure that would force Nestlé into modifying its aggressive marketing practices in Third World countries. At the time, Nestlé was considered to be, "the most egregiously unethical actor" in the infant formula debate.[19] INFACT distributed letters, brochures, and various reports to show consumers how Nestlé was creating infant malnutrition and deaths in Third World countries. A sample INFACT letter encouraging membership and support of the boycott is shown as Exhibit 4. Consumers across the World stopped buying Nestlé products. INFACT stated that the purpose of the boycott was to, "halt the unethical and dangerous promotion of infant milk formula in Third World countries, through widespread public education and generation of grass-roots pressure against the offending corporations."[20] The boycott was not to be stopped until Nestlé met several of INFACT's demands:

- Stop the use of "milk nurses"
- Stop distributing free samples/supplies of the formula to medical facilities and homes
- Stop promoting formulas to the health professionals and through health care institutions
- Stop direct promotion and advertising to consumers, as recommended by the World Health Organization

The boycott against Nestlé was structured to address Nestlé's social irresponsibility and not against Nestlé's product. Consumers and advocates believed the product was of high quality and value if used properly. Boycotters were not arguing against Nestlé's infant formula. They were arguing Nestlé's lack of responsibility as evident in the company's mass media/marketing practices.

Nestlé tried to protect itself by filing a lawsuit against the Third World Action Group. The lawsuit was filed in the World Court in Bern, Switzerland. The trial in Bern backfired when the judge stated that legally, Nestlé's was correct but morally and ethically, they were wrong. This added fuel to the eventual boycott movement. The ultimate result was that the World Health Organization drew up a code for ethical marketing practices in Third World nations.

The World Health Organization and the WHO Code

In 1981, the World Health Organization (WHO) met with the World Health Assembly and adopted as a recommendation the International Code of Marketing of breast milk substitutes. The code states that advertising of infant formula or bottles directly to the public is prohibited, and shall be provided only by certified health care workers who provide only ethical information. The code was set up for all countries to sign and abide, and although most countries did sign in the 1980's, the United States did not sign until 1994.

Criticism worsened when internal documents were leaked to the press, which showed that Nestlé perhaps tried to co-opt some of WHO's officials and attempted to secretly finance an anti-boycott campaign. Exhibit 5 shows the editorial memo that appeared in the *Toronto Star*.[21] Nestlé's rebuttal appears in Exhibit 6.[22]

In 1988, the Action for Corporate Accountability (ACA) renewed the boycott against Nestlé, which continues to present day. The United Nations Children's Fund (UNICEF) provides a current report, "Cracking the Code," which details the most up-to-date Nestlé violations of the WHO code.[23]

Discussion Questions

1. How would you evaluate Nestlé's ability to add value resulting from competence and virtue resulting from character?
2. What kind of research was Nestlé legally required to do when making decisions about its formula placement and positioning? What kind of research would have

been ethically appropriate? How could that research have been conducted in such a way as to avoid the problems that occurred?

3. What kinds of positioning decisions were made that had ethical consequences in marketing the formula?

4. How should Nestlé have handled positioning in a way to maintain its integrity and credibility?

5. In its use of "milk nurses," Nestlé misled less educated members of the population as to the health benefits and risk of using formula. In what ways could the company have employed sales people in a developing nation that was less misleading?

6. What would a business model founded on integrity look like in this case and how would this have helped grow the business?

E x h i b i t **1 Laws, Court Rulings, and Regulations That Affect Business**

- **Environment**
  Clean Air Act, 1963
  Water Quality Act, 1965
  Air Quality Act, 1967
  National Environmental Policy Act, 1970

- **Equal Employment Opportunity**
  Title VII of the Civil Rights Act, 1964, as amended by the Equal Employment Opportunity Act, 1972
  Age Discrimination in Employment Act, 1967
  Pregnancy Act, 1978
  Americans with Disabilities Act, 1990

- **Consumerism**
  Meat Inspection Act, 1906
  Federal Food, Drug, and Cosmetics Act, 1938, as amended by presidential executive order creating the Office of Consumer Affairs, 1964
  National Traffic and Motor Vehicle Safety Act, 1966, as amended
  Fair Packaging and Labeling Act, 1966
  Consumer Credit Protection Act, 1968
  Toy Safety Act, 1969
  Truth-in-Lending Act, 1969
  Consumer Product Safety Act, 1972

- **Energy**
  Federal Energy Administration Act, 1974
  Energy Policy and Conservation Act, 1975

- **Economics**
  Chrysler Loan Guarantee Act, 1979
  Deregulation of airlines and trucking, 1979–1981
  FCC allows AT&T to sell nonregulated services, 1979
  Federal Reserve Bank permits banks to pay interest on checking accounts, 1980
  AT&T divests itself of local telephone companies, 1984
  S&L bailout acts
  Bank Regulation Act, 1991

- **Labor**
  Occupational Safety and Health Act, 1970

- **Other Laws**
  Interstate Commerce Act, 1887
  Sherman Antitrust Act, 1890
  Pure Food and Drug Act, 1906
  Sixteenth Amendment (income tax), 1913
  Clayton Act, 1914
  Federal Trade Commission Act, 1914
  Federal Communications Act, 1934
  Wagner Act, 1935
  Social Security Act, 1936
  Robinson-Patman Act, 1936
  Fair Labor Standards Act (Wage and Hour Act), 1938

Source: Adapted from Terry W. McAdam, *Business and Society Review,* Summer, 1973.

E x h i b i t **2 Categories of Social Responsibility**

- **Product Line**
  Internal standards for products
  Average product life
  Product performance

- **Marketing Practices**
  Sales practices
  Accuracy of advertising claims—specific government complaints
  Consumer complaints about marketing practices
  Fair pricing
  Packaging

- **Employee Education and Training**

  Policy on leaves of absence

  Dollars spent on training

  Career training and counseling

- **Corporate Philanthropy**

  Contribution performance

  Selection criteria for contributions

  Procedures for performance tracking of recipient institutions or groups

  Programs to permit and encourage employee involvement in social projects

  Extent of employee involvement in philanthropy decision making

- **Environmental Control**

  Measurable Pollution

  Violations of government (federal, state, local) standards

  Cost estimates to correct current deficiencies

  Extent to which various plants exceed current legal standards

  Resources devoted to pollution control

  Effort to monitor new standards as proposed

  Programs to keep employees alert to spills and other pollution-related accidents

- **External Relations**

  Support of minority and community enterprises

  Investment practices

  Government relations

  Specific input to public policy through research and analysis

  Political contributions

  Disclosure of information

  Comparisons of policy and performance with those of other countries and against local standards

- **Employee Relations, Benefits, and Satisfaction with Work**

  Comparison of wage and other policies with competition and/or national averages

  Comparison of operating units on promotions, terminations, hires

  Performance review system and procedures for communication with employees whose performance is below average

  Promotion policy—equitable and understood

  Transfer policy

  Termination policy

  General work environment and conditions

  Fringe benefits as percentage of salary at various salary levels

  Evaluation of employee benefit preferences

  Evaluation of employee understanding of current fringe benefits

  Union/industrial relations

  Confidentiality and security of personnel data

- **Employment and Advancement of Minorities and Women**

  Current hiring policies in relation to requirements of affirmative action programs

  Percent minorities and women employed in major facilities in relation to minority labor force available locally

  Number of minorities and women in positions of high responsibility

  Promotion performance of minorities and women

  Special recruiting efforts for minorities and women

  Opportunities for the physically handicapped

- **Employee Safety and Health**

  Work environment measures

  Safety performance

  Services provided for safety equipment, instruction, and special safety programs

  Comparisons of health and safety performance with competition and industry in general

  Employee health measures

Source: Adapted from Terry W. McAdam, *Business and Society Review,* Summer, 1973.

E x h i b i t   **3 Responsibilities of Business**

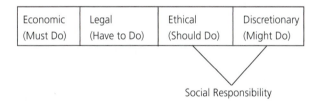

Economic (Must Do)	Legal (Have to Do)	Ethical (Should Do)	Discretionary (Might Do)

Social Responsibility

Source: ACADEMY OF MANAGEMENT REVIEW by AB CARROLL. Copyright 1979 by ACAD OF MGMT. Reproduced with permission of ACAD OF MGMT in the format Textbook via Copyright Clearance Center.

E x h i b i t   **4 Benjamin Spock, M.D.**

Rogers, Arkansas

Dear Friend,

In asking for your help in the boycott of Nestlé products, I speak for myself and for the Infant Formula Action Coalition.

Nestlé, the largest food processor in the World, is actively encouraging mothers in the developing countries in Africa, Asia and South America to give up breast feeding and turn to powdered milk formula instead.

But in such countries water is contaminated, sterilization procedures are unknown, illiteracy makes proper preparation impossible, and poor people try to stretch the powdered milk supply by overdiluting their babys formula.

The tragic results are widespread malnutrition and severe infant diarrhea that often ends in death.

Despite Worldwide protest, Nestlé continues to put profits first and refuses to halt this traffic with death.

So we are trying, by boycott, to compel Nestlé to do what they don't do out of decency.

INFACT and I ask you to do two things: Boycott all Nestlé products, and send a generous contribution to help us spread the word.

Most Sincerely,

Benjamin Spock, M.D.

Source: INFACT, Fall, 1978, in Neil Harrison, "Nestlé Alimentana S.A—Infant Formula," 1980, p. 43.

E x h i b i t   **5 The Lid Is Blown Off Nestlégate**

By Michele Landsberg

Nestlé S.A. is a giant multinational corporation that prides itself on an image of rosy-cheeked Swiss propriety and benevolence. But secret Nestlé documents leaked to the *Washington Post* last week tell another story, a story of corporate deviousness that reminds me of nothing so much as the blandly conscienceless carryings-on of the Watergate gang.

The documents show Nestlé engaged in a grim battle to discredit the anti-Nestlé boycott and to undermine the World Health Organization's plans to draw up an ethical marketing code. The code, due next spring, is designed to curb the aggressive and often unscrupulous marketing of baby formula in the Third World, where millions of babies suffer and thousands die from the now notorious Baby Bottle Syndrome.

Now we learn that Nestlé has co-opted some of the WHO's highest officials and has surreptitiously financed anti-boycott propaganda which masquerades as impartial journalism.

Leaked Memo

In one of the leaded memos, Nestlé Swiss vice-president, E.W. Saunders, says that one of WHO's assistant directors has "been very active" on Nestlé's behalf, and another "can be counted on as a sure friend." At least two of these reliable friends found a friendly home on the Nestlé payroll, or the payroll of a Nestlé-dominated umbrella group, immediately after leaving WHO.

Even more startling is Nestlé's involvement with Herman Nickel, the Washington editor of *Fortune* magazine. Nickel, who wrote a supposedly impartial, pro-Nestlé article in *Fortune,* picked up a $5,000 fee from a conservative Washington foundation which was being funded by Nestlé to the tune of $25,000.

The foundation, called the Ethics and Policy Centre, is headed by an ex-adviser to Ronald Reagan, one Ernest Lefever. It was Lefever who met with Nickel and asked him to write the article. Nickel, this stalwart of journalistic integrity, also agreed to let a panel, including a baby formula manufacturer, "review" his article before publication.

Saunders' memo, now so deliciously available for public scrutiny, talks about plans to finance a pro-Nestlé film through Lefever's foundation and to further "encourage" Nickel's impartial journalistic efforts by flying him to Switzerland for a nice visit.

While Nickel was preparing his *Fortune* article, Nestlé executives were "concerned that Nestlé should not be seen to be the dominant subscriber to the centre," confides the memo. But not to worry. The company's Washington lawyer, "informs us that there are ways in which this matter can be satisfactorily handled."

I don't know about you, but when I hear phrases like that, words like CREEP and John Mitchell and money-laundering leap into my mind.

Nickel's article in *Fortune* turned out to be the only piece in any major publication to support Nestlé's Third World marketing tactics and to attack the boycott. Saunders urges "maximum exploitation" of the *Fortune* article, and indeed, Lefever's foundation reprinted it.

Stunningly Scurrilous

I've read the article. It's called "The Corporation Haters" and uses the stunningly scurrilous phrase that the boycotters are "Marxists marching under the banner of Christ."

The boycott is spearheaded in North America by the National Council of Churches and supported by thousands of church and charitable organizations. Nickel contends, however, that the National Council of Churches is a hotbed of leftist radicals and Marxists in clerics' clothing, and that the boycott is merely a hoke-up excuse for a radical attack on big business.

Nickel's article is loaded with character assassination and straight misinformation. He simply brushes aside the substantial evidence of health experts around the World about the devastating effects of Nestlé's mass marketing.

But that's okay. Nickel's "objectivity" won't be fooling anybody anymore. And neither will Nestlé's constant hand-on-heart avowals that it will be happy to abide by any code drawn up by WHO.

Thanks to Nestlé's own documents, we see how desperately the company is trying to influence WHO to write a "soft" pro-industry code, and to what lengths Nestlé is willing to go to continue its lucrative Third World activities unhindered.

I phoned Nestlé's public relations office in New York to ask if they had any statement they wished to make on the affair of the leaked memos.

"Gee, no, I mean, you're the only one who's asked," the Nestlé account executive told me. I believe they call that stonewalling. Welcome to Nestlégate.

Source: Michele Landsberg, "The Lid is Blown Off Nestlégate," *Toronto Star,* January 12, 1981.

E x h i b i t **6 Nestlé Rebuttal of Misleading Allegations**

On January 12, 1981, Michele Landsberg wrote an article that appeared in the *Toronto Star* challenging the allegations leveled at Nestlé. The article made the following points:

1. *"Secret Nestlé documents...tell...a story of corporate deviousness."*

   This claim represented Ms. Landsberg's interpretation and not the facts.

2. *"Nestlé has co-opted some of the WHO's highest officials."*

   Similar to labor unions and other non-government agencies, Nestle maintains a dialogue with WHO. There is no substance to the claim that Nestlé "co-opted" any WHO official.

3. *"(Nestlé) . . . has surreptitiously financed anti-boycott propaganda."*

   Nestlé had no influence over *Fortune,* which used the phrase "Marxists marching under the banner of Christ," a phrase which, in the managing editor's opinion, was "justified by the evidence."

4. *"Nestlé's Vice President, E.W. Saunders, says that one of the WHO's assistant directors has 'been very active' on Nestlé's behalf, and another 'can be counted on as a sure friend'."*

   Mr. Saunders has not made this comment.

5. *"At least two of these reliable friends found a friendly home on the Nestlé payroll, or the payroll of a Nestlé-dominated umbrella group."*

   The International Council of Infant Food Industries (ICIFI) consists of 14 members and is not dominated by Nestlé. Dr. Stanislas Flache was appointed Secretary General of ICIFI (with the prior knowledge of WHO Director General Halfdan Mahler) after he retired from the UN having completed 20 years service. The purpose of Dr. Flache's appointment was to improve co-operation between UN agencies and industry. This goal was hindered by activist's smear campaign that made false claims that WHO officials were on Nestlé's payroll.

6. *"Nickel's article in* Fortune *turned out to be the only piece in any major publication to support Nestlé's Third World marketing tactics and to attack the boycott."*

   The *Fortune* article did not reference Nestlé marketing policy. Periodicals and newspapers such as the *Wall Street Journal, Barron's, Business International* and scientific and medical authorities, have criticized the unsubstantiated activists' attacks on infant formula manufacturers.

7. *"Even more startling is Nestlé's involvement with Herman Nickel, the Washington editor of* Fortune *magazine."*

   Ms. Landsberg claimed this allegation is libelous since Mr. Nickel had contacted other infant formula manufacturers, clergymen and social critics before he contacted Nestlé.

Ms. Landsberg concluded that scientific evidence and research discredits the claim that Nestlé's "mass marketing" harmed infants.

Source: Adapted from Nestlé S.A., "Nestlé Response to Toronto Star," January 13, 1981.

Endnotes

1. James M. Higgins and Julian W. Vincze, *Strategic Management,* Dryden Press, 1993, p. 136–137.
2. Adapted from Terry W. McAdam, *Business and Society Review,* Summer, 1973.
3. Fred R. Davis, *Strategic Management,* Prentice Hall, 1999, p. 155.
4. Milton Freidman, "The Social Responsibility of Business is to Increase Its Profits," *New York Time Magazine,* September 13, 1970, p. 126–127.
5. Archie B. Carroll, "A Three Dimensional Conceptual Model of Corporate Performance," *Academy of Management Review,* October, 1979, p. 497–505.
6. J.B. Barney and M. H. Hanson, "Trustworthiness as a Source of Competitive Advantage," *Strategic Management Journal,* 1994, p. 175–190.
7. S. Preece, C. Fleisher, and J. Toccacelli, "Building a Reputation Along the Value Chain at Levi Strauss," *Long Range Planning,* 1995, p. 88–98.
8. L. Martinez-Mont, "Sweat Shops are Better Than No Shops," *Wall Street Journal,* June 25, 1996, p. A14.
9. Neil Harrison, "Nestlé Alimentana S.A—Infant Formula," 1980, p. 8.
10. James E. Post and Edward Baer, "Analyzing Complex Policy Problems: The Social Performance of the International Infant Formula Industry," *Research in Corporate Social Performance and Policy,* Volume 2, JAI Press, 1979.
11. James E. Post and Edward Baer, "Demarketing Infant Formula: Consumer Products in the Developing World." *Journal of Contemporary Business* 7, no. 4, 1978, p. 17–35.
12. James E. Post and S. Prakash Sethi, "Public Consequences of Private Action," p. 39.
13. Kathy Winstead and Philip Cateora, *International Marketing,* Eighth Edition, http://www.pace.edu/lubin.
14. "FTC Policy Statement on Deception," Federal Trade Commission, Washington DC, October 14, 1983, http://www.lawpublish.com.
15. James E. Schatz and Paul M. Laurenza, "Advertising Law Primer," http://www.oppenheimer.com.
16. Kathy Winstead and Philip Cateora, *International Marketing,* Eighth Edition, htp://www.pace.edu/lubin.
17. D.B. Jelliffe, "Commerciogenic Malnutrition? A Time For Dialogue," *Food Technology,* February, 1971.
18. David O. Cox, "The Infant Formula Issue: A Case Study," in Epstein, Edwin M., and Preston, Lee E., eds., *Business Environment and Public Policy: The Field and its Future,* St Louis: American Assembly of Collegiate Schools of Business, 1982, p. 82.
19. Katie Allison Granju, "The Story of the WHO Code," Attachment Parenting: The Instinctive Care for Your Baby and Young Child, http://www.breastfeeding.com/reading_room/code.html.
20. Douglas A. Johnson, INFACT, "Nestlé Boycott," in Neil Harrison, "Nestlé Alimentana S.A—Infant Formula," 1980, p. 41.
21. Michele Landsberg, "The Lid is Blown Off Nestlégate," *Toronto Star,* January 12, 1981.
22. Nestlé S.A., "Nestlé Response to *Toronto Star,*" January 13, 1981.
23. Mary Assunta, Third World Network, "International Boycott Against Nestlé Continues," February, 1997, http://www.ThirdWorldtraveler.com/people/stevetwt/Boycotts/Nestléboycott_cont.html.

Index

Note: Page numbers in *italics* identify an illustration or figure.